MEMORY, MASCULINITY AND NATIONAL IDENTITY IN BRITISH VISUAL CULTURE, 1914–1930

To the memory of my grandmother for unconditional love, endless affection and kind understanding.

Memory, Masculinity and National Identity in British Visual Culture, 1914–1930

A Study of 'Unconquerable Manhood'

GABRIEL KOUREAS

ASHGATE

Published by
Ashgate Publishing Limited
Gower House
Croft Road
Aldershot
Hampshire GU11 3HR
England

Ashgate Publishing Company
Suite 420
101 Cherry Street
Burlington, VT 05401-4405
USA

Ashgate website: http://www.ashgate.com

British Library Cataloguing in Publication Data
Koureas, Gabriel
Memory, masculinity and national identity in British visual culture, 1914-1930 : a study of 'unconquerable manhood'
1. Masculinity - Great Britain - History - 20th century
2. Masculinity in art 3. National characteristics, British
4. Memory - Social aspects - Great Britain - History - 20th century 5. War memorials - Great Britain - History - 20th century 6. World War, 1914-1918 - Monuments - England
7. Great Britain - History - George V, 1910-1936 - Historiography
I. Title
305.3'1'0941'09041

Library of Congress Cataloging-in-Publication Data
Koureas, Gabriel.
Memory, masculinity, and national identity in British visual culture, 1914-1930 : a study of 'unconquerable manhood' / Gabriel Koureas.
p. cm.
Includes bibliographical references and index.
ISBN-13: 978-0-7546-6017-0 (hardcover : alk. paper)
1. Masculinity in popular culture--Great Britain--History--20th century. 2. World War, 1914-1918--Social aspects--Great Britain. 3. Memorialization--Great Britain--History--20th century. 4. War memorials--Social aspects--Great Britain. 5. National characteristics, British--History--20th century. 6. Psychic trauma--Great Britain--History--20th century. 7. Great Britain--History--George V, 1910-1936. I. Title.

HQ1090.7.G7K68 2007
305.310941'0904--dc22

2006021584

ISBN: 978-0-7546-6017-0

Printed and bound in Great Britain by MPG Books Ltd, Bodmin, Cornwall.

Contents

List of Illustrations

3 Abjection, Idealisation, Trauma and Acting-Out of Masculinities in the Inter-War Years

Acknowledgements

The long road of completing this project has been full of adventure and discovery and sometimes, angry Poseidons. Many people helped in keeping my *Ithaka* in my mind and make the arrival there possible.

Singling out people for their contributions, encouragement and support is difficult. However, one person needs a very particular mention for her constant and wonderful support from the moment this project was conceived. Annie Coombes believed in the possibility of this project and her guidance, comments and most importantly, moral support have been invaluable. Words cannot describe my gratitude.

Many years back, growing up in a culture that did not allow for difference, I was introduced to the poetry of Constantinos Cavafy and the possibilities that it offered for a less rigid understanding of the world. I thank my high school teacher, Anna Farmakas, for that superb gift she gave me at a young age.

This work would not have been possible without the financial assistance of the Arts and Humanities Research Board. Special thanks also to Erika Gaffney, commissioning editor at Ashgate, for seeing the relevance of this book to present global events, and the anonymous reader who offered many helpful comments.

I thank the many archivists and librarians that provided me with my source material at the Imperial War Museum, the National Inventory of War Memorials, the Army Museum Chelsea, the Wellcome Institute, the People's Museum, the Modern History Archives, the Henry Moore Institute Archives, the British Library, Birkbeck Library and the Senate House Library.

The staff and students at Birkbeck College provided a stimulating environment in which this project could be nurtured. In particular, I thank the members of the reading group for inspiring discussions and in particular, Patrizia di Bello and Christine Boyanoski. Many people offered constructive and helpful advice on papers delivered at various conferences. I thank in particular, Fae Brauer, Michael Hatt, Claudine Mitchell, Debra Kelly, Valerie Holman, Paul Gough, Graham Dawson, Jo Labanyi, Urszula Szulakowska and Angela Weight.

Special thanks go to Sarah Masters for editing the final draft, and to Maggie Millman for reading an earlier draft. Many thanks also to Jacqui Cornish, senior desk editor at Ashgate for all her work during the final stages of production. Any omissions are entirely my own responsibility.

Friends and family had to endure my constant absorption in this project. They provided a much needed diversion, support and encouragement. Miriam Davies, Gregoris Gregoriou, Constantinos Phellas, Myranda Havouzaris and Roisin Nield have always been there to listen. Miriam Orriss provided a much needed healing and comforting space during very intense periods. My parents, Andreas and Maroulla, were as always exceptionally understanding, loving and supportive. Very special thanks go to David Sidonio for so many things that will take forever to list. I hope one day you understand.

Finally, one person did not live to see this project completed. I dedicate this work to *γιαγια* for unconditional love, endless affection and kind understanding. I do miss you.

List of Abbreviations

ILN	*Illustrated London News*
IWGC	Imperial War Graves Commission
IWM	Imperial War Museum
IWM North	Imperial War Museum North
LNWR	London and North Western Railways
MCU	Middle Class Union
MGC	Machine Gun Corps
MSS	Modern Records Centre, University of Warwick
NIWM	National Inventory of War Memorials, Imperial War Museum
NMOS	National Museum of Struggle
NUR	National Union of Railwaymen
PRO	Public Records Office
RA	Royal Academy
RAMC	Royal Army Medical Corps

List of Abbreviations

Introduction

On Sunday, 2 November 1997 a group of men holding a pink triangle, the mark of homosexual men in the concentration camps of the Second World War, gathered in front of the Cenotaph in London. They were commemorating the lesbian, gay and bisexual people who had died in World War I and II. The ceremony was organised by *OutRage!* The existence of gay war veterans has never been acknowledged by the ex-services association the British Legion or by the official state-sponsored Remembrance Day ceremony. The British Legion denounced the commemoration as 'distasteful' and 'offensive', and 'bound to offend many former soldiers'.[1]

This incident raises issues about the relationship between sexuality and national identity and in particular why the British Legion bans any association between war commemoration and homosexuality. It also raises questions concerning the kinds of masculinities that the commemorative ceremonies of the First World War are projecting and whether these could be said to promote a hegemonic version of masculinity.

This book focuses on two main concerns: memory, both personal and collective, and definitions of masculinity. Personal and collective identity can only ever be presumed, claimed and reclaimed[2] and as such it has to be reaffirmed, especially in periods of uncertainty, turmoil and change. We often call on memory to legitimise identity, to construct it or reconstruct it. Two issues seem to be historically tied to the formation of identity. The first is the threat of some imaginary outsider; experiences of humiliation, real or imaginary, are linked to the threat of the imaginary outsider and the 'tendency to reject, to exclude, is a response to this threat'.[3] The second issue is the incidence of violent and traumatic events. Collective identity is rooted in events that are violent, and 'collective memory is a kind of storage of such violent blows wounds and scars'. The First World War provided the violent event on which national identity was cemented in order to reconstruct and stabilise post First World War society. A host of other events, and for the purpose of this book, the working-class man and the shell-shocked returning soldier, deemed in much of contemporary literature as lacking masculine qualities, provided the necessary threat around which British post-war society could be reconstructed.

1. *OutRage!* is a political activist group that promotes direct action in advancing gay rights. Information can be found at *www.outrage.nabumedia.com*
2. Ricoeur, Paul, 'Memory and Forgetting', in Kearney, Richard and Dooley, Mark (eds), *Questioning Ethics. Contemporary Debates in Philosophy* (London: 1999), p. 7.
3. Ibid., p. 8.

The concept of the performativity of gender is central to the arguments presented in this book: gender is produced as a ritualised repetition of conventions, and this ritual is socially compelled in part by the force of a compulsory heterosexuality. A gender identity depends on performative acts that give the illusion of naturalness.[4] This illusion is then used to establish a hegemonic masculinity which is expressed within a web of power relations that are in a continual state of flux and transformation.[5] Unveiling ceremonies commemorating those who fell during the war provided the performative acts that were able to give an illusion of naturalness in a period when previously uncontested norms of masculinity were under dispute.

Cultural memory, very much like masculinities, is a field of contested meanings in which society interacts with cultural elements to produce a sense of belonging to a nation or 'imagined communities'.[6] Michael Lambek and Paul Antze have argued that memory always depends on cultural vehicles for its expression, in particular the symbols, codes, artefacts, rites and sites in which memory is embodied and objectified.[7] This book concentrates on various 'sites of memory': Memorials and architecture, photographic images and albums, the museum space, souvenirs, union banners and spectacles, popular culture and political activism. In doing so the book interrogates Pierre Nora's assertion that 'if what they defended were not threatened, there would be no need to build them'.[8] These sites need to be seen as 'technologies of memory', cultural objects through which memories are produced, shared and given meaning, and not simply 'vessels of memory' in which memory passively resides.[9]

I have concentrated on memorials to the First World War in relation to the broader aspects of the visual culture of the period and have not attempted to address any specific medium in order to reveal the way in which memories, public or private, are shared, produced and given meaning.[10] However, I don't attempt to provide an inventory of the commemorative representations of the war. The

4. Butler, Judith, 'Melancholy Gender/Refused Identification', in Berger, M. *et al.* (eds), *Constructing Masculinity* (London: 1995), p. 31.
5. See Connell, R. W., *Masculinities* (London: 1995); Roper, M. and Tosh, J., 'Historians and the Politics of Masculinity', in Roper, M. and Tosh, J. (eds) *Manful Assertions. Masculinities in Britain since 1800* (London: 1991); Brod, H. and Kaufman, M., 'Introduction', in Brod, H. and Kaufman, M. (eds), *Theorising Masculinities* (London: 1994); Whitehead, S. and Barrett, F., 'The Sociology of Masculinity' in Whitehead, S. and Barrett, F. (eds), *The Masculinities Reader* (Oxford: 2001).
6. Anderson, Benedict, *Imagined Communities. Reflections on the Origins and Spread of Nationalism* (London: 1994).
7. Antze, Paul and Lambek, Michael, 'Introduction', in Antze, Paul and Lambek, Michael (eds), *Tense Past. Cultural Essays in Trauma and Memory* (London: 1996), p. xvii.
8. Nora, Pierre, 'Between Memory and History: *Les Lieux de Mémoire*', *Representations*, 26, Spring 1989, p. 12.
9. Sturken, Marita, *Tangled Memories. The Vietnam War, the AIDS Epidemic, and the Politics of Remembering* (Berkeley: 1997), p. 5.
10. I use the term visual culture in the manner in which Jessica Evans and Stuart Hall define it; see Evans, Jessica and Hall, Stuart, *Visual Culture: The Reader* (London: 1999), pp. 1–9.

focus is on understanding power relations between and within male sociality, and establishing how at a precise historical moment the definitions of contested masculinities might have functioned in post-war reconstruction.

Commemorative events, or commemorations, can be seen as attempts at closure and imposition: 'like the sharp report of a field gun at a military commemoration and the ringing silence that follows it: this is the sound of remembrance, this is the silence.'[11] Benedict Anderson refers to the tombs of the unknown soldiers as emblems of the modern culture of nationalism precisely because they are either empty or contain unidentified bodies.[12] Within the British cultural context, Patrick Wright sees commemorations as acting to erase the realities of war and transpose such realities with the 'introduction of order, solemnity and meaning where there was chaos, disorder and loss'.[13]

The realities of war were not the only thing to threaten certain middle and upper-class values; the events of the Russian Revolution also had a part to play, and this book highlights the need to understand the impact of international events on national cultures and the absence of such recognition from studies of the British commemoration of the First World War.[14]

Recent studies of the commemoration of the First World War argue that a consensual effort amongst all classes[15] promoted a universal[16] need to express the enormity of the losses incurred during the war. However, this book will argue

---

11. Sider, Gerald and Smith, Gavin, 'Introduction', *Between History and Histories: The Making of Silences and Commemorations* (Toronto: 1997), p. 7.
12. Anderson, Benedict, *Imagined Communities*, p. 6.
13. Wright, Patrick, *On Living in an Old Country. The National Past in Contemporary Britain* (London: 1985), pp. 136–7.
14. Ashplant, T. G., Dawson, G. and Roper, M., 'The Politics of War Memory and Commemoration. Contexts, Structures and Dynamics', in Ashplant, T. G., Dawson, G. and Roper, M. (eds), *The Politics of War Memory and Commemoration* (London: 2001), p. 15. See also Marwick, Arthur, 'Two Total Wars, the Cold War and Postmodernism: the Arts in Europe, 1910–2000', in Emsley, C. (ed.), *War, Culture and Memory* (Milton Keynes: 2003), p. 203.
15. Gregory, Adrian, *The Silence of Memory. Armistice Day 1919–1946* (Oxford: 1994); King, Alex, *Memorials of the Great War. The Symbolism and Politics of Remembrance* (Oxford, 1998), pp. 141–9; Lloyd, David, *Battlefield Tourism. Pilgrimage and the Commemoration of the Great War in Britain, Australia and Canada, 1919–1939* (Oxford: 1998), chapter 2.

    For works that question the all inclusiveness of the commemoration of the First World War, see Moriarty, Catherine, 'Private Grief and Public Remembrance: British First World War Memorials', in Evans, M. and Lunn, Ken (eds), *War and Memory in the Twentieth Century* (Oxford: 1997); Bushaway, Bob, 'Name Upon Name: The Great War and Remembrance', in Porter, R. (ed.), *Myths of the English* (Oxford: 1992). For the case of France, see Sherman, Daniel, 'Art, Commerce, and the Production of Memory in France after World War I', in Gillis, John (ed.), *Commemorations* (Princeton: 1994). See also Brower, Brady M., 'Strategic Remembering. The Boundary Politics of Mourning in Post-Great War France', *Rethinking History*, 1/1 (1997), pp. 21–33.

    The above are discussed in more detail in Chapter 1 of this book.
16. Winter, Jay, *Sites of Memory, Sites of Mourning* (Cambridge: 1995), p. 104.

that such expression, in particular the idea of simplicity, seen by recent studies as facilitating the grieving process,[17] was an aesthetic language embedded in middle and upper-class aesthetic sensibilities. As such, the notion that there was a universal language of commemoration becomes questionable. The memorials, and the ritual that accompanied their ceremonial unveiling, need to be seen as part of a spectacle that attempted to erase and subsume any revolutionary feelings and radical ideas from the collective memory. As Terry Eagleton has commented, 'we live within societies whose aim is not simply to combat radical ideas but to wipe them from living memory'. The ultimate aim, according to Eagleton, has been to 'bring about an amnesiac condition in which it would be as though such notions never existed, placing them beyond our very powers of conception'.[18]

Studies of the commemoration of the First World War in Britain so far have not attempted to examine the relationship between those ideal versions of masculinity projected in the commemoration of war and the masculinities they attempted to erase from any memory of the war.[19] This book will argue that it is only by understanding the power relations associated with such a process that one can challenge the assumed all inclusiveness of the commemoration of the war and reveal a means by which the unveiling ceremonies, through formalism and performativity, attempted to establish acceptable norms of masculinity. Such norms, we will discover, were informed by the pre-war masculinities of the public school education system.

In this respect, the book contributes to those debates around the First World War that see the war either as a watershed that signalled the transformation of the cultural traditions of the past, or as a perpetuation of old traditions.[20] The commemoration

17. Ibid.
18. Eagleton, Terry, *The Ideology of the Aesthetic* (Oxford: 1990), p. 7.
19. As Frank Mort has noted, the study of the relationship between sexuality and national identity remains relatively underdeveloped. See Mort, Frank, *Dangerous Sexualities: Medico-moral Politics in England since 1830* (London: 2000, [1987]), p. xx. This is even more the case of the relationship of commemoration, sexuality and national identity. For an insight into Germany in relation to the First World War, see Mosse, George, *Nationalism and Sexuality. Respectability and Abnormal Sexuality in Modern Europe* (Madison: 1988); Mosse, George, *Fallen Soldiers. Reshaping the Memory of the World Wars* (Oxford: 1990). Mosse, however, conflates homosexuality with fascism. For a criticism of his approach, see Hewitt, Andrew, *Political Inversions. Homosexuality, Fascism and the Modernist Imaginary* (Stanford: 1996).

    For an insight into France in relation to the First World War, see Sherman, Daniel, 'Monuments, Mourning and Masculinity in France after World War I', *Gender & History*, 8/1 (April, 1996).

    For a discussion of Britain, see Bourke, Joanna, *Dismembering the Male. Men's Bodies, Britain and the Great War* (London: 1996); Dawson, Graham, *Soldier Heroes. British Adventure, Empire and the Imagining of Masculinities* (London: 1994)

    For a discussion of the relationship between sexuality and national identity, see Parker, A., Russo, M., Sommer, D., Yaeger, P., 'Introduction', in Parker, A. *et al.* (eds), *Nationalisms and Sexuality* (London: 1992).
20. For Jay Winter, the commemoration of the First World War in particular looked to pre-war years for its inspiration in the use of traditional motifs in memorials. For Winter, the use of

of the war to a very great extent relied on the use of an ideal masculinity and on an aesthetic language that were both informed by pre-war standards. It denied agency to those new power relations that emerged during the war. This practice of looking to the past was not simply aimed at providing comfort through familiarity; it was also designed to impose control over what was perceived as unacceptable behaviour.

The unacceptable behaviour that so threatened sensibilities was seen as a manifestation of two distinct, contested masculinities: working-class masculinity, which was perceived as the antithesis of public school values of self-sacrifice, devotion to duty, emotional strength and self-sufficiency, and the former servicemen whose memories revealed fractures in what was perceived as an impenetrable masculinity. The trauma of war and the memories of comradeship provided such discontinuities. Studies of the commemoration of the First World War make no allowances for the enormity of the loss felt by the servicemen and the opportunities offered by the commemorative machine to address their loss and trauma. This book argues that the traumatic memories of the combatants[21] offer a means of resisting the received memory of the war projected by the commemoration ceremonies.

The male body, particularly bodily memories, provided a vehicle not only for traumatic memories but also for memories of comradeship. It provided not only a site of destruction and disgust, but also an expression of *esprit de corps* and desire. Recent work on masculinities in wartime Britain has avoided the possibility that servicemen at the Front might have harboured a desire for one another.[22] The construction of sexuality needs to be seen as not relying solely on desire, but on the possibilities of desire. The desiring self has to be understood as constructed through and contingent on the extreme circumstances of the Front, in what has been described as a 'new world of largely nongenital tactile tenderness'.[23] This book will argue that

traditional forms becomes a 'way of remembering which enabled the bereaved to live with their losses'. Such motifs are seen as possessing a special 'power to mediate bereavement'. Winter defines traditional motifs as an eclectic set of classical romantic, or religious images and ideas. Winter, Jay, *Sites of Memory, Sites of Mourning*, p. 5.

21. Although this books deals specifically with male trauma in war, it does not attempt to gender trauma into what Margaret Higonnet calls a 'privileged, masculine form of testimony'. On the contrary it recognises the importance of the work of Higonnet and the trauma experienced by women, usually nurses, at the Front. Moreover, it recognises the importance of testimony in allowing alternative, non-hegemonic masculine narratives to be constructed. See Higonnet, Margaret, 'Authenticity and Art in Trauma Narratives of World War I', *Modernism/Modernity*, 9/1 (2002): 91–107.

22. See for example Bourke, Joanna, *Dismembering the Male*, pp. 24–5; Ferguson Niall, *The Pity of War* (London, 1998), caption for illustration No.6.

23. Das, Santanu, '"Kiss me, Hardy": Intimacy, Gender and Gesture in World War I Trench Literature', *Modernism/Modernity*, 9/1 (2002): 51–74. On sexuality and the First World War in relation to war poets see, Caesar, Adrian, *Taking It Like a Man. Suffering, Sexuality and the War Poets* (Manchester: 1993); Taylor, Martin, 'Introduction', in Taylor, M. (ed.), *Lads. Love Poetry of the Trenches* (London: 1989), pp. 15–57; on cross dressing at the front in relation to new found forms of intimacy see Boxwell, David, 'The Follies of War: Cross-Dressing and

the coexistence of disgust and desire in the traumatic memories of the servicemen in some way reflected the complications in the politics of masculinity. The strict definitions of masculinity at the time, as manifested in the authorities' insistence on separating shell shock from sexuality, made it impossible for traumatised combatants who may have experienced different forms of masculinity at the Front, to mourn their comrades. It also made it impossible for them to come to terms with the return to the pre-war codes of masculinity that the commemoration of the war attempted to impose. The result was an acting out of masculinities in the inter-war years. The complications of the politics of masculinity can also be found in the insistence of the commemorative machine on re-installing the pre-war tropes of masculinity that had relied on clearly defined boundaries for their existence. Such boundaries were also a prominent feature in unveiling ceremonies, designed to separate spectators from the spectacle.

The book is divided into different unveilings: the Cenotaph, the *London and North Western Railway Memorial*, the *Machine Gun Corps Memorial* and the Imperial War Museum. Each unveiling is juxtaposed to several veilings: the disorderly crowds, unrest, trauma, desire and war. The first chapter focuses on the Cenotaph and the aesthetic language of simplicity promoted in the Royal Academy conference and exhibition of war memorials and emphasised in the architectural work of Edwin Lutyens, who designed the Cenotaph.

Chapter 2 examines a period of industrial unrest, the 1919 strike by the National Union of Railwaymen and the unveiling of the *London and North Western Railways Memorial* at Euston Station. The establishment of a hegemonic masculinity is discussed through the ceremonial figure of the soldier in uniform. The masculinities projected by these cultural artefacts are subsequently contrasted with the masculinities that the unveiling of the memorial was attempting to subsume and erase.

A memorial which departs from the traditional figure of a soldier in uniform provides the focus for Chapter 3. The *Machine Gun Corps Memorial* and the controversies to which it gave rise are discussed in relation to the traumatic memories of the servicemen and the possibilities offered by the commemoration of the First World War to resolve the men's grief and trauma. The chapter discusses various cases of unresolved trauma in the inter-war years. The diaries and memoirs of the servicemen and details of their medical histories expose new forms of male sexuality which challenge and threaten the notions of masculinity accepted at that time.

The Imperial War Museum, the main focus of Chapter 4, has received very little critical attention. Its installation and first exhibition reveal how the museum space was used to define a 'consensual past'[24] and, most importantly, to promote certain

Popular Theatre on the British Front Lines, 1914–18', *Modernism/Modernity*, 9/1 (2002): 1–20; Fussell, Paul, *The Great War and Modern Memory* (Oxford: 1975).

24. Coombes, Annie E., 'The Recalcitrant Object: Culture Contact and the Question of Hybridity', in Barker, F., Hulme, P., Iversen, M. (eds), *Colonial Discourse/Postcolonial Theory* (Manchester: 1994), p. 91.

ideal masculinities. Recognising the unstable positioning of masculinities during the post-Armistice period, the museum curators chose to place particular emphasis on the instruments of war rather than the personal memories and souvenirs collected by the former servicemen. The machinery of warfare becomes the cultural icon of the period, transforming killing machines into aesthetic objects.

The veilings and unveilings are discussed in terms of binaries which offer not contradictions but also ways of understanding the discourses surrounding the commemoration of the First World War.[25] The veil has traditionally been associated with the female figure and with connotations of the exotic and the oriental. Ludmilla Jordanova has argued that the idea of unveiling men is 'comic, implausible and unthreatening, presumably because their bodies are not the symbolic carriers in modern society either of creative or destructive forces'.[26] In the years between the two World Wars the male body did indeed become a symbolic carrier of destructive and disruptive forces as exemplified by the insistence in veiling the male body in the shroud of the military uniform. The unveiled/veiled male bodies revealed the precariousness of 'unconquerable manhood'.

25. Sedgwick Kosofsky, Eve, *Epistemology of the Closet* (London: 1990), p. 11.
26. Jordanova, Ludmilla, *Sexual Visions: Images of Gender in Science and Medicine between the Eighteenth and Twentieth Centuries* (London: 1989), p. 54.

Chapter 1

Ritual, Ceremonial, Order and the Aesthetics of Simplicity

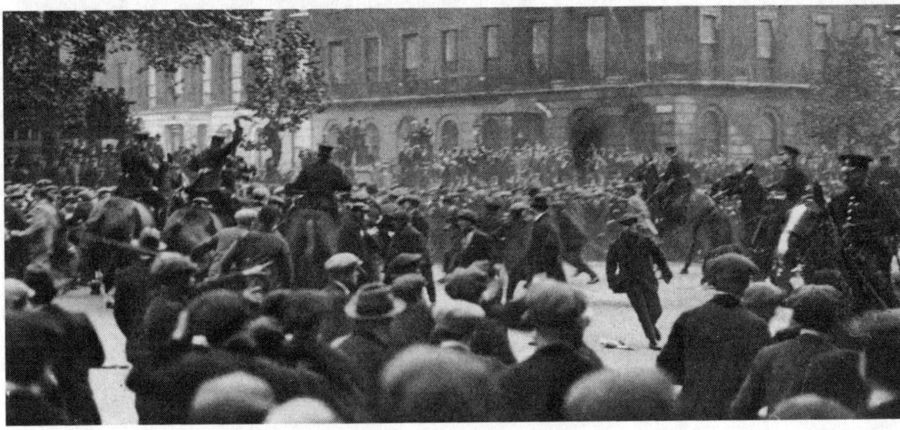

Figure 1.1 Unemployment Rioting in Whitehall. *Illustrated London News*, 23/10/1920

The images depicted in *illustration 1.1* and *illustration 1.2* reflect diametrically opposite representations of crowds. *Illustration 1.1* shows the crowds in Whitehall rioting on the eve of the unveiling of the Cenotaph, while *Illustration 1.2*, of the unveiling ceremony the following day, shows a crowd which is now orderly and contained. Julia Kristeva has argued that when 'revolt exists, our spectacle-oriented society' submerges and renders it impossible by 'distraction-culture, performance-culture, show-culture'.[1] This chapter will investigate the submerging and transformation of the rioting crowd within the visual culture of the commemoration of the First World War and in particular within the promotion of a particular aesthetic language.

A few days after the unveiling of the Cenotaph, Edwin Lutyens, the architect of the monument, received a letter from the Prime Minister, Lloyd George, which said that: 'The Cenotaph by its very simplicity expresses the memory in which

---

1. Kristeva, Julia, 'Revolt Today?', in Kearny, R. and Cooley, M. (eds), *Questioning Ethics. Contemporary Debates in Philosophy* (London: 1999), p. 220.

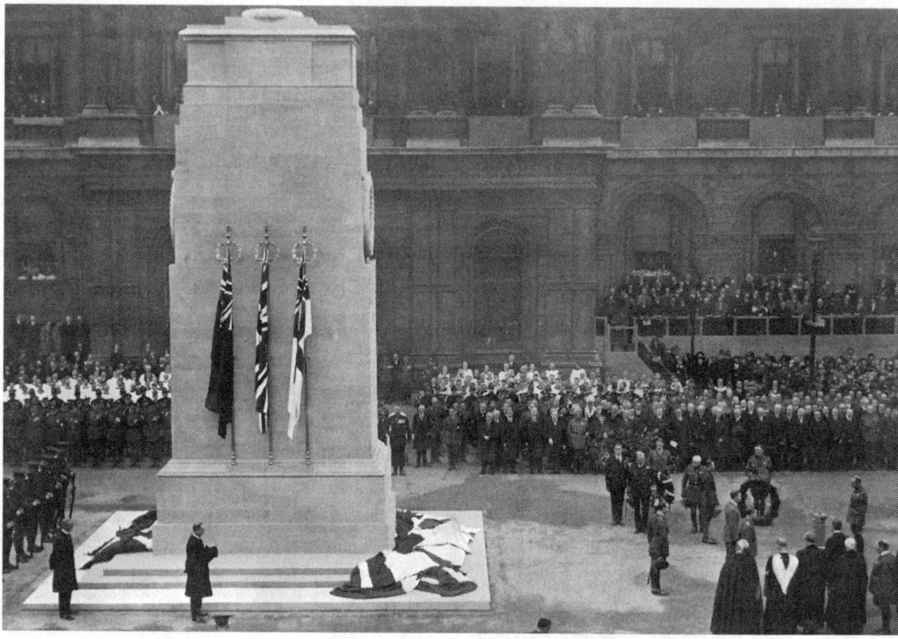

Figure 1.2 The Cenotaph after the unveiling. *The Sphere*, 12/11/1920

the people hold all those who so bravely fought and died in the country.'[2] Lloyd George's letter encapsulates the idea of the universality of simplicity in articulating memories of the war. The notion of simplicity was an aesthetic concept which derived from middle and upper-class artistic sensibilities, and this chapter will reveal how the site of the Cenotaph, its design, the ceremonial unveiling of the monument, and in particular the silence accompanying this unveiling, 'calls one's attention to struggles between classes'.[3] Central to the argument is the fact that the period immediately after the First World War represented a 'crisis' period for the middle classes, something which tends to have been 'expunged from our historical memory'.[4] Most importantly, during the years immediately prior and after the First World War the middle classes identified themselves within cultural debates as the 'constitutional classes', or the 'public', a position which was seen as directly opposed to the working classes.[5] Another major threat for the middle classes was the returning servicemen who came to represent the iconography and

2. Letter from Lloyd George to Edwin Lutyens, 17/11/1920, quoted in Hussey, *The Life of Sir Edwin Lutyens* (London: 1950), p. 394.
3. Sider, Gerald and Smith, Gavin, 'Introduction', *Between History and Histories: The Making of Silences and Commemorations* (Toronto: 1997), p. 7.
4. McKibbin, Ross, *Classes and Cultures. England 1918–1951* (Oxford: 1998), p. 50.
5. Ibid., p. 58.

ideology of the Bolshevist Revolution, and the imaginary potential damage this could inflict on British society and in particular the middle and upper classes. This chapter aims to show that the commemoration of the First World War, and public expressions of grief, were framed by 'dominant narrative forms' which were 'mobilised on behalf of conflicting political positions'.[6] The writer G. K. Chesterton[7] claimed that if he wanted to write a history of modern England, he would hang it on the making of the war memorial in the town where he lived.[8] Whose history *was* this, and how was it being promoted?

Defining the Ideal Memorial

On June 26, 1918, the Royal Academy of Arts held a conference which was attended by 'a number of distinguished officials representing the Church, Government Departments and artistic institutions'.[9] The aim of the conference was not only to promote the interests of artists in acquiring commissions for war memorials,[10] but also, as this chapter will argue, to set standards of aesthetic judgment and taste for the construction of memorials. These aesthetic values were promoted as universal and according to Alex King, were able to present memorials as a 'worthy offering to the dead'.[11] What King does not take into account, is that by promoting these aesthetic values as universal, the conference was laying down a set of parameters which represented a distinct section of the population, the middle and upper classes. By doing so, the conference and subsequent exhibition provided what Ashplant *et al.* have recently identified as the 'micro-politics of

---

6. Ashplant, T. G., Dawson, G. and Roper, M., 'The Politics of War Memory and Commemoration. Contexts, Structures and Dynamics', in Ashplant, T. G., Dawson, G. and Roper, M. (eds), *The Politics of War Memory and Commemoration* (London: 2001), pp. 3–85, p. 14.
7. Chesterton was amongst those whom C. F. G. Masterman, Director of the Department of Information (Propaganda), called on for support. See Hynes, Samuel, *A War Imagined. The First World War and English Culture* (London: 1990), p. 26.
8. Quoted in Inglis, Ken, 'The Homecoming: The War Memorial Movement in Cambridge, England', *Journal of Contemporary History*, 27 (1992), p. 585.
9. Royal Academy of Arts, *Annual Report* (London: 1918), p. 66. The representatives amongst others included, the Earl of Plymouth, Lord Desborough; Lord Henry Bentinck, MP; Lieut. Col. Sir Arthur Leetham (for the Army Council); Sir Alfred Mond MP (First Commissioner of Works); Sir Lionel Earle (Secretary, Office of Works); Sir Frederick Kenyon (Director, British Museum); C. J. Holmes (Director, National Gallery); the Deans of Canterbury, York, Bath and Ely; Brig.-Gen. Fabian Ware; Messrs R. C. Norman (Chairman, LCC); H. T. Hare (PRIBA) and Earl Ferrers (Master, Art Workers' Guild). The conference was chaired by Edward Poynter, and a large number of the members of the Royal Academy were present.
10. Alex King argues that artists recognised the professional benefits to be reaped from the large demand for memorials, and attempted to make the most of these benefits through professional organisation and propaganda. See King, Alex, *Memorials of the Great War. The Symbolism and Politics of Remembrance* (Oxford: 1998), p. 107.
11. Ibid., p. 120.

aesthetic form' and the 'range of identifications' that can be instigated by such aesthetic forms.[12] As Terry Eagleton has argued, the construction of the modern notion of the aesthetic artefact is inseparable from the construction of the dominant ideological forms of modern class-society and, indeed, from a whole new form of human subjectivity appropriate to that social order.[13] As such, the aesthetic forms promoted by the conference and exhibition, and which were meant as the carriers of the memory of the war and the resolution of the grief of the bereaved, sustained what John Gillis has recognised as 'subjective positions' for commemorations, imposing specific 'social boundaries' for sustaining power within a specific group in society.[14] But the question remains, why was there the need for an imposition of social barriers?

The conference at the Royal Academy of Arts opened with a speech by Sir Edward Poynter, president of the Academy, outlining the attitude of the Royal Academy towards the erection of war memorials and the aesthetic qualities that should govern their conception and execution.[15] According to Sir Edward, the most important point to consider in the design of war memorials was that 'simplicity, scale, and proportion needed to be aimed at rather than detail'.[16] What constituted a 'good war memorial' was the 'imaginative and intellectual quality of the work'. It was this quality that gave the memorial 'its final value' by 'unifying the efforts of the public'.[17]

The role of the memorial committees in setting up local memorials was seen as important in determining and guiding the efforts of the public. Recent commentators have attributed a large degree of inclusiveness[18] to memorials of the First World War because the memorial committee was 'rarely free to act in complete autonomy' and remained answerable to the general public whose 'support was vital for funding and the memorial's meaning'.[19] However, funding was where

12. Ashplant *et al.*, 'The Politics of War Memory and Commemoration', p. 37.
13. Eagleton, Terry, *The Ideology of the Aesthetic* (Oxford: 1990), p. 3.
14. Gillis, John, 'Introduction', in Gillis, John (ed.), *Commemorations* (Princeton: 1994), p. 4.
15. Royal Academy of Arts, *Annual Report*, p. 65. A circular in the form of 'suggestions' for war memorials was issued by the Royal Academy to all interested parties before the conference. The suggestions concerned the design and site of the war memorials, and the materials used to construct them.
16. Other points to consider were that a professional artist needed to be employed, and the site and materials for the memorial carefully chosen, in order to do justice to the subject matter. Account needed to be taken of the amount of money available, but most importantly, of the character and availability of local materials. Ibid., p. 66.
17. Ibid.
18. Alex King argues that the commemoration of the war was 'essentially inclusive' because it was a 'socially comprehensive activity', and that although most memorials followed aesthetic and iconographic precedents, they were not left to speak for themselves in an established symbolic language. See King, *Memorials of the Great War*, pp. 246–7.
19. Moriarty, Catherine, 'Private Grief and Public Remembrance: British First World War Memorials', in Evans, M. and Lunn, Ken (eds), *War and Memory in the Twentieth Century* (Oxford: 1997), p. 127.

the representation of a whole community stopped. The various social and political sectors were not always represented and only in few instances could the make-up of the committees be described as truly representative. Committee members in some instances were 'public representatives who would most likely form a powerful and influential committee'.[20] How, then, could memorial committees claim to be expressing the grief felt by all sectors of the community, and was it possible for the memorials of the First World War to have universal[21] and democratic[22] appeal? What was proposed at the conference, and subsequently became a unifying factor, was the development of an aesthetic language for war memorials. However, it should not be overlooked that this language still only belonged to a small section of the population, the middle and upper classes, who made up the audience of the Royal Academy conference.

The conference delegates were in unanimous agreement with Sir Edward on the need to unify the efforts of the public. Collective representation and a unified aesthetic were the means of providing this. The Earl of Plymouth, Lord Desborough,[23] argued that the question of the control of war memorials was one which 'universally affected our lives'. He urged the Royal Academy members and other experts to 'take every possible step to keep before the public the pre-eminent claims of art in the matter of patriotic commemoration'.[24] Lord Crawford[25] voiced fears that the individualism of the English nation would re-emerge after the collective effort of the war, and that the Royal Academy needed to 'induce collective effort' in the 'permanent records'[26] of the achievements of the war. What was at work here was the construction of a system of artistic control through the establishment of hegemonic aesthetic notions of what constituted an appropriate war memorial. The establishment of such ideas required the

20. The committee in Islington, for example, comprised a number of councillors, MPs, clergy, heads of charity and the local Hospital Extension Committee. Metropolitan Borough of Islington, Minutes of Proceedings, 26 May 1919 quoted in King, *Memorials of the Great War*, p. 30.

    Sometimes members were elected at a public meeting, but in many instances they were chosen by the proposer of the scheme or another individual with influence. A few operated in virtual autonomy, and in some cases persuasive individuals dominated the decision making. See Moriarty, 'Private Grief and Public Remembrance', p. 127.
21. For the universality of the appeal of First World War memorials, see Winter, Jay, *Sites of Memory, Sites of Mourning. The Great War in European Cultural History* (Cambridge: 1995).
22. Inglis, K. S., 'War Memorials: Ten Questions for Historians', *Guerres Mondiales et Conflicts*, 42/167 (1992), p. 7.
23. Lord Desborough was president of the Volunteer Training Corps during the period of the First World War.
24. Royal Academy of Arts, *Annual Report*, p. 68.
25. Lord Crawford was an art collector and the Conservative Party Chief Whip from 1911.
26. Royal Academy of Arts, *Annual Report*, p. 68.

organisation of 'strong body of artistic opinion' which would 'temper enthusiasm with discretion'.[27]

Sir Alfred Mond hoped that the move would 'succeed in saving the country from the erection of unsightly objects intended to commemorate the war'.[28] He may also have been referring to the shrines that emerged during the war, which originated from the Church of England's wartime evangelism and support from the press. The movement to built shrines was mainly targeted at women,[29] and, as such, found opponents who saw the unmanliness of the shrines as offensive, leading the nation away from the 'manly faith of true Protestantism'.[30] By implication, Sir Alfred Mond not only established what constituted an acceptable form of commemoration, but also defined the masculinisation of the memorial designs away from the realm of the feminine qualities which shrines symbolised This was particularly poignant in a period when, as Alison Light has argued, masculinity and the ideas of the nation were perceived as being 'feminised'.[31] Most importantly, as Margaret Higonnet *et al.* note, after the First World War, messages of reintegration are expressed within a rhetoric of gender which assigns distinct social positions to men and women.[32]

A press release issued by the Royal Academy of Arts and dated November 20, 1918 also promoted the need for the memorials to incorporate aesthetic values that could represent the nation's feelings towards the war. The representatives of the Royal Academy encouraged the notion that memorials should express the 'emotion of the present' without losing touch with the past, and that 'instead of being a rock of offence to future generations, they should be objects of veneration'.[33] Most importantly, what the various establishments represented at the conference wanted was for the war memorials to express the ideals of courage and patriotism of those who had died, without sacrificing 'any of that older beauty' which was 'England's legacy from an immemorial past'.[34] In this way the aesthetics of beauty came to reflect a national identity and form a bridge connecting the period before and the period after the First World War. The press release signals an issue that interests scholars today: the effect that the war had

27. Ibid.
28. Ibid.
29. King, Alex, *Memorials of the Great War*, p. 55.
30. *Church Family Newspaper*, 10 November 1916, quoted in ibid., p. 53.
31. Light, Alison, *Forever England. Femininity, Literature and Conservatism between the Wars* (London: 1991), p.10. See also Kent, Susan Kingsley, *Making Peace. The Reconstruction of Gender in Interwar Britain* (Princeton: 1993).
32. Higonnet, Margaret *et al.*, 'Introduction', in Higonnet, M., Jenson, J., Michel, S., Collins Weitz, M. (eds), *Behind the Lines. Gender and the Two World Wars* (New Haven: 1987), p. 4.
33. Royal Academy, *Annual Report*, p. 70.
34. Royal Academy, *Annual Report*, p. 68.

on the birth of modernism. Paul Fussell[35] and Modris Eksteins[36] see the war as playing a fundamental role in breaking the cultural traditions of the pre-war era whereas for Jay Winter the commemoration of the war in particular looked to pre-war years for its inspiration in the use of traditional motifs in memorials. For Winter, the use of traditional forms becomes a 'way of remembering which enabled the bereaved to live with their losses'. Such motifs are seen as possessing a special 'power to mediate bereavement'.[37] However, these same motifs also served another purpose. As Ashplant *et al.* argue, by concentrating on the 'metanarrative of the birth of the modern [it] obscures a more contextualised discussion of aesthetic forms'.[38] By defining what was beautiful and acceptable, the conference was attempting to create a spontaneous consensus.

As a result of the conference, the Royal Academy hosted an exhibition on war memorials jointly with the Victoria and Albert Museum.[39] The purpose of the exhibition was to assist 'the promoters of War Memorials and others who may be interested in the subject, by providing them with a successful survey of modern works by competent artists'. Memorial committees often sought advice on engaging artists, and the Leicester memorial committee called on the services of the architect Edwin Lutyens, giving him a 'free hand as to the form' the memorial should take.[40]

It is also important at this point to see the exhibition within the wider context of the museum and exhibition space at the time. Annie Coombes comments that ethnographic collections and exhibitions helped to promote support for class unity.[41] Tony Bennett argues that the Victoria and Albert Museum, which opened in the nineteenth century provided a means of displaying new instruments for the moral and cultural regulation of the working classes and 'exposing [the working

35. Fussell, Paul, *The Great War and Modern Memory* (Oxford: 1975).
36. Eksteins, Modris, *Rites of Spring. The Great War and the Birth of the Modern Age* (Oxford: 1989).

    Samuel Hynes stresses both the continuity and change, pointing to modernist elements in culture prior to 1914 and the persistence of older cultural forms after 1918. According to Hynes, the war is not the sole instigator of change but still relates to a new way of seeing the world. Hynes, Samuel, *A War Imagined*.
37. Winter defines traditional motifs as an eclectic set of classical romantic or religious images and ideas. Winter, Jay, *Sites of Memory*, p. 5.
38. Ashplant, T., *et al.*, 'The Politics of War Memory and Commemoration', p. 37.
39. The exhibition was organised by a special committee appointed by the executive committee selected at the conference. The members of the executive committee included the President of the Royal Academy, architects and sculptors such as J. S. Sargent RA and Capt. F. Derwent Wood ARA. All the sculptors who became members of the committee went on to receive important commissions for war memorials. The minutes of the committee no longer survive at the Royal Academy Archives. Royal Academy, *Annual Report*, p. 66.
40. Leicester Memorial Committee, 'The Arch of Remembrance', IWM, Ephemera, Memorials, Box C.
41. Coombes, Annie E., 'Ethnography and the Formation of National and Cultural Identities', in Hiller, Susan (ed.), *The Myth of Primitivism. Perspectives on Art* (London: 1991), p. 197.

classes] to the improving influences of the middle-classes'.[42] Within this context and in the absence of any attendance figures, one assumes that the few working-class members of the memorial committees that visited the exhibition of war memorials would have assimilated such educational influences from the middle classes.

The war memorial exhibition was divided into two sections: a retrospective section, and a modern section indicating the importance that traditional forms played in informing the construction of a new aesthetic in the commemoration of the war.[43] The material was selected on the 'principle that all the works and designs shown should have some direct reference to war, or should provide some definite suggestion for the treatment of War Memorials'. Visitors could obtain further information from a 'Bureau of References', including 'lists of qualified artists'[44] that could have been employed for the design of memorials.

The retrospective section of the exhibition included 'not only works of art which have served as memorials in the past, but others which may be regarded as offering useful suggestions to the designers of such memorials in the various crafts at the present time'.[45] It therefore melded English tradition and history with the future production of memorials. There were also exhibits which provided some association with contemporary realities, thereby reflecting the temporary nature of the exhibition without breaking any ties with the past and tradition. One example of this was carpet weaving; an internal memo from the curator justified the inclusion of carpet weaving by saying that it 'was important to have a pattern of a carpet which might be used, for example as a model for a sanctuary carpet' but most importantly in view of 'the taking-up of carpet-knotting by disabled soldiers'.[46] This is one of the very few times that the disabled ex-servicemen are acknowledged by the commemorative machine.[47]

---

42. Bennett, Tony, 'The Exhibitionary Complex', in Greenberg, R., Ferguson, B., Nairne, S. (eds), *Thinking About Exhibitions* (London: 1996), pp. 92–5.
43. Part of the modern section was later transferred to the Royal Academy.
44. Royal Academy, *War Memorials Exhibition*, 20 October to 29 November 1919, Catalogue, no pagination.
45. Letter from Cecil Smith to the Right Rev Bishop Ryle, Dean of Westminster, Victoria & Albert Museum Archives, Nominal File, Exhibition of War Memorials July–Oct 1919, Letter dated 12/05/1919. Such items included a knotted English carpet displaying the Royal Arms, dating back to the sixteenth century.
46. Ibid.
47. The implications of the idealisation of the male body in the commemoration of the war will be discussed in more detail in Chapter 3.

    The implications of disability for returning ex-servicemen are discussed by Joanna Bourke, who argues that those maimed by the war struggled to create new lives that challenged their status as physically disabled people but that this challenge was not met with support from the government and society at large. According to Bourke, any respect that had been given initially to the disabled ex-servicemen, ended by the late 1920s.

The exhibition and its aims also gave rise to some reservations relating to standardisation and the uniformity of the memorials. In an internal memo to the director of the Victoria and Albert Museum, the curator, A. Kendrick voiced his own fears. Firstly, he pointed out, the 'standardisation of Art' had traditionally favoured only a few artists and architects and continuing this practice would lead to 'an inevitable tendency to sameness in the result'. Secondly, local interest in the memorial would not be enhanced 'by the fact that a well known artist in London was responsible for the memorial'. Thirdly, the museum's involvement in recommending particular artists meant that other artists with whom the museum was in touch would be ignored. The consequence of this was that 'these people would naturally be annoyed at the idea that advice given in the Museum would tend largely to withdraw from them any opportunities they may have had of being entrusted with local memorials'.[48]

Kendrick's fears and reservations proved to be justified. The majority of the memorial committees favoured a few 'London artists' including the architect Edwin Lutyens. Their advice and designs became much sought after, as in the case of the Leicester memorial committee who sought Lutyen's advice on the basis of his design for the Cenotaph in London.[49] The standardised designs for memorials, such as the Celtic Cross, the soldier in various military stances and the Cenotaph, were later reproduced throughout Britain.

The exhibition received mixed reviews. Art reviewers and influential magazines such as *Country Life* seemed to be in agreement that the purpose of the exhibition was not 'supplying material which may actually be used as memorials' but to provide 'suggestions which may be of assistance'. They also seemed to agree with the idea of breaking the exhibition into sections and juxtaposing old and new designs for memorials. The *Architects Journal*, which represented the views of the architectural profession, wrote: 'With great appropriateness, a model of the *Wellington Memorial* by Alfred Stevens stands near the entrance of the modern section: the spirit of the past presiding over the efforts of the present.'[50] Anchoring the works in the past provided not only a safeguard for their aesthetic qualities, but also offered a link and continuation with the past, something which the war seemed to have disrupted.

Where the critics differed was on the quality of the work displayed in the modern section of the exhibition and the ideal design for a memorial. There were several reasons for this discrepancy, but most prominent was the difficulty of finding an artistic language to express the devastation of the war. Most

See Bourke, Joanna, *Dismembering the Male. Men's Bodies, Britain and the Great War* (London: 1996), p. 15.

48. Internal Memo from the curator, A. Kendrick to Cecil Smith, 02/06/1919, Victoria & Albert Museum Archives, Nominal File, Exhibition of War Memorials July–Oct 1919. The memo was marked confidential, indicating the sensitivity of its content.

49. Leicester Memorial Committee, 'The Arch of Remembrance'.

50. *Architects Journal*, 16 July 1919, Victoria & Albert Museum Archives, Nominal File, Exhibition of War Memorials July–Oct 1919, press cuttings.

importantly, the critics felt that the designs lacked monumentality. *Country Life* criticised the work in the modern section as displaying 'absence of character, conviction, often even craftsmanship'.[51] The critic toned down his criticism, however, by arguing that the real problem lay in finding a language, a convention, in which the artist 'can naturally express his own emotions', and that 'simplicity and common sense' were what was needed. In fact, the only consensus amongst critics seemed to be on the importance of simplicity in the design of war memorials.[52] *The Times* affirmed that the most important aspect to take into consideration for the memorials was simplicity, the use of appropriate material, and a return to basics and order.[53]

Kenneth Silver, commenting on reactions to the war in France, argued that purity and simplicity reflected a new 'post-war spirit of traditional order, proportion, clarity and discipline'[54] which established the 'triumph of French taste' and a 'glorious manifestation of the post war sense of national identity'.[55] He referred to the Purist movement and its use of simplicity and tradition as taking an 'anti-revolutionary stance' that gave voice to a 'very real fear abroad in post-war France'.[56] This book will argue that the notion of simplicity as promoted within the construction of war memorials in the period after the First World War formed a similar but distinct aesthetic to the reconstruction debates in France. The British aesthetic of simplicity was, as in the case of Purism in France, an anti-revolutionary aesthetic that saw tradition as its main inspiration. Unlike its French counterpart the British aesthetic of simplicity was entrenched in class ideology and did not aspire to cultural progress. The British commemoration of the war also offered a vehicle for reconstruction and a means of accepting the civil unrest that followed the war. As Bob Bushaway argues, the theme of remembrance permeated British society and resulted in the 'denial of any political critique' of the war and of post war society. Popular expectations which elsewhere took the form of revolution or nationalism, in Britain were subsumed within the overarching theme of remembrance.[57]

51. Clutton-Brock, A., 'The War Memorials Exhibition at the Victoria and Albert Museum', *Country Life*, 19 July 1919.
52. Ibid.
53. *The Times*, 16 July 1919.
54. Silver, Kenneth, *Esprit de Corps. The Art of the Parisian Avant-Garde and the First World War, 1914–1925* (London: 1989), p. 368.
55. Ibid., p. 367.
56. Ibid., p. 390.
57. Bushaway, Bob, 'Name Upon Name: The Great War and Remembrance', in Porter, R. (ed.), *Myths of the English* (London: 1992), pp. 136–67, p. 137. Adrian Gregory has criticised Bushaway's approach as using 'traditional Marxist analysis of false consciousness' leading him to overemphasize the use of commemoration as a 'force of integration beneficial in averting political polarisation' thus over-determining the use of memory in its relationship to politics. See Gregory, *The Silence of Memory*, p. 3.

Simplicity was also recommended by a number of other publications published at this time. A writer for the Civic Arts Association,[58] A. C. Benson, argued that memorials should not only 'remind us' but also 'kindle emotion and imagination'. This could be achieved, according to Benson, through 'beauty, dignity, simplicity and force.' He also made the connection between the 'simplicity' of those who fell and the simplicity of the memorial itself: 'We are not likely to forget the war; but, what we may forget is that the result of it is the outcome of modest, faithful, loyal services done with no flourish or vanity, by thousands of very simple, straightforward people.'[59]

In the same article Benson identified certain characteristics, such as modesty, faithfulness and loyalty, which he attributes to the middle classes and to the middle-class man in particular.[60] These values were promoted within the discourse of the commemoration of the war and incorporate what Terry Eagleton describes as the 'aestheticisation of power'. Eagleton argues that the ultimate binding force of the bourgeois social order are the habits, pieties, sentiments and affections governing their lives, and that power is inscribed into these subjective experiences.[61]

It is precisely these subjective experiences that the commemoration of the First World War sought to promote. The unveiling ceremonies functioned as what Pierre Nora describes as 'sites of memory'.[62] In many cases these sites represented the most significant public event to take place in years and were attended by entire communities, with shops closing and other activities suspended for the duration. The ceremonies included elaborate processions, and were carefully orchestrated to convey certain notions and codes of behaviour, such as self-sacrifice, comradeship, devotion to the good of others, and manliness. The memorial committees ensured that all sections of the community were represented at the ceremony and there was a special enclosure for the bereaved, although they were obliged to apply for a certain number of tickets in advance. A local government or military official was usually given the responsibility of describing the local war effort and the background to the memorial. This allowed the authorities to announce how the memorial was to be interpreted and to explain the iconography of the memorial.

58. The Civic Arts Association was part of the Civic Societies Movement. Alex King argues that the movement promoted a non-party activism in the cause of urban improvement and the improvement of social conditions. See King, *Memorials of the Great War*, pp.101–2.

59. Benson, A. C., *Lest We Forget* (London: 1917), p. 15.

60. From the nineteenth century onwards these characteristics usually centred on notions of self-discipline and the 'cult of the Great Man'. See Pears, Iain, 'The Gentleman and the Hero: Wellington and Napoleon in the Nineteenth Century', in Porter, R. (ed.), *Myths of the English*, p. 217 and Dawson, Graham, *Soldier Heroes. British Adventure, Empire and the Imagining of Masculinities* (London: 1994) in relation to the cult of the soldier hero in early twentieth century Britain.

61. Eagleton, Terry, *The Ideology of the Aesthetic*, p. 20.

62. Nora, Pierre, 'Between Memory and History: *Les Lieux de Mémoire*', *Representations*, 26 (1989): 7–25.

According to Moriarty, the ceremonial was an opportunity for 'visiting dignitaries to reiterate the meaning of war'.[63]

It was during these unveiling ceremonies that the aesthetic of simplicity was promoted, integrated and accepted by those present as a means of conveying the memory of war. It was an aesthetic that was imposed hegemonically. As an abstract idea simplicity very much emphasised difference rather than alleviated it. This contrasts to Alex King's arguement that 'memorials were symbolic objects that transcended differences amongst participants through the practical activities and not the abstract ideas that were associated with them'.[64]

The *Gateshead Memorial* provides an example of abstract ideas of simplicity becoming an integral part of the commemoration in order to promote ideas of class unity and control. The souvenir programme accompanying the unveiling of the memorial states that all classes, 'from the Mayor of the Borough to the humblest members of the community were alike in their willingness to back their country's cause', and that the 'dweller in the low street was as sensitive to the varying fortunes of the War as the villa or suburban terrace resident'. However, this became problematic with the end of the war and the Armistice celebrations. The inhabitant of the 'low streets' was 'more openly demonstrative and picturesque' than the 'suburban terrace resident' and the 'noble' Gateshead Cenotaph was erected to rectify this anomaly in taste and uncontrolled emotions.[65] With its 'classic design' – supplied by yet another London architect and sculptor[66] – the Cenotaph becomes the antidote to the execrable taste of the inhabitants of the 'low streets', confirming the fears of the Victoria and Albert Museum curator that a handful of London artists would take over the memorial design business, leading to 'an inevitable tendency to sameness in the result'.[67]

The aesthetic of simplicity permeated the commemoration of the war. The memorial in Arbroath, for example, was described as symbolising the 'simplicity, the constancy' and the 'repose of those it commemorates'.[68] The *Balydon Memorial* was meant to bring consolation to the bereaved through its beauty and simplicity.[69] The *Crompton Memorial* was described as 'entirely free from any superfluous detail'.[70] The *LNWR Euston Memorial* was described as presenting a 'dignified and

63. Moriarty, Catherine, 'Private Grief and Public Remembrance', p. 130.
64. King, Alex, 'Remembering and Forgetting in the Public Memorials of the Great War', in Forty, A. and Kuchler, S., (eds), *The Art of Forgetting* (Oxford: 1999), p. 148.
65. Gateshead Memorial Committee, *Gateshead and the Great War. A Retrospective and a Reminder*, IWM, Ephemera, Memorials, Box C, p. 24.
66. The architect of the memorial was John Spink and the sculptor for the soldier and bronze panels was Richard Goulden. See ibid., p. 12.
67. Internal Memo from Kendrick to Cecil Smith, Marked Confidential, Victoria & Albert Museum Archives, Nominal File, Exhibition of War Memorials July–Oct 1919, 02/06/1919.
68. Arbroath War Memorial Committee, IWM, Ephemera, Memorials, Box C.
69. Balydon War Memorial Committee, IWM, Ephemera, Memorials, Box C.
70. Crompton Memorial Committee, IWM, Ephemera, Memorials, Box C.

imposing affair' through the 'austerity of the obelisk'.[71] The simplicity and classic design may not have provided a vehicle for the grief of the bereaved or transcended social differences but the memorials, through their aesthetic consideration, provide an interesting exercise in social reconstruction and harmony as promoted by civil institutions.

The idea of simplicity as promoted during this period can be traced back to 1916. In a pamphlet published by the Civic Arts Association, Arthur Clutton-Brock[72] argued that memorials should speak simply and precisely. 'Please give us war memorials, simple and expressive. That is all we want',[73] he begged. This was not just a plea for simplicity of design, but a plea for simplicity in the inscription,[74] language and lettering of the monument. The plea for simplicity particularly applied to village memorials, which needed to be seen to be humble and to 'have been made by the villagers in order to express their own native sorrow and pride'. This has important implications for the way that the association saw the memorials, especially village memorials, as central to their design. Alex King has demonstrated the ways in which the civic movement aimed to consolidate social harmony through the aesthetic improvement of urban environments.[75] Clutton-Brock promoted war memorials as a means of social harmony. The social harmony in this instance moved away from the confines of the urban environment, which the civic association was aiming to improve, and into the British countryside, a place that has always played an important role in defining and shaping British identity and often became 'a national mythology mobilised at times of political tension to figure some essence of true Englishness'.[76]

Nick Mansfield has argued recently that it is easy to assume that a sense of national interest predominated during this period, and to underestimate the extent of class conflict that existed in the countryside.[77] As such, the designs and unveilings of war memorials in villages could provide an exercise in social harmony. The unveiling of the *Skirling Memorial* offers a glimpse into the way in which this was constructed through aesthetic notions of simplicity. The memorial was unveiled by Lady Carmichael, a member of the committee. The souvenir programme for the unveiling ceremony comments that the architect, 'guided by the counsel of Lord and Lady Carmichael', created a 'graceful and tasteful monument'. The

71. Euston Memorial, NIWM, File 2087.
72. Arthur Clutton-Brock was also the art critic of *The Times*.
73. Clutton-Brock, A., *On War Memorials* (London: 1916), p. 5.
74. The Victoria and Albert Museum published a booklet with suggested inscriptions for memorials. See Victoria and Albert Museum, *Inscriptions Suggested for War Memorials* (London: 1919).
75. King, Alex, *Memorials of the Great War*, pp. 101–2.
76. Potts, Alex, '"Constable Country" Between the Wars', in Raphael, Samuel (ed.), *Patriotism: The Making and the Unmaking of British National Identity. Vol. 3, National Fictions* (London: 1989), p. 160.
77. Mansfield, Nick, 'Class Conflict and Village War Memorials, 1914–24', *Rural History*, 6/1 (1995), p. 71.

monument, which takes the form of a Mercat Cross, sits on an oval pedestal.[78] The souvenir programme describes the ceremony as 'simple and impressive', noting that 'the silent crowd gathered at the foot of the cross, surrounded on all sides by the green hills in clear atmosphere and calm sunshine, while near by lay the autumnal fields thickly studded with sheaves of yellow'.[79] The 'eternal' countryside provides not only the backdrop but also the rhetoric to the memorial committee. The sublime language used to describe the countryside also lends itself to the construction of an aesthetic language for the memorial. Both aim for a seamless past that is rooted in a sense of Britishness. It is worth noting that Skirling is in Scotland, but at the unveiling Lord Carmichael had no qualms about stating that 'the cement, that binds all the structure together, is English, and shows us, I hope that "auld enemies" may become close friends'.[80] In the same way that a Scottish regional identity is subsumed within the Englishness of the stone, any ideological differences are subsumed within the idea of self-sacrifice that the memorial is meant to inspire. The only way of achieving this 'working together' was, according to Lord Carmichael, to '[keep] clearly before us the example set by the men whom we are honouring this afternoon'.[81]

Consensus on the 'right public opinion' is problematic from the start, as in Ernesto Laclau's view it constitutes a 'contingent universality'. Laclau, drawing on Gramsci's theory of hegemony, argues that if the hegemony of a particular social sector depends for its success on presenting its own aims as the universal aims of the community, then this sector constitutively requires political mediation and specific relations to modes of representation.[82] During the period after the First World War, Laclau argues, the notion of 'organised capitalism' prevailed.[83] The commemoration of the First World War was part of a 'laborious construction' which aimed to establish the dominance of the middle classes at a time when, according to Antonio Gramsci, 'cracks opened up everywhere in the hegemonic apparatus'.[84] These cracks will be examined in more detail in order to establish the relationship between events taking place in Russia at that time, the commemoration of the war in Britain and the 'hegemonic framing of the memory'[85] of the First World War.

78. Skirling Memorial Committee, p. 3.
79. Ibid.
80. Ibid.
81. Ibid., p. 7.
82. Laclau, Ernesto, 'Identity and Hegemony: The Role of Universality in the Constitution of Political Logics', in Butler, J., Laclau, E., and Zizek, S. (eds), *Contingency, Hegemony, Universality. Contemporary Dialogues on the Left* (London: 2000), p. 51.
83. Ibid., p. 52.
84. Gramsci, Antonio, *Selections from the Prison Notebooks*, Hoare, Q. and Nowell Smith, G. (eds) (London: Lawrence & Wishart, 1971), p. 80f.
85. Ashplant, T. *et al.*, *The Politics of War Memory and Commemoration*, p. 53.

Bolshevism and the Returning Ex-Servicemen

While the exhibition on war memorials was underway the *Illustrated London News* (*ILN*) documented the destruction of Tsarist monuments in Russia by the Bolshevists. But what was being documented? Was this merely photo-reportage of a series of events taking place in a foreign country, or were the visual images intended to symbolise a more deeply rooted fear within British society?

What the *ILN* was reporting was Lenin's *Plan for Monumental Propaganda.*[86] Lenin's plan was conceived and implemented in April 1918. According to Christina Lodder, Lenin was making an 'imaginative and visionary leap by realising the potential of visual propaganda'[87] and in particular the use of monuments and the unveiling rituals. But to what extent did the events in Russia influence the commemoration of the First World War in Britain and did the erection of memorials in Britain serve as a means of visual propaganda? The obvious difference between the two situations lies in the fact that Russia in the 1920s was operating under a totalitarian regime which relied on coercion, while Britain was a liberal democracy which required public consent to promote particular beliefs and ideologies. This section, however, will aim to show that the events in Russia provided a catalyst for the fears of the middle and upper classes in Britain towards the working classes. The argument follows the assertion from Ashplant *et al.* that any analysis of war memory and commemoration must 'also be sensitive to the dynamics of change that are operating trans-nationally, and the ways in which they impact 'within national contexts'.[88]

Lenin's *Plan for Monumental Propaganda* was announced in the Soviet press in April 1918. It consisted of two parts: the systematic demolition of Tsarist monuments, and the replacement of these structures with 'monuments to outstanding persons in the field of revolutionary and social activity, philosophy, literature, science and art'.[89] The demolition of the Tsarist monuments represented an iconoclastic act to expunge the memory of the Tsarist regime and the social order that prevailed, and impose a new social order. As Victor Misiano comments in Laura Mulvey's and Mark Lewis' film *Disgraced Monuments*, 'all successful

86. Lodder, Christina, 'Lenin's Plan for Monumental Propaganda', in M. Cullene-Brown and B. Taylor (eds), *Art of the Soviets. Painting, Sculpture and Architecture in a One-Party State 1917–1992* (Manchester: 1993), p. 18.

87. Ibid.

88. The need for a trans-national view of war memory and commemoration also contradicts Jay Winter's universalising view of First World War grief and commemoration across Europe. See Winter, Jay, *Sites of Memory*.

For an opposing view see Ashplant, T. *et al.*, *The Politics of War Memory and Commemoration*, p. 15. Also Marwick, Arthur, 'Two Total Wars, the Cold War and Postmodernism: the Arts in Europe, 1910–2000', in Emsley, C. (ed.), *War, Culture and Memory* (Milton Keynes: 2003), p. 203.

89. Quoted in Lodder, Christina, 'Lenin's Plan for Monumental Propaganda', p. 20.

revolutions end with statues coming down'.[90] However, Lenin knew that this iconoclastic act in itself was not sufficient to erase the memories of the old regime, and that he needed to reclaim the sites of the old monuments and the memories they conveyed. He was anxious that part of the second stage of the Plan should be achieved in time for the May Day celebrations in 1918. The monuments, which were to be set up 'in suitable corners of the capital', would 'serve the aim of extensive propaganda' rather than immortalisation. Most importantly, there would be a ceremonial unveiling of the monuments.

The ceremonies to unveil the new monuments were scheduled for Sundays, to ensure maximum attendance. There would be speeches and music to make the ceremonies 'an act of propaganda', with short biographies of the person celebrated in the memorial and brochures to provide a permanent record.[91] In this way, the ritualised dismantling of the old regime's symbols and their replacement by revolutionary symbols became a feature of the reconstruction of society. What, then, was the significance of the *ILN* feature? The answer lies in the way the revolution was perceived in Britain and especially the way in which the masculinity of the working-class man was viewed by particular sections of the community. This is captured in the reconstruction debates that will be discussed in what follows.

The problems that Britain would face at the end of the war were widely debated during the war years. The Ministry of Reconstruction[92] was set up in 1917 specifically to deal with these problems, which were seen as 'picking up the broken threads' and 'renewing the old habits and traditions'.[93] The Ministry identified its main objective as the increase of industrial output, but recognised three potential challenges to this aim: first, the war had 'greatly altered the attitude of the worker'; second, the returning soldier did not intend to return to the 'low paid conditions of life which characterised a part of British industry before the war'; third, and most alarmingly for the industrialists, 'large changes in the relations of employers and employed were inevitable'.[94] The Ministry argued that the only way forward was for the confidence of the returning soldiers

---

90. *Disgraced Monuments* (1992), directed by M. Lewis and L. Mulvey. Quoted in Forty, Adrian, and Kuchler, Susanne (eds), *The Art of Forgetting* (Oxford: 1999), p. 10.

    More recently, the destruction of the monuments of Saddam Hussein by the 'allied forces' in Iraq provides another instance of iconoclasm and the attempt to erase and reclaim the memories of Hussein's regime. The covering of the statue of Saddam first by the American flag and subsequently by the Iraqi flag, followed by the toppling of the statue, became symbolic of the collapse of Baghdad into the hands of the American forces.

91. Lodder, Christina, 'Lenin's Plan for Monumental Propaganda', p. 22.

92. See Morgan, Kenneth, *Consensus and Disunity. The Lloyd George Coalition Government 1918–1922* (Oxford: 1979), for a detailed discussion of the work of the Ministry of Reconstruction.

93. Ministry of Reconstruction, *The Aims of Reconstruction* (London: 1918), p. 3.

94. Ibid., p. 9.

to be re-gained and their 'co-operation enlisted'.[95] It appealed to the patriotism of the ex-servicemen, calling on them to understand 'how their work' was 'needed for the sake of the future of the country in the same way as they learned to understand the purpose and meaning of their military duties'.[96] The Ministry was effectively constructing an idealised memory of the war, erasing from public memory any examples of unrest.

While the Ministry of Reconstruction was formulating government policy in relation to the problems that Britain would face at the end of the war, a series of five articles was launched in *The Times*, attacking the working class and what they perceived to be the real threat emanating from the current of industrial unrest sweeping across the country. The anonymous author, who claimed that he wrote the articles because he was a 'patriotic Englishman', criticised the fact that the government's reaction to the industrial unrest was to set up a commission of enquiry.[97] He claimed that the government had ignored the real movements that were at work, which 'aimed at the complete overthrow of the existing economic and social order', and that Britain was witnessing a 'revolutionary ferment', spread by 'the intellectually inclined young men of the well-paid wage-earning class,' and inspired by a 'string of theories incompatible with the present organisation of society.' Even more alarming than this, to the author of the series, was the fact that these men could contemplate and spread such theories in the middle of a 'dangerous war'. They were 'prepared to risk their country's independence for the delights of universal disorder'. They couldn't be patriotic because the 'revolutionist knows no country and he is blind to most facts'. This was evidenced by the absence of any mention of war in the 'petty magazines' and 'periodical fly-sheets' of the revolutionaries. The 'pacifism' to which these publications referred was in its way 'a revolutionary movement', the author of *The Times* articles warned. However, these revolutionary men should not be confused with the pacifist or the conscientious objector, both of whom were distinguished by their middle-class or bourgeois associations. They were working-class men with 'oratorial skills' and 'disciples of the teaching of Karl Marx' and, according to *The Times*, were 'inordinately proud of themselves' and 'loquacious'.[98]

95. Ibid.
96. Ibid.
97. The government responded to the outbreak of strikes in the spring of 1917 and the general growing discontent among the working class. In June 1917 Lloyd George appointed eight commissions to enquire into the industrial unrest and to make recommendations to the Government. The reports gave detailed examples of the widespread unhappiness among the working classes. Particularly important among the findings were the high prices, especially in food, restrictions of personal freedom because of the enforcement of the Defence Of The Realm Act, restrictions on alcohol, lack of housing and dilution of labour. See Bentley, Gilbert, *British Social Policy, 1914–1939* (London: 1970), p. 11.
98. This is based on a series of articles published in *The Times* starting on 25 September 1917. The author of the articles is not named. See *The Times*, 25 September 1917.

The working-class background of the revolutionaries was much to blame for their attitudes. According to the author, the nation was divided into two distinct communities. The series of articles sets out the 'relational identities'[99] of the two communities and of 'Old England' as the legitimising identity,[100] constructed through tradition and historical institutions. The 'Labour Nation' was earning a considerable amount of money, and although it contributed to the war effort in terms of providing soldiers and finances, its contribution in comparison with the rest of the society was 'light'. What the author referred to as 'Old England' still functioned, and was the Old England of the nineteenth century. It was a community that included both rich and poor, while the 'Labour Nation' by contrast had in many instances more money in its disposal. What is interesting here, is the characteristics that the author uses to define 'Old England': an attachment to 'individualistic theories', 'saving habits', and a 'willing submission to the authority of Parliament'.[101] The series clearly sets the parameters of two 'imagined communities',[102] each with its own distinct stereotype: the overpaid, selfish working-class man, and the selfless, hardworking and underpaid middle-class man who gave rise to an 'anti-working class folklore'.[103] Such attitudes were widespread and reflected in the writings of the Liberal cabinet minister C. F. G. Masterman, who argued that the 'municipality pays its scavengers and street cleaners substantially higher salaries than it pays its elementary school teachers'.[104]

It was not only the press, however, who were preoccupied with the events in Russia. The government was becoming increasingly agitated about the way that the Russian Revolution was developing, especially in relation to the repercussions it might have for Britain. Special reports commissioned by the government were sent back to Britain on a regular basis throughout the Russian Revolution and immediately afterwards, and formally published in 1919.[105] The individual reports paint a horrific picture of the destruction that was wrought by the Revolution. It is worth noting, however, the emphasis that the reports place on certain emblems and sections of the community. For example, the report of September 3, 1918,

99. Hall, Stewart, 'Cultural Identity and Diaspora', in Rutherford, J. (ed.), *Identity: Community, Culture, Difference* (London: 1990).

100. Castells, Manuel, *The Power of Identity* (Oxford: 1997), p. 8.

101. The above are based on the first two articles of the series published on September 25 and 26 1917 in *The Times*.

102. Anderson, Benedict, *Imagined Communities. Reflections on the Origins and Spread of Nationalism* (London: 1994).

103. McKibbin, Ross, *Classes and Cultures*, p. 57.

104. Masterman, Charles, *England After the War. A Study* (London: 1922), p. 76, quoted in McKibbin, Ross, ibid., p. 57. McKibbin argues that *no* municipality paid its dustmen more than its elementary schoolteachers: even in 1920 the income of a male elementary schoolteacher was more than twice that of a local authority labourer.

105. Parliamentary Reports, 'A Collection of Reports on Bolshevism in Russia', No.1 (1919), April 1919, Cmd8, Vol. Liii.

describes the destruction of the British Embassy by revolutionary troops. The report highlights the manner in which the Cross of St. George was taken from the body of Captain Cronie, one of the Embassy staff, and subsequently 'worn by one of the murderers', and the refusal on the part of revolutionaries, despite requests by clergymen, to 'repeat prayers over the body'.[106]

The reports also stress the fact that it is the bourgeoisie who are suffering the wrath of the revolutionary government. One report claims that 'thousands of Russians, belonging to the officer and wealthy classes' were arrested daily and that some of these were shot.[107] Worst of all was the humiliation that the bourgeoisie were subjected to, which forced them into compulsory labour, performing jobs such as 'discharging coal' and 'cleaning water-closets in the soldiers' barracks'.[108] There were also detailed reports of mass murders and mutilated bodies: 'No. 62 arrested without accusation ... Body afterwards found covered with straw and dung, beard torn from face with flesh, palms of hands cut out, and skin incised on forehead.'[109] All these accounts pointed to one thing: Bolshevism needed to be stopped because the 'civilisation of the whole world was threatened'.[110]

The element of fear contained in the reports from Russia was also evident in the letters pages of the *Daily Telegraph*. During August and September 1920 a series of letters from the newspaper's middle-class readership questioned the concept of reconstruction and asked whether the war had given birth to a new world.[111] The readers of the *Daily Telegraph* saw society as suffering from a 'nervous strain' which had 'led to the loss of balance';[112] the world was 'chaotic' and in 'need of equilibrium'; the war had instigated a 'social and political avalanche';[113] the people had 'lost their anchorage' and 'were now adrift'; most people felt 'irritable and excited and frightened at shadows'.[114] The war was also seen as having instigated 'nervous distrusts and expectancy' and given rise to a 'wave of social insanity' which tended to 'subvert and demolish all law, order and authority'.[115]

The chaos, nervous tension, irritability, distrust and other ailments identified by the *Daily Telegraph* readers as being wrought on society by the war seemed to be aimed at a particular section of the population – namely, the working-class soldier who had

106. Sir R. Paget to Mr A. Balfour, 03/09/18, Report No.3, Parliamentary Reports, ibid.
107. Sir M. Findlay to Mr Balfour, 17/09/1918, Report No. 6, Parliamentary Reports, ibid.
108. Mr G., Report No. 12, n.d., Parliamentary Reports, ibid.
109. Sir C. Elliot to Earl Curzon, 22/02/1919, Report No. 44, Parliamentary Reports, ibid.
110. Sir M. Findlay to Mr Balfour, 17/09/1918, Report No. 6, Parliamentary Reports, ibid.
111. The articles and letters were published in 1920 in a volume. All subsequent citations are from this. Courtney, W. L., *Is it a New World? A series of Articles and Letters contributed by Correspondents to the Daily Telegraph, August–September, 1920* (London: 1920).
112. Courtney, W. L., in ibid., p. 3.
113. W. J. C., in ibid., p. 25.
114. G. N. Barnes MP, in ibid., p. 58.
115. 'Spectator', in ibid., p. 71.

been at the Front. These men were now seen as showing 'extraordinary demands' and wanting to 'impose their will on the community'.[116] Selfishness, materialism and greed were their main failings. They were seen as incapable of understanding the need for 'fortitude, endurance, self-sacrifice, and vigilant discipline', all of which came from a public school ethos and from the 'Old World'.[117] 'Playing the game' and its virtues of 'fortitude, endurance, self-sacrifice and vigilant discipline'[118] were necessary to achieve the aims of reconstruction. Without these virtues, Britain was at the mercy of the 'atrocities of Bolshevism'.[119] George Mosse has argued that the public school system developed during the nineteenth century offered an 'education in manliness as the preparation for a governing elite'. The qualities of endurance, discipline, obedience and self restraint which the readers of the *Daily Telegraph* assigned to the middle-class man and saw as lacking in the working-class man, were duties inculcated in the 'chapel and the playing fields' of public schools – the latter, providing a 'fit and masculine body and experience of fair play', and the former, providing 'proper morality'.[120]

The government's fears about the way the economy was functioning and the need for the soldier to adjust to civilian life were of particular concern to British industry as a whole. Even before the war ended, the Royal Society of Arts had tried to predict the problems for society of the returning soldier. In a lecture delivered in May 1918, Major Sir Robert Armstrong-Jones (MD, RAMC) argued that the war 'disturbed the mind and altered the course of thought of whole continents'. The civil population was suffering from an 'excitement' or a 'mental erethism'. Most alarming, for the speaker, was the fact that any sense of privilege during the war had been curtailed and 'equality ruled'. This state of things, according to Armstrong-Jones, was bound to leave a 'permanent memory and mould the character of the young'.[121]

Armstrong-Jones also foresaw production problems and labour unrest. These, he saw as stemming largely from 'socialist *doctrinaires*' which thrived on 'stirring up suspicion and strife between master and workman'. The way forward, he suggested, was for class feeling 'to be avoided at all costs'.[122] In the discussion that followed Major Armstrong-Jones's speech, the Chairman of the Royal Society of Arts, Lord Sydenham, highlighted the effects of the war on the 'attitude of labour'. As with

116. W. J. C., in ibid., p. 25.

117. Sir Sidney Low, in ibid., p. 107.

118. Ibid.

119. Lucas Malet, in ibid., p. 101.

120. Mosse, George, *The Image of Man. The Creation of Modern Masculinity* (Oxford: 1996), pp. 134–5. The literature on the formation of middle-class masculinities in the public school is extensive. See Rutherford, Jonathan, *Forever England. Reflections on Masculinity and Empire* (London: 1997), pp. 14–15. See also Mangan, J. A. and Walvin, J. (eds), *Manliness and Morality. Middle Class Masculinity in Britain and America* (Manchester: 1987).

121. Armstrong-Jones, Robert, 'The Mental Effects of the War and their Lessons in Regard to Medical and Social Reconstruction', *Journal of the Royal Society of Arts*, LXVI (1918), p. 434.

122. Ibid., p. 447.

Armstrong-Jones, he found that the greatest threat came from the spread of Socialist theories, and warned that: 'If, however, Socialist theories were ever translated into action, the result would be national bankruptcy and national ruin.'[123]

The attacks on Bolshevism continued in the press. Various authors wrote of the 'menace' and the 'sickness'[124] of Bolshevism, whose ultimate goal was to create a 'world revolution'.[125] Bolshevism was described as a 'barbarous tyranny' based on 'destruction, injustice and disorder' and, most importantly, 'chaos'.[126] Others saw Bolshevism as a disease for which a cure had to be sought. Canon E. A. Burroughs claimed in a letter to the Editor of *The Times* that a 'definite and appropriate policy towards Bolshevism' was needed. Military intervention was not the way forward because the 'Bolshevist bacillus' was already in the 'blood of the whole world'.[127] To counteract it, one needed to find a 'stronger, kinder bacillus to fight it in the very veins of the world's spiritual life'. This needed to be in the form of a 'Christian revival all the world over'.[128]

Fear of Bolshevism also spread to the House of Commons. There were numerous questions on whether the Government was taking 'any definite steps to deal with Bolshevism'.[129] The idea of Bolshevism as a disease was also rife in these quarters. Winston Churchill commented: 'Bolshevism is not a policy; it is a disease. It is not a creed; it is a pestilence.' As such, 'it breaks out with great suddenness; it is violently contagious; it throws people into a frenzy of excitement; it spreads with extraordinary rapidity; the mortality is terrible'.[130] In order to survive, this pestilence needed to find 'new areas to ravage and new populations to devour'.[131] The cure, or antidote, was a 'social guardian of morality'. Susan Sontag commenting on the way that illness is used as a metaphor for social ills and often adopts military jargon, has argued that it reflects a 'simplistic view of the world that can turn paranoid'.[132]

123. Lord Sydenham, 'The Mental Effects of the War and their Lessons in Regard to Medical and Social Reconstruction – Discussion', *Journal of the Royal Society of Arts*, LXVI (1918), p. 450.
124. *The Times*, 'Mr Barnes MP on Bolshevism', 11 January 1919 and *The Times*, 'Leading Article', 10 January 1919.
125. 'Leading Article', *The Times*, 10 January 1919.
126. Benson, E. F., 'The Meaning of Bolshevism', Letter to the Editor, *The Times*, 22 January 1919.
127. Burroughs, E. A. B. (Hertford College, Oxford), 'Counter-Bolshevism. The Remedy of Idealism', Letter to the Editor, *The Times*, 5 April 1919.
128. Ibid.
129. This is just one of the many questions put forward in the House of Commons. Terrell, G., MP, *Hansard*, 113/1719, 17 March 1919.
130. Churchill, W., MP, *Hansard*, 116/1526, 29 May 1919.
131. Ibid., cl. 1527.
132. Sontag, Susan, *Illness as Metaphor. AIDS and Its Metaphors* (London: 1991), p. 69.

    In the context of the AIDS epidemic, medical and military terminologies were used interchangeably to describe the way that the disease attacked the body's immune system.

The paranoia that surrounded fears of the Russian Revolution spreading like an illness to Britain resulted in calls from the House of Commons for the 'urgent, the imperative viscosity for preventing this poisonous virus from penetrating further into the veins of the world'.[133] MPs also equated Bolshevism with anarchy, arguing that 'we must call this danger by its proper name, which is anarchy'. Their references to disease, poison, penetration, and anarchy provided a terrifying and apocalyptic view of the future if Bolshevism was allowed to spread in Britain. The MPs also called for a policy of containment for those most at risk. One of the groups most at risk was the working-class man, especially the returning ex-serviceman. The government instigated the arrest of a number of ex-servicemen who were subsequently brought to trial.[134]

The fear of the 'disease' of Bolshevism spreading amongst the working-class man was also closely monitored by The Directorate of Intelligence, who produced weekly reports for the Cabinet on 'Revolutionary Feeling' in Britain, which were then summarised for a yearly report. The report for the year 1919 stressed the difficulties the country was facing:

> November 11, 1918, was a sinister date … for on that day there were attempts at revolution in both Switzerland and Holland, and there were many people in this country who thought that the weeks following the Armistice might be very critical for the stability of England.[135]

There were of course steadying influences which could potentially dampen any revolutionary feeling. The report identified amongst others the popularity of the Royal Family and sport. Other government departments identified further steadying influences. In a note to the Cabinet, the Minister of Labour, G. Roberts, on the suggestion of Sir Stephenson Kent, recommended that 'it is desirable that all orders restricting amusements, should be withdrawn as far as possible on the signing of the Armistice, and that horse-riding, football and other sports should be encouraged'. Marching processions were also seen as beneficial: 'As such processions appear to be possible under the Demobilisation scheme, it is suggested that they should take place.' What was most important however was that 'public opinion should be stirred to the highest pitch'.[136] Norton Griffiths, another member of the Directorate of Intelligence shared this view. He urged:

> One of the best methods of counteracting this [revolutionary feeling], in my opinion is that every brass band in the country should be let loose as often as possible, and to encourage

133. Rapper, MP, *Hansard*, 119/1247, 12 August 1919.

134. An example is the case of David Ramsey, who was brought to trial after delivering a seditious speech which insinuated that 'having been taught to shoot, the workers should use that knowledge against the masters'. *The Times*, 10 March 1919.

135. 'A Survey of Revolutionary Feeling in the Year 1919', Directorate of Intelligence, Special Report No.13, PRO, Cab 24/96, CP462.

136. 'Note by the Minister of Labour', 11 November 1918, PRO, Cab 24/69, GT6259.

> flag waving – one form of letting 'steam' off. ... Parading in all the principal towns in celebration should take place – in short, everything possible should be done to work up a high patriotic feeling from the results of victory.[137]

The government machine was not the only body to see the antidote to civil unrest as lying in the strengthening of patriotic feeling. Several readers of the *Daily Telegraph* saw the need for a 'new machinery of propaganda'[138] which was necessary because of the 'disappearance of so many familiar landmarks' and the 'apparent uselessness of experience as a guide'.[139] Crucially, the unveiling of the Cenotaph and the war memorial movement served to fill the gaps left behind by the disappearance of familiar landmarks, and provided the machinery of propaganda that was so badly needed during the reconstruction period. Such monuments were also able to provide a focal point for the uncontrollable crowds of the demonstrators to gather in perfect formation. These death rituals, as Nigel Llewellyn argues, restore the social fabric which death threatens with fragmentation and disintegration.[140] They re-erect social differences obliterated by the impartial facts of death and decay. Through their reverence to the dead, they also transform the movement and perceived force of the crowd by containing it and subsuming it within the confines of acceptable behaviour. The ceremonial and ritual of the unveiling of the Cenotaph, as well as the aesthetics of its design, will be discussed in this light in the next part of this chapter, along with the contribution they made to a hegemonic framing of the memory of the First World War.

Ceremonial, Ritual and Simplicity

The design of the Cenotaph was described by *The Times* on Armistice Day in 1920 as:

> Simple, massive, unadorned it speaks of the qualities of the race, which were in the forefront of the battle of the Allies.[141]

This view still informs present day commentary on the Cenotaph:

---

137. From Norton Griffiths to Austen Chamberlain, 'Suggestions to Prevent the Spread of Revolutionary Ideas in the UK', 1 November 1918, PRO, Cab 24/68, GT6195.

138. Sir Sidney Lee, in Courtney, W. L. (ed.), *Is it a New World?*, p. 165.

139. Courtney, W. L., in ibid., p. 2.

140. Llewellyn, Nigel, *The Art of Death: Visual Culture in the English Death Ritual c.1500–c.1800* (London: 1991), p. 102; see also Whaley, Joachim, 'Introduction', in Whaley, Joachim (ed.), *Mirrors of Mortality. Studies in the Social History of Death* (London: 1981); Cannadine, David, 'War and Death, Grief and Mourning in Modern Britain', in Whaley, Joachim (ed.), ibid.

141. *The Times*, 11 November 1920.

> Lutyens's Cenotaph is a mark of genius largely because of its simplicity. It says so much because it says so little. It is a form on which anyone could inscribe his or her own thoughts, reveries, sadness.[142]

The memorial was invested with simplicity from its early days as a wooden, temporary structure erected for the Peace Celebrations of July 1919. Even the wooden structure itself was described as 'simple, grave and beautiful in design'. *The Times* wrote that the Cenotaph 'has been universally recognised as a just and fitting memorial of those who have made the greatest sacrifice'.[143] The following year, after the wooden temporary structure had been replaced by a permanent marble memorial, praise for the Cenotaph continued. The 'common sense' of the design was applauded, particularly the way that it was able to convey its message 'simply' and 'precisely' like 'a Greek epitaph'.[144]

Roland Barthes, analysing the structure of myth in society, has argued that the 'form does not suppress the meaning, it only impoverishes it, it puts it at a distance' in order to 're-invest it with a different meaning'.[145] The new meaning, the myth that surrounded the Cenotaph, was hinted at in the quote from *The Times*. Through its simplicity, its unadorned surfaces and its sheer size, the Cenotaph conveyed the 'qualities of the race'. Its simplicity and directness 'revealed its purpose', which, according to *The Times*, was to 'provide a common focus' for the 'sincerest devotional thoughts and most sacred memories'. Most importantly, the memorial would prove 'that we have not forgotten the war and the noble cause for which it was fought'. The phenomenon of the popularity of the Cenotaph was described by *The Times* as 'thoroughly spontaneous'. The paper told its readers that 'it has to be seen in order to be understood' and advised the provincial municipal authorities to provide facilities for 'chosen parties of mourners from the provinces to come to London'.[146] Thus, was the myth of the Cenotaph formed. In this section the popularity of the Cenotaph will be discussed within two parameters: firstly, in terms of the spectacle and ritual that accompanied its unveiling and its perceived inclusivity; secondly, in relation to the architectural work of Lutyens and the aesthetic of simplicity.

The main preoccupation for those reporting on the Armistice celebrations was the inclusiveness and equality of the ceremony. Sir Philip Gibbs,[147] writing in the

---

142. Winter, Jay, *Sites of Memory, Sites of Mourning*, p. 104.
    Other recent commentaries provided similar views on the universality of the Cenotaph. See Greenberg, Allan, 'Lutyens's Cenotaph', *Journal of the Society of Architectural Historians*, XLVIII (March 1989): p. 12; King, Alex, *Memorials of the Great War*, pp. 145 and 147.
143. *The Times*, 26 July 1919.
144. *The Times*, 11 November 1920.
145. Barthes, Roland, *Mythologies* (London: 1993), p. 118.
146. *The Times*, 15 November 1920.
147. Gibbs was a journalist and official war correspondent on the Western Front for the *Daily Chronicle* during the First World War. According to Samuel Hynes, Gibbs was probably the most widely read and most influential of English journalists. His war reports offered a

ILN at the time of the burial of the Unknown Soldier, commented that the act of transporting the Unknown Soldier from his grave in Flanders to the heart of London symbolised a way in which all 'great and humble people' could be made 'equal in reverence to the virtue of the Common Man'.[148] This 'Common Man' represented all classes and was present among the crowds who gathered to pay tribute to the Unknown Soldier. Gibbs argues that these men were thinking of 'cynical things' and 'sometimes angry words' but is quick to add that during the ceremony such thoughts were erased. Rather, he believes that their thoughts had returned 'to the days in Flanders and the Fields of the Somme, to old things they have never told, even to each other'. As the two minutes' silence began, even these memories were silenced: 'Remembrance, ghosts, pities, subconscious and unuttered thoughts came to each living brain in all that multitude, and *may not be told*. [My italics]'[149]

Gibbs' commentary on the burial of the Unknown Soldier and the inclusiveness and equality of the ceremony attributed to it by the idea of an unknown soldier needs to be seen in the context of the reconstruction debates discussed in the previous section and in particular the accusations that the working-class ex-servicemen were somehow selfish, undisciplined and generally lacking the qualities that characterised the middle-class man. Gibbs may have been attributing agency to the working-class man in offering him a voice to express his discontent, but if so, then this agency is soon withdrawn. The 'unuttered thoughts cannot be told', Gibbs writes. The two minutes' silence becomes not just symbolic but a reality.

The leading article in *The Times* on Armistice Day 1920 also applauded the inclusiveness of the Cenotaph. The Cenotaph's inscription, the article pointed out, did not refer to a single individual: 'not to a General whose genius inspired the troops, nor to a warrior whose prowess was renowned among his fellows.' The inscription referred to a body of people who were 'equal in both death and glory'. The Unknown Soldier, according to *The Times*, embodied these elements, and as such was the 'emblem of the plain man', of the 'masses of the people'. The Cenotaph was seen as a 'public sign of the undying admiration and gratitude' that the dead 'have excited in the hearts of all'.[150] However, this was not a symbol of mourning that was all-inclusive. *The Times* noted that the Cenotaph would become a focal point for the widows and the parents of the dead, but excluded the surviving servicemen. These servicemen were also excluded from the ceremony of the burial of the Unknown Soldier in Westminster Abbey. Places for the ceremony

---

positive view of even the most 'disastrous circumstances'. These were published in his book *The Battle of the Somme*. By the end of the war, however, his views were greatly altered. His most famous book, *The Realities of War* offers a revisionary history of the war and its consequences. See Hynes, Samuel, *A War Imagined*, pp. 283–4.

His book *The New Man* will be discussed in relation to middle-class perceptions of working-class masculinities in Chapter 2.

148. Gibbs, Philip, *ILN*, 20 November 1920.

149. Gibbs, Philip, ibid.

150. *The Times*, 11 November 1920.

were allocated according to the following priorities: women who had lost their husband and one or more sons, mothers who had lost 'only sons' or all their sons and, finally, widows.[151]

With the exception of disabled soldiers and those representing particular units, combatants were excluded from the ceremonies. This, it could be argued, epitomises the way in which they were treated on their return from the Front. One particular class of combatants, the working-class man, was identified as being the cause of the industrial unrest that followed the end of the war and will be discussed in more detail in the next chapter. In contrast to the disorderly rioting strikers and uncontrollable Bolshevist crowds depicted in government reports, women represented an 'orderly crowd'.[152]

The ritual of the burial of the Unknown Soldier and the unveiling of the Cenotaph were repeatedly portrayed as 'simple' and 'striking'. G. K. Chesterton called it a 'tale that could be told in any future society, and remain simple and striking'.[153] *The Times* described the unveiling ceremony as expressing in its 'sublime simplicity the very heart of the whole people'.[154] Ceremonies held in later years were given similar endorsements. The 1921 ceremony, for example, was described as having drawn 'its beauty from simplicity'.[155] Simplicity was also presented as a national characteristic: 'Field Marshal Sir Douglas Haig who carried no staff and rode by with an air of complete simplicity which formed a strong contrast to the stern intensity of Marshal Foch.'[156] It was also seen as part of the ritual, a factor that did not go unnoticed by the press. G. K. Chesterton argued that 'ritualism is the only possible alternative to dogma'. Dogma, he claimed, was problematic: 'Dogma is so deep and vital that its verbal definition invariably leads to disputes and absurd misunderstandings.' Ritual, on the other hand, with its 'silent symbol of gesture and action', was more appropriate in the case of the Armistice celebrations.[157]

Rituals depend on crowds for their effectiveness, and at the same time the crowds had a role as catalysts for the ideals being projected by the rituals. In the 1920 Armistice Day celebrations, *The Times* correspondent referred to the importance of distinguishing between crowds that are uncontrollable, the 'mob' or 'herd', and crowds that are receptive and controlled. The mob is 'incontinent and undisciplined, causeless in its rage and fear'. However, such 'low instincts' were not apparent among the crowds attending this ceremony; rather: 'Here all was planned and as in a great piece of music, all of us were members of the orchestra; we had, each, his part in the expression of the grief.'[158]

151. *The Times*, 16 November 1920.
152. *The Times*, 12 November 1920.
153. G. K. Chesterton, *ILN*, 20 November 1920.
154. *The Times*, 12 November 1920.
155. *The Times*, 12 November 1921.
156. *The Times*, 21 July 1919.
157. G. K. Chesterton, *ILN*, 20 November 1920.
158. *The Times*, 12 November 1920.

Commenting on the representativeness of the spectacle in a given society, Guy Debord has argued that the 'spectacle epitomises the prevailing model of social life' and serves as the 'total justification for the conditions and aims of the existing system', as well as 'the presence of that justification'.[159] As such the spectacle of the unveiling of the Cenotaph provided the representation of the hegemonic order of the time within British society and a justification for its power at a time when that very power was becoming questionable and threatened by the multiplicity of factors discussed so far.

Silence

Sir Percy Fitzpatrick, who had served as High Commissioner in South Africa during the First World War, submitted a memorandum to the Cabinet in early November 1919, concerning the planned Armistice celebrations:

> During the War, we in South Africa, observed what we called the 'Three minutes' pause'. Silence, complete and arresting, closed upon the city – the moving, awe inspiring silence of a great Cathedral where the smallest sound must seem a sacrilege ... Only those who have felt it can understand the overmastering effect in action and reaction of a multitude moved suddenly to one thought and one purpose [...] When we are divided it [silence] may serve to remind us of the great things we hold in common.[160]

Sir Fitzpatrick's observations provide an insight into the ways in which silence was used to unite a divided nation – South Africa – and its possible application in Britain, another divided country.

Gestures and silence were the main characteristics of the ritual of Armistice Day. One example is provided in the following passage from *The Times*:

> The sense of unity and of Eternity came through the eye as well as the ear, when all heads were bare and there were thousands of faces lit by the quiet sunlight, the sense of multitudes none could number, set free from time and place, because they were gathered together in the one commemorative act.[161]

The description sets the parameters of the ritual very clearly. The baring of the heads and the faces lit by the sunlight constituted a commemorative act which provided its own temporality for the participants. Paul Connerton has argued that performatives during commemorative ceremonies are encoded in set postures, gestures and movements. Their strength lies in their sparseness. In contrast to language and its potential for producing statements that can be negotiated through ambiguity,

159. Debord, Guy, *The Society of Spectacle* (New York: 1994), p. 12.

160. Sir Percy Fitzpatrick, memorandum submitted to Lord Milner for the attention of the War Cabinet: PRO CAB 24/CP45 (4 Nov. 1919), quoted in Gregory, Adrian, *The Silence of Memory*, p. 9.

161. *The Times*, 12 November 1920.

indeterminacy and uncertainty, gestures and movement defy hermeneutic puzzles.[162] In this way they also defy resistance and translation.[163]

Silence provided both a censoring and at the same time an inscribing process for those attending the ceremony. *The Times* commented that thoughts and feelings 'came over us in one wave with the wave of sound and grew stronger with the silence'.[164] The implication is that contained within that silence were numerous private thoughts, including 'Forgetfulness of self'. Forgetfulness of self, implying, in turn, oneness, unity and membership of 'one body politic', was the ultimate thought, according to *The Times*.[165] Most importantly, silence represented a symbol of the 'English spirit' during the war, a spirit that needed to be restored.[166] Not everybody, however, accepted the silence unconditionally. The socialist newspaper, the *Daily Herald*, interpreted silence as forgetting. It stressed the importance of remembering the reasons for the country going to war; the main reason being the 'peace and happiness of the world' which should never again be allowed to 'fall in to the murderous hands of a few cynical old men'.[167]

The silence imposed on those attending the Armistice celebrations is best understood within the context of the class conflict that followed the First World War. Empty tombs, Benedict Anderson points out, are 'saturated with ghostly national imaginings'.[168] Within the British cultural context, Patrick Wright sees the establishment mode of remembrance in relation to the Cenotaph as being both militarist and nationalist in its detail. The dead are 'raised' and repositioned in the 'heart of the nation', erasing their historical diversity and establishing the single unity of the nation to which they are assimilated.[169] Other nations were to follow the British example of entombing the Unknown Soldier. From London to Baghdad, Inglis observes, 'every Unknown was immured in politics'.[170]

For the combatants, the silence offered a tense, ambivalent, moment. The writer R. H. Mottram considered the stillness 'uncanny'. It provided a sense of anticipation, waiting for the 'sound and movement that had been so vital and is now hushed for

162. Connerton, Paul, *How Societies Remember* (Cambridge: 1989), p. 59.

163. Translation is used here to signify the possibility of articulating the operations of agency in the construction of historical memory. See Coombes, Annie E., 'Translating the Past: Apartheid Monuments in Post-Apartheid South Africa', in Brah, A., and Coombes, A. E. (eds), *Hybridity and Its Discontents. Politics, Science, Culture* (London: 2000), p. 175.

164. *The Times*, 12 November 1920.

165. Ibid.

166. *The Times*, 11 November 1920.

167. *Daily Herald*, 11 November 1919.

168. Anderson, Benedict, *Imagined Communities*, p. 6.

169. Wright, Patrick, *On Living in an Old Country. The National Past in Contemporary Britain* (London: 1985), pp. 136–7.

170. Inglis, Ken, 'Entombing Unknown Soldiers: From London and Paris to Baghdad', *History and Memory*, 5/1 (1993), p. 18.

ever'.[171] Mottram sees the silence as the antithesis to the actual memories of war, which he remembers as being noisy and kinetic. He goes on to recall the trenches and the smells, the noises, the wounded and their mutilated bodies.[172] These are the memories that the aesthetic of simplicity and the ritual and ceremonial fail to address. By their silence they suppress these traumatic memories.

Mottram sketches a scene. It is Armistice Day and two ex-servicemen find themselves in a hotel room together. 'This was not by appointment' comments Mottram. They had each made excuses to slip out from their offices in order to get away from everyone. 'Their trouble was that they simply could not bear it.'[173] They both ended up in a room in a hotel overlooking the town war memorial and from there watched the Armistice celebrations. They did not want to be part of the crowd down below. Mottram describes the two friends fidgeting. He writes: 'it was all very well for the major part of the crowd below' which was composed mostly of women and children. For them, it was a 'fit and touching ceremony'.[174] To the two friends, on the other hand:

> [I]t was different. There, across their lives, like a great scar across the face, was the War – something you could neither obliterate, explain, nor turn to any useful end. Every year came this funeral of part of themselves, unavoidable, saddening in its associations. They turned away from the window. Their island of birth and upbringing forbade the expression of any feeling, but Skene, the more vocative by profession, silently handed Dormer his pouch.[175]

The silence allowed competing thoughts to emerge, but did it permit competing languages to do so? Adrian Gregory argues that the success of the competing languages depended to a great extent on their ability to define the groups to which these languages appealed.[176] In the incident above, Mottram describes the two ex-servicemen feeling that they did not belong within the crowd because their thoughts and experiences did not fit within the silences and the ritual that was taking place in front of the memorial. Most importantly, the masculine codes to which they had to conform did not permit them to express any emotions in public.

The Cenotaph

The iconic status with which the Cenotaph came to be associated also applied to its creator, Sir Edwin Lutyens, his architectural work as a whole and ideas on Britishness and the class system that his work appeared to incorporate. Following the Peace celebrations in France, the British government decided to organise a similar event in Britain and to erect its own national monument to peace. It was perhaps inevitable

171. Mottram, R. H., *Ten Years Ago. Armistice and Other Memories* (London: 1928), p. 7.
172. Ibid., pp. 27–9.
173. Ibid., p. 170.
174. Ibid., p. 173.
175. Ibid., p. 174.
176. Gregory, Adrian, *The Silence of Memory*, p. 12.

that Alfred Mond, Commissioner of Works for the British government, should turn to Lutyens for advice.[177]

Lloyd George met Lutyens to discuss the design, stipulating that it was to be of the 'un-denominational type already approved by the Government'.[178] Christopher Hussey quotes a letter that Lutyens sent to his wife Emily during a visit that he made to the Western Front in 1917 in connection with his work for the Imperial War Graves Commission. In the letter, Lutyens vents his emotions on the destruction reaped by the war:

> The battlefields – the obliteration of all human endeavours, achievement, and the human achievement of destruction, is bettered by the poppies and wild flowers – they are as friendly to an unexploded shell as they are to the leg of a garden seat in Surrey.[179]

The association between Lutyens' work on the Cenotaph and other memorials, and his architectural work, starts to emerge. Hussey points out that the garden seat mentioned in Lutyens' letter refers to a commission he was undertaking for Gertrude Jekyll's garden in Munstead. Jekyll, a garden designer, often collaborated with Lutyens on gardens for his clients. The story goes that Gertrude Jekyll had asked Lutyens to build her a garden seat, 'a massive affair consisting of an immense balk of timber supported by masonry,' but that when it was finished, their friend Charles Liddell remarked that it looked like the Cenotaph of Sigismunda. Lutyens, who was not familiar with the word cenotaph, learned that it meant an empty tomb, and shortly afterwards 'jokingly explained to Herbert Jekyll that the new object in the garden was 'a Cenotaph for Bumps [Miss Jekyll]'.[180] This anecdote shows the way in which simplicity was associated with a certain class in society and, as such, informed the way in which the Cenotaph could be inscribed by different groups of people within post-war society.

Country Life magazine became a key champion of Lutyens' career and designs. The magazine, published by Edward Hudson, first appeared in 1897 and helped to launch an English way of life that was predominantly based on a romanticised view of the countryside. Lutyens' work began to receive prominent exposure through *Country Life* and Hudson himself commissioned three houses – *Deanery Gardens,*

177. For a detailed discussion of the proceedings of the Committee, see Greenberg, Alan, 'Lutyens's Cenotaph', p. 7.

    Alan Greenberg observes that Lutyens was chosen because of his work for the Imperial War Graves Commission.

178. Quoted in Hussey, Christopher, *The Life of Sir Edwin Lutyens* (London: 1950), p. 391.
179. Lutyens to Emily Lutyens, 12 July 1917, quoted in ibid., p. 372.
180. Lutyens, Robert, *Sir Edwin Lutyens. An Appreciation in Perspective – By His Son* (London: 1942), p. 29.

    One also needs to ask to what extent the majority of the people understood the word 'Cenotaph' at the time, in light of the fact that Lutyens himself was not familiar with it. On a personal note, I undertook a small survey of BA students to find out how many understood the meaning of the word 'Cenotaph'; almost seventy-five per cent admitted that they didn't know.

Lindisfarne Castle and *Plumton Place* – as well as the *Country Life* offices in Covent Garden. According to Clive Aslet, the key to *Country Life*'s success was twofold: firstly, it reflected the interest of the middle classes in country houses and secondly, it spoke to those who already owned country houses and who were flattered that the surroundings they had previously taken for granted should become the focus of admiring interest.[181] John Cornforth argues that Hudson's personal patronage of Lutyens was balanced by the architect's significant influence on the development of the style and approach of the magazine. The photographer Charles Latham added to his exposure by showing off Lutyens' austere interiors and exteriors to great effect in his photographs.[182]

In the years preceding the First World War, simplicity became synonymous with 'Good Taste'. Not only did it encompass aesthetic/political considerations, but it also reflected practical concerns. Norman Shaw argued that the objects in a house should be 'little more than a background'. It is disconcerting, Shaw wrote, 'when you find that your host and hostess are less noticeable than their wall paper and their furniture'; wallpaper needed to be 'pure and simple'. The following extract shows his distaste for bold patterns:

> When ill and in bed, what it is to have always in evidence a patterned wall-paper, a thing that transforms a wall into a labyrinth of curving lines by which the mind is fascinated and rendered anxious and feverish. Surely, we might be spared the destruction![183]

The practical benefits of simplicity, for Shaw, included the minimal work and labour required to run a household: 'the simpler our houses are made both inside and out, the more successful they will be'. Shaw asked his readers to plan their houses 'with an absence of everything that goes to make work and labour'.[184] The austere, simpler values of Lutyens and Hudson were increasingly adopted by the rest of Britain as the servant shortage began to make itself felt after the First World War.

Simplicity also represented a way of life as well as a design issue; one which embodied Spartan values. Clive Aslet notes that a small but growing number of homeowners chose not to sleep in a bedroom at all. Lord Leverhulme, for example, slept all year round under a sleeping shed attached to the roof of his house. In January 1910, a correspondent wrote in *Country Life*: 'The sleeping shed at the foot of the garden, which has become a feature of so many country houses in the last years, represents the climax of a grand revolt against the confined and air-proof bedrooms

181. Aslet, Clive, *The Last Country Houses* (London: 1982), p. 42.

182. Cornforth, John, 'Lutyens and Country Life', in *Lutyens. The Work of the English Architect Sir Edwin Lutyens (1869–1944)*, Exhibition Catalogue, Hayward Gallery (London: 1981), p. 26.

183. Shaw, Norman, 'The Home and Its Dwelling Rooms' in Sparrow, Shaw (ed.), *The British Home of Today. A Book of Modern Domestic Architecture and the Applied Arts* (London: 1904), p. cii.

184. Shaw, Norman, 'The Modern Home' in Sparrow, Shaw (ed.), *The British Home of Today. A Book of Modern Domestic Architecture and the Applied Arts* (London: 1904), pp. 102–3.

of a former-age.'[185] According to Aslet, 'simplicity, or what was thought of as such', had become 'something of a cult'.

Patrick Wright and Michael Bommes have argued that in producing a national heritage, 'a particular conception of the past is produced, privileged, installed and maintained as a public and traditional consensus'.[186] For Wright and Bommes, the soul of Britain was epitomised by the country house, which combined its own 'historic interest' with the 'natural beauty' of its surroundings and represented the perfect naturalisation of a dominant view of the nation.[187] Evidence of this can be seen in some of the contemporary reviews used to describe Lutyens' houses.

Lawrence Weaver, one of the main champions of Lutyens' architecture,[188] casts an image of Lutyens as the quintessential British architect. Weaver notes the way that British architecture was inspired by Greek architecture and argues that the work of Lutyens, although informed by the 'Greek spirit', retained its British 'nationality'. The 'Greek spirit' for Weaver is an 'affair of ideals rather than mouldings'.[189] Lutyens adapts these ideals to the English climate and tradition in order to present 'one outstanding quality style'; a style which, according to Weaver, contains both 'unity' and 'simplicity': 'The function of architecture is not to apply ornament to buildings, but to create a building, an artistic unity so pervading that it shall be impossible to detach any one quality.'[190] Weaver believes that Lutyens' work avoids the 'over-accentuation of parts', resulting in a 'feeling of breadth and completeness'. These principles, according to Weaver, apply to three houses in particular – *Middlefield, Great Shelford*, and *Dormy House*.

Weaver describes *Middlefield* (1908) as the 'most austere' of Lutyens' houses, relying on the 'qualities of mass, symmetry and proportion'. The windows and doors are the only parts to feature any external mouldings and even these are of an 'extreme simplicity'. One looks in vain for 'relief in a carved tympanum here or a keystone there'. It would be quite possible to charge the design with a certain 'baldness', in Weaver's view, if it were not for the fact that it is precisely this austerity that is the building's real strength:

---

185. Quoted in Aslet, Clive, *The Last Country Houses*, p. 71.
186. Wright, Patrick and Bommes, Michael, '"Charms of Residence": the public and the past', Richard Johnson *et al.* (eds), *Making Histories: Studies in History Writing and Politics* (London: 1982), p. 253.
187. Ibid., p. 276.
188. Two writers in particular became the main champions of Lutyens' work in *Country Life*. Lawrence Weaver joined the magazine in 1909 and began the series called Lesser Country Houses, which was devoted to newly built houses. During the First World War Weaver promoted the 'ideal memorial' through *Country Life*.

    Christopher Hussey shared Hudson's enthusiasm for Lutyens and combined a historical approach with an enthusiasm for contemporary architecture. Hussey also wrote on memorials and particularly featured the work of the Canadian sculptor, Tait McKenzie.
189. Weaver, Lawrence, *House and Gardens by Sir Edwin Lutyens RA* (London: 1925 [1913]), p. xxiv.
190. Ibid., p. xl.

> It has been always the finest types of small domestic architecture, which disappoint the unthinking critic by lacking gold on their garments, buildings which have won their place in our affections by the very fact of being 'simple persons'.[191]

Houses like *Middlefield,* according to Weaver, reflect the people that inhabit them and, as such, have the 'gift of repose'. This repose comprises several factors: 'The perfect suavity' of the lines of the roof, which are kept in 'harmonious and unbroken planes', the 'masculine tower-like bulk of the chimneys', the windows 'few but large', and the dormers which 'grow organically out of the roof.' The materials used in its construction add to its 'extraordinary repose': the scale of the house is made greater by the smallness of the bricks. The same simplicity that informs the exterior is carried into the interior: 'The fittings throughout are of the plainest', writes Weaver. The architect is seeking to give the building its own character and achieves this through a combination of 'mass, proportion, textures and colour. *Dormy House* (1906) provides such an example. To Weaver, it is the 'apotheosis of architectural common sense: 'It starts with a basis of absolute simplicity and continues to the chimney-tops in the same spirit.' The qualities of 'masculine repose' and 'quiet rhythm' which characterise it, are 'qualities of which it is impossible to tire'.

The same qualities permeate traditional Britishness, which has at its heart the British countryside. 'We are still a country nation', declares Christopher Hussey; 'our common ideals are those of countrymen: a healthy body, a little home, the prize in sport and in labour to the strong and swift'.[192] Science is greeted with suspicion: political science is directed 'towards burdening the strong for the relief of the weak', while medical science, is aimed at 'preserving the weak to the detriment of the strong'. The result is that 'our population is growing unwieldy and the proportion of deficients, increases'.[193]

This is the point at which eugenic discourse enters the discussion.[194] According to Hussey, the countryside provides an unlimited supply of 'vigorous men' who travel to the cities to maintain the British Commonwealth. He sees in the tall chimneys evidence of the Empire's status: 'Every tall chimney represents a Tower of London.'[195] Chimneys become symbolic structures, carrying with them connotations of manliness and success, along with a romanticised idea of the countryside. Weaver quotes the words of Henry Ryecroft: 'hold by the open fire as you hold by whatever else is best in England,'[196] in order to assert

---

191. Ibid., p. 232.
192. Hussey, Christopher, *The Fairy Land of England* (London: 1924), p. 5.
193. Ibid.
194. For a discussion of the Eugenics Society in Britain, see Searle, Geoffrey, *Eugenics and Politics in Britain, 1900–1914* (Leyden: 1976); Soloway, Richard, *Demography and Degeneration. Eugenics and the Declining Birthrate in Twentieth-Century Britain* (Chapel Hill: 1990).
195. Hussey, Christopher, *The Fairy Land of England*, p. 6.
196. Ryecroft, Henry, *The Private Papers*, quoted in Weaver, Lawrence, op.cit., p. 277.

that: 'Most people who are not hypnotised by the desire to order their lives on scientific lines will cordially agree that nothing can be the same as a beautiful core of glowing fuel.'[197] Lutyens' designs were particularly praised for their chimneys. The American architect Frank Lloyd Wright said of Lutyens' architecture that it idealised and dramatised the big chimney with a 'success unequalled' and that the chimneys emitted the 'Old English feeling of dignity and comfort'.[198]

The dignity and Englishness of the chimney and the fireplace in Lutyens' architecture also feature in a house which the Independent MP Noel Pemberton Billing commissioned *(Illustration 1.3).* The dancer Maud Allan had brought a libel case against Billing for implying in his paper the *Vigilante* that Maud was a lesbian. In the article in question, entitled 'Cult of the Clitoris', Billing suggested that the Germans were holding a 'Black Book' containing the names of 47,000 'sexual perverts', including cabinet minister Herbert Asquith and his wife, and Maud Allan, who at the time was appearing in Oscar Wilde's *Salome*.[199] The resulting libel trial defined what constituted acceptable norms of behaviour, associated with the 'healthy mind of England'.[200] Pemberton Billing's promotion of the hearth as the quintessential English accessory to the home reinforces the notion of acceptable and unacceptable sexual boundaries, while Lutyens' designs, especially the 'masculine repose' of his chimneys, define the acceptable masculine behaviour of a particular class.

The *Viceroy's House* in India provides a further example of simplicity and the way in which it can embody a sense of class, race and nation. In an article in *Country Life,* travel writer Robert Byron elaborates on the way that the building blends the 'theatricality' of Islam with the intellectual, three-dimensional tradition of solid form and exact proportion of Europe. Byron argues that Lutyens 'expressed in his medium the splendour of a political idea'. The dome of the building represents the 'climax, the shroud of imperial suggestion'. This is achieved, according to Byron, by the fact that 'not a window nor a door, nor a hint of utilitarianism, interpolates upon the monumental affirmation of temporal power.' Most importantly, the dome 'is a slap in the face of the modern average

197. Weaver, Lawrence, ibid.

198. Frank Lloyd Wright, quoted in Edwards, Brian, *Goddards. Sir Edwin Lutyens* (London: 1996), p. 20.

199. Bland, Lucy, 'Trial by Sexology? Maud Allan, Salome and the "Cult of the Clitoris" Case', in Bland, Lucy and Doan, Laura (eds), *Sexology in Culture. Labelling Bodies and Desires* (Oxford: 1998), pp. 183–4. See also, Medd, Jodie, '"The Cult of the Clitoris": Anatomy of a National Scandal', *Modernism/Modernity*, 9/1 (2002), pp. 21–49.

200. Lucy Bland has argued that the trial was significant because of the use of sexological theories in a public forum. Billing, who defended himself in court (he was a trained barrister, as well as an actor), used theories from sexologists such as Krafft-Ebing and Havelock Ellis to prove his allegation that Maud Allen was a lesbian. The term 'clitoris' used in the libellous article was also drawn from such theories. See Bland, Lucy, ibid.

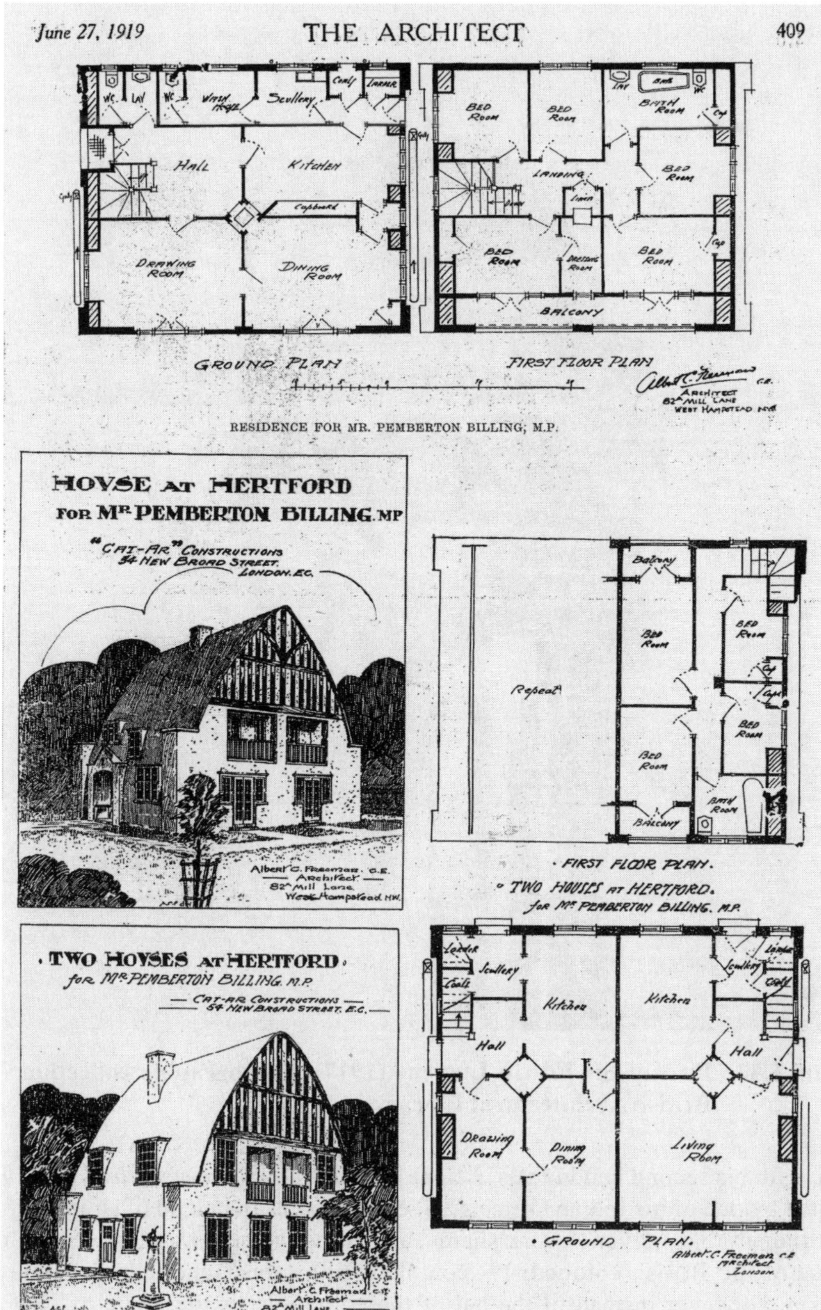

Figure 1.3 Design for Pemberton Billing, MP – *Architect*, 27/06/1919, p. 409. Photographic collection. The British Architectural Library

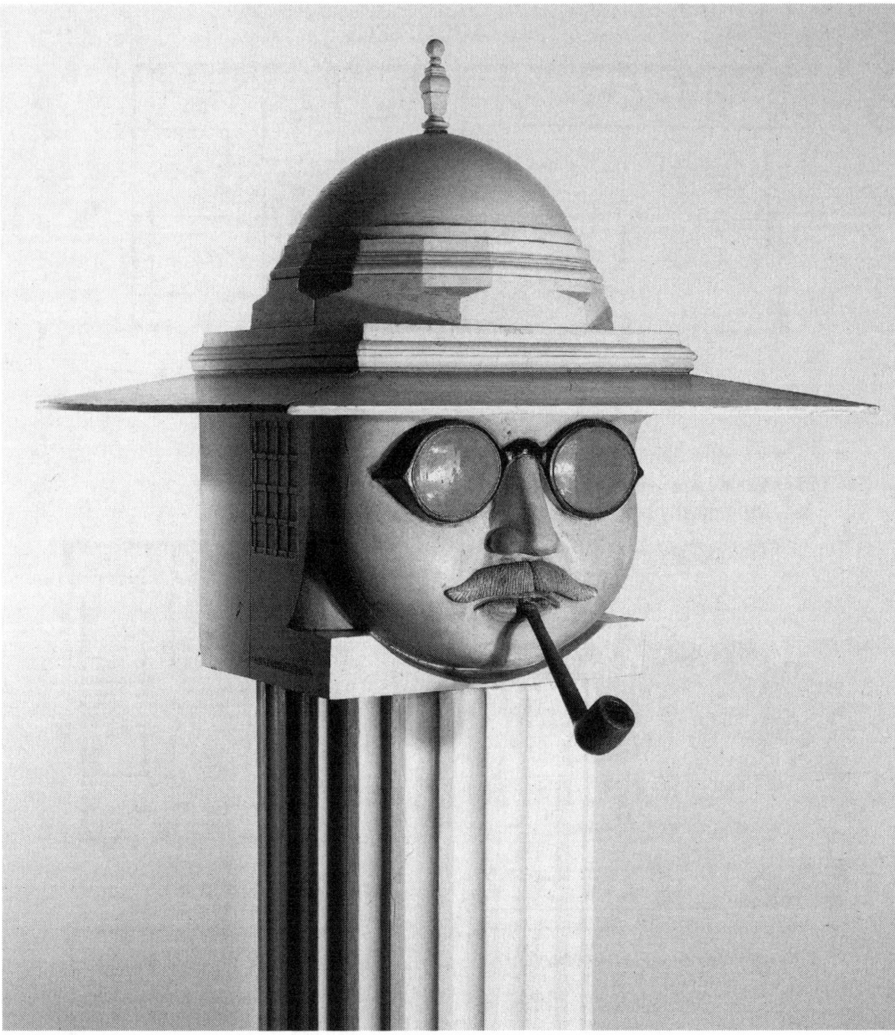

Figure 1.4 Bust of Sir Edwin Lutyens (1917). Photographic collection. The British Architectural Library

man, with his second hand ideals'.[201] The caricature of Lutyens *(Illustration 1.4)*, created by one of his Indian Office staff, encapsulates the blend of simplicity and imperialism that Lutyens' work shares, and fuses the Greek influences with the image of the British colonialist – complete with moustache, tobacco pipe and glasses. However instead of the hat of the colonialist is the dome of *Viceroy's House* epitomising British imperial identity.

201. Byron, Robert, quoted in Lutyens, Robert, *Sir Edwin Lutyens*, p. 47.

Simplicity and Uniformity: The Imperial War Graves

Simplicity, equality and uniformity were also characteristics that were central to the debates around the establishment of the Imperial War Graves Commission (IWGC), the Stone of Remembrance and its inscription.[202] The design of the stone, like the design of the Cenotaph, relies on *ενταασις*, or a system of optical corrections. It is within this system that, one could argue, the simplicity of the stone breaks down. The 'complex' geometry, as Hussey describes it, which derives from the study of the Parthenon, is meant to imbue the monument with an aura of simplicity. However, the Greek word *ενταασις* translates as tension. Tension is at the heart of the simplicity attributed to both the stone and the Cenotaph.[203]

This tension was also apparent in the debates within the House of Commons on whether the war graves should be uniform in design, or should be individual. According to the IWGC, uniformity provided 'artistic effect', and 'nothing more impressive' could be imagined. Colonel Burn MP (Conservative) argued that uniformity meant that 'a general, a private soldier and an unknown soldier', could be seen lying next to each other, 'all the same'.[204]

Others believed that uniformity was not synonymous with equality. Viscount Wolmer argued that 'uniformity is not and never can be equality'.[205] He found it particularly alarming that the designs proposed by the IWGC put an emphasis on militarism. For Viscount Wolmer, this was a memorial '*not* [my italics] to freedom, but to rigid militarism':[206] uniformity threatened individuality, and individuality needed to be preserved. Viscount Wolmer read out to other Members of Parliament from letters he had received on the matter: 'I hate to be buried like a dog', one combatant had written to his mother before he died. 'The tombstones resemble milestones,' a mother had written. Another letter urged the Government to direct its attention to only those graves 'where there are no relations'. The correspondent added that 'it is so natural that we should look on our dead as belonging primarily to us as individuals'.[207]

The debate ended with Winston Churchill arguing the case for uniformity of style. His speech provides an eloquent example of how the personal memory of the dead turned into a quest for national pride and identity. Churchill argued that the need for uniformity was foremost a practical consideration, due to the unprecedented numbers of dead. The enormous task the IWGC had to tackle could only be achieved through standardisation. The standardisation that fed the war machine during the war became the driving force behind the uniformity in the

202. The War Graves Registration Commission, instigated by Sir Fabian Ware, was recognised by the War Office in 1915 and the Imperial War Graves Commission was established in 1917. Imperial War Graves Commission, *Annual Report, 1920–21* (London: 1921).

203. Hussey, *The Life of Sir Edwin Lutyens*, p. 388.

204. Colonel Burns MP, *Hansard*, cl. 1948, 4 May 1920.

205. Ibid., cl. 1941.

206. Viscount Wolmer, MP, *Hansard*, cl.1942, 4 May 1920.

207. Turton, Edmund, MP, *Hansard*, cl. 1953, 4 May 1920.

graveyards. A uniform shape for each stone would also give maximum space for inscriptions, while using the same materials for each would contribute to their durability. A crucifix could not provide this durability and if a variety of designs were to be introduced, durability would be sacrificed. Durability and permanence became focal points for Churchill. The permanence of the memorial became a way of repaying the soldiers for the loss of their lives. Each headstone would be inscribed with the name, regiment and place where the combatant had died.[208]

Churchill's position came to be endorsed not only in the manner by which the dead were remembered in the cemeteries of the Imperial War Graves Commission, but also in the way in which those who had died were acknowledged on war memorials. Various authors have commented that the inscriptions exemplified a new era of remembrance which was more democratic than previous eras, and which preserved the name of the common soldier for future generations to see.[209] However, one also needs to consider how their individual lives had been erased from the discourse of the commemoration and replaced by a brief moment in their lives: their active service at the Front, represented by the name of their regiment and the place where they fell. The only visible reminder of their past is in their name; a name which has lost its original identity and now carries a new military status. As Judith Butler puts it:

> But do names really 'open' us to an intersubjective ground, or are they simply ruins which designate a history irrevocably lost? Do these names really signify for us the fullness of the lives that were lost, or are they so many tokens of what we cannot know, enigmas, inscrutable and silent?[210]

This may be the reason that visitors to the *Vietnam Veterans Memorial* felt compelled to add photographs, letters, and other memorabilia – building a picture of the person behind the name.[211] In the case of the *NAMES Project Quilt*, the panels embroidered by friends and family often incorporated the life stories of their loved ones who had died. Unlike the memorabilia that mourners bring each day to the *Vietnam Veterans Memorial* and which each day is removed by the memorial curators, the personal tributes incorporated in the Quilt are not extraneous to its

---

208. Churchill, W., MP, *Hansard*, cl. 1969, 4 May 1920.
209. See for example Laqueur, Thomas, 'Memory and Naming in the Great War', in Gillis, John (ed.), *Commemorations* (Princeton: 1994), p. 155 and Inglis, K. 'War Memorials: Ten Questions for Historians', p. 7.
210. Butler, Judith, 'Review Essay: Spirit in Ashes', *History and Theory*, 27/1 (1988), p. 69.
211. On the Vietnam War Memorial the names are not listed alphabetically. According to Marita Sturken, read alphabetically, the names become anonymous – not individuals, but statistics. Read chronologically, however, they create a narrative framework charting the story of the conflict. By walking along the wall, one effectively is walking through the history of the war. The fact that visitors have to look up a name in the index and then find it on the wall also gives them an active role in the story. Sturken, Marita, *Tangled Memories. The Vietnam War, the AIDS Epidemic, and the Politics of Remembering* (Berkeley: 1997), p. 61.

formal act of memory but 'snapshots of the soul that none touches up, censors or edits'.[212]

In contrast with the uncensored, unedited panels of the *NAMES Project Quilt*, Churchill was arguing for a 'collective' and 'corporate' tribute to the dead. The 'simplicity' and 'symmetry' of the proposed designs, to him represented the collectivity and corporeality of the sacrifice. This was due, to an extent, to the way in which the cemeteries would be maintained and funded. 'They will be supported and sustained by the wealth of this great nation and Empire, as long as we remain a nation and an Empire', Churchill announced. The sense of 'beauty', 'dignity', and 'repose', and the feelings of 'reverence' and 'comfort' which according to Churchill characterised these cemeteries, were also synonymous with nationhood and Empire.[213] The proposed amendment for non-uniformity of the IWG was removed on the grounds of not wanting to 'divide the Committee'[214] and Churchill called on those who objected to the scheme, to make 'one further sacrifice' and allow it to go ahead.

What the IWGC debates highlighted, was that during the post-Armistice period, the concept of simplicity in the commemoration of the First World War was an aesthetic idea embedded within middle- and upper-class artistic sensibilities. As such, the design of war memorials cannot be seen as providing a universal language for the expression of a nation's grief. As this chapter has argued, the promotion of simplicity needs to be considered within the broader context of the commemoration of the war, particularly the unveiling ceremonies and the silence they imposed on those witnessing the event.

The main voice that these ceremonies was attempting to silence was the class conflict that was developing in British society. This chapter has already concentrated on the Russian Revolution, and the influence that the ideology and iconography of the revolution had on the attitude of the middle and upper classes towards the returning working-class servicemen. The next chapter will discuss in more detail the ways in which the middle classes saw themselves as 'the public', most importantly, the 'constitutional classes', and how they dealt with the threat of what they perceived as the organised working classes. It will also look at the National Union of Railwaymen's strike of 1919, including the hegemonic masculinities that were promoted during the strike, and the possibilities that the *LNWR Euston Memorial* offered for the grieving process of the relatives of those who had died and those who had returned from the war front.

---

212. See for example Hawkins, Peter, 'Naming Names. The Art of Memory and NAMES Project AIDS Quilt', in Greenberg, R., Ferguson, B., Nairne, S. (eds), *Thinking About Exhibitions* (London: 1996), pp. 140–1.
213. Churchill, W., MP, *Hansard*, cl. 1971, 4 May 1920.
214. Remnant, Sir J., MP, *Hansard*, cl. 1972, 4 May 1920.

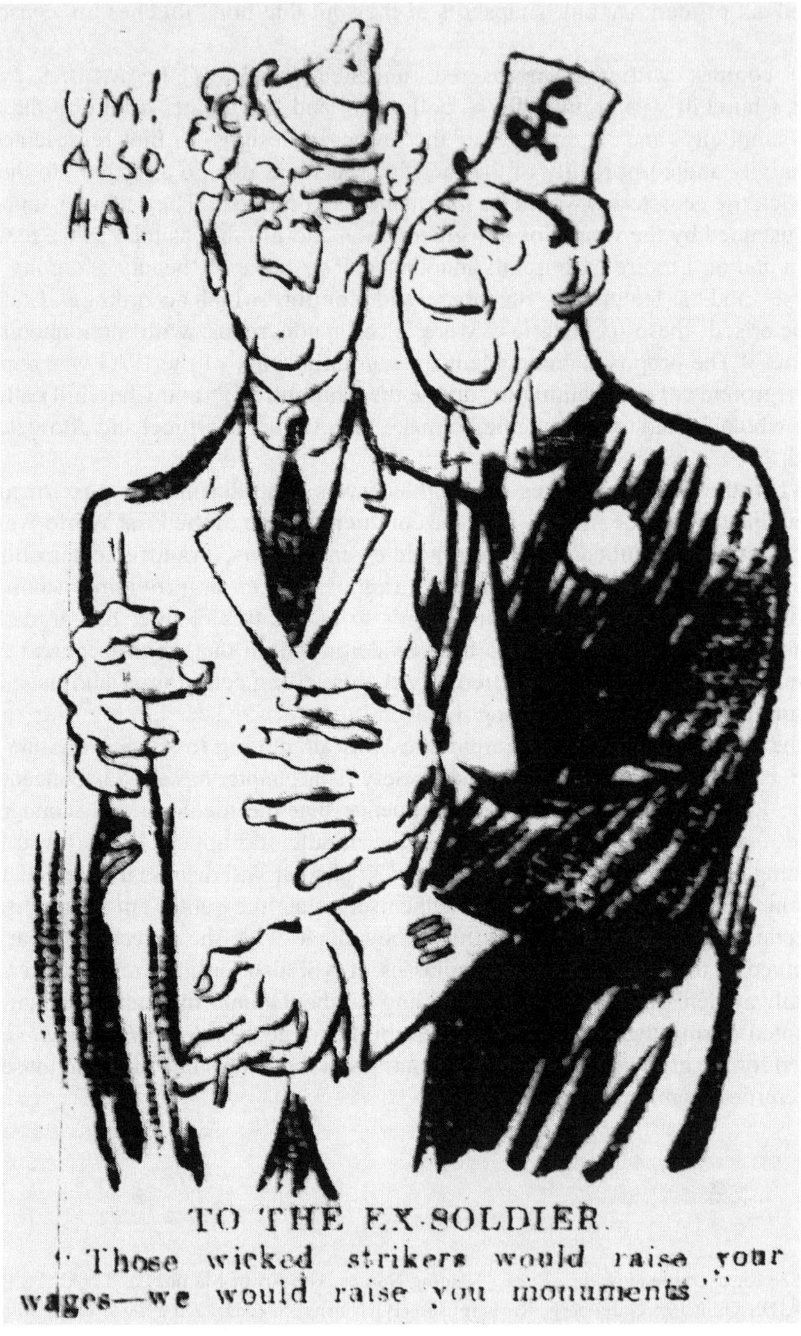

Figure 2.1 To the Ex-Soldier. *Daily Herald*, 30/09/1919

Chapter 2

Class Conflict, the New Man and the Picturesque Soldier

> Those wicked strikers would raise your wages – we would raise you monuments[1]

This quotation comes from a cartoon that was published by the *Daily Herald (Illustration 2.1)* during the 1919 National Union of Railwaymen (NUR) strike. In the cartoon, an overweight man in high collar and top hat, displaying a prominent pound sign, the symbol of capitalism, is seen clasping the returning working-class ex-serviceman in an embrace. The cartoon makes a direct association between the commemoration of the war and the silencing that this commemoration sought to achieve following the displays of civil unrest after the war and the demands from working-class ex-servicemen for better pay and conditions.

The cartoon raises certain issues that this chapter will attempt to address in relation to the visual culture of the commemoration of the war. The main issue is the absence of such images from the collective memory of the First World War, raising questions about the 'unequal struggle to install particular memories at the expense of others which are marginalized and forgotten'.[2] Any images of the NUR strike were quickly erased from the cultural memory of the commemoration of the First World War, to be replaced by images of the soldier in uniform.

So, what effect did these images have on notions of masculinity at that time? In this chapter we will discover that the commemoration of the war promoted hegemonic notions of masculinity which sought to subsume and control working-class ex-servicemen. Having a particular influence on these power relations was the emergence of the 'New Man', as featured in Philip Gibbs' book *The New Man* (1913). At a point when class boundaries were beginning to break down, Gibbs' book set out to re-establish masculine norms that showed clear distinctions between the different classes. These norms were based on notions of self-sacrifice, chivalry and obedience, all qualities associated with the middle-class man, as opposed to the working-class man who represented greed, disobedience and 'un-gentlemanly' behaviour. These characteristics also featured in the representation of the working-class strikers by the press and the middle-class volunteers drafted in to replace the

---

1. *Daily Herald*, 4 October 1919.
2. Ashplant, T. G., Dawson, G. and Roper, M., 'The Politics of War Memory and Commemoration. Contexts, Structures and Dynamics', in Ashplant, T. G., Dawson, G. and Roper, M. (eds), *The Politics of War Memory and Commemoration* (London: 2001), p. xi.

workers on strike, and served to 'reproduce and legitimate social inequalities' and to 'naturalise hierarchically ranked social distinctions'.[3]

The same comparisons were evident in the ceremonial speeches given at the unveiling of the *London and North Western Railway Memorial* at Euston Station, at which honours were awarded to those soldiers who had shown particular displays of courage during the war. The bestowal of honours was one of the ways in which the working-class man could be subsumed and assimilated within established norms of masculinity. Benedict Anderson has argued that a nation mobilises its people to die in its defence by interpellating them as members of an imagined community.[4] According to Ashplant *et al.*, war commemoration is a vital stage in that process. This chapter will argue that the unveiling ceremonies, through their formalism and performativity, reinforced the hegemonic norms of masculinity that had been challenged during the war and the post-Armistice period.

A further issue that will be addressed in this chapter concerns the possibilities that arise from excluded memories and narratives. In discussing the construction of Anzac memories, Alistair Thomson analyses the case of Fred Farrall, a working-class soldier who only gained access to a language distinct from the Anzac legend of the history of the First World War when he joined the Communist Party in the 1930s. It was his membership of the Communist Party that gave him the opportunity to express his revulsion at the war.[5] This chapter will examine these excluded memories, taking into account the effect that the Central Labour College, which was mostly funded by the NUR, and the union banners and posters produced during the strike had on British society at the time. As we will discover, the banners and posters of the 1919 strike provided a form of counter-culture to the visual culture of the commemoration of the war.

The National Union of Railwaymen Strike of 1919

> The Government intend to meet the blow at the public with all the resources at the disposal of the state, and they look to the nation, without distinction of class, for it affects everybody, cheerfully to bear the deprivations which this indefensible strike will inevitably entail, and to support them in maintaining the fabric of social order upon which the prosperity of this country depends.[6]

3. Hebdige, Dick, 'The Impossible Object: Towards a Sociology of the Sublime', *New Formations*, 1 (1987), p. 60.
4. Anderson, Benedict, *Imagined Communities. Reflections on the Origins and Spread of Nationalism* (London: 1994), pp. 9–10.
5. Thomson, Alistair, *Anzac Memories: Living with the Legend* (Oxford: 1994), pp.170–3.
6. '"Prime Minister's Denunciation", An Anarchist Plot of Few', *The Times*, 29 September 1919. This was part of a telegram sent by Prime Minister Lloyd George to the Chairman of the Carnarvonshire County Council at Carnarvon concerning his inability to give a speech in Carnarvon due to the outbreak of the strike.

Like the War with Germany, it must be a fight to the finish.[7]

The strike by the National Union of Railwaymen (NUR) began on 26 September, 1919 and lasted nine days. It started 'quite unexpectedly – as a thief in the night', Lloyd George wrote in a letter to his wife. Kenneth Morgan comments that both the workers and the management regarded the strike as an industrial disruption of unprecedented magnitude and seriousness and 'its atmosphere seemed a prelude to open class war'.[8] The unions achieved total solidarity throughout Britain and rail services were paralysed. According to Bernard Waites, the strike brought the 'conflict imagery of industrial relations before a huge public', and was the first time that the government had taken 'the field against a body of workers with all the paraphernalia of press propaganda and military preparations.' The NUR strike also needs to be seen against the climate of trade disputes during the post-Armistice period which culminated in the Emergency Powers Act in 1920, which allowed the British government to declare a state of emergency if strike action should threaten to interfere with the 'essentials of life'.[9]

The conduct of the NUR strike, Waites argues, was a testament to the discovery of public opinion during the war, the refinement of the press's techniques of persuasion, and the government's role as a 'creator of opinion'.[10] We will start by examining the machinery of propaganda that came into force at the very start of the strike, and in particular the class discourses that permeated the pages of the national press.

Noreen Branson has argued that the government's actions during the strike implied that it was 'preparing for insurrection'. In some stations such as Woking, machine guns were positioned, although the Cabinet turned down a proposal from Winston Churchill to place machine guns at the entrances of railway tunnels.[11] The use of troops in strike situations was an ongoing debate within the government at the time. The Directorate of Intelligence pointed out in their report for the year 1919 that the publication by the left-wing paper the *Daily Herald*, of a secret government circular relating to the use of soldiers during the strikes and the gathering of

7. 'Leader Article', *The Times*, 29 September 1919.
8. Morgan, Kenneth, *Consensus and Disunity. The Lloyd George Coalition Government 1918–1922* (Oxford: 1979), p. 60.
9. In 1919 the number of trade disputes recorded by the Ministry of Labour reached 1,413 and involved nearly 2.6 million workers. See Bourke, Joanna, *Working-Class Cultures in Britain, 1890–1960* (London: 1994), p. 178.
10. Waites, Bernard, *A Class Society at War. England 1914–1918* (Oxford: 1987), p. 72.
11. Branson, Noreen, *Britain in the Nineteen Twenties* (London: 1975), p. 31.

    To understand the government's reaction to the strike, one needs to look further into its make-up and the public support it received during this period, particularly the increase in public support for the Conservative Party. Employers who had formerly been Liberal supporters increasingly began to identify with the Conservative Party. This shift was encouraged by the fact that a growing number of industrialists were looking to the Conservatives for protection from the strikers. 43% of Conservative MPs and 35% of Liberal MPs were listed as company directors in 1918. At least thirty MPs were directors of railway companies. Ibid., pp. 8–9.

intelligence from soldiers, 'provoked great resentment against the Government'.[12] A discussion on the leaked document at the House of Commons reveals to some extent the government's attitudes towards working-class men who were still at the front waiting for demobilisation.[13]

Winston Churchill declared the leak of the circular by the *Daily Herald* as an incitement to cause 'trouble and mischief at this crucial time in the Army and among the workmen'. He criticised the newspaper for wanting to 'provoke an outbreak in the form of a mutiny or general strike in the hope that a general smash up and overthrow of society may result', and concluded that the purpose of this exposure was to 'weave them [all working-class men] together and rouse them all at once to make a general overthrow on the Russian model'.[14]

Other government officials found the publication of the circular equally offensive, as they considered it undignified and unmanly for the press to spy on their men. The Labour MP Colonel Wedgwood accused the government of adopting the same oppressive tactics as the Soviet Government in extracting information out of working-class men in the Army.[15] The dialectical irony of these accusations could not have been more pronounced. Extreme fear of Bolshevism had resulted in the British government adopting the same behaviour as those they accused.

The Liberal MP Lieut. Commander Kenworthy, recognising the dilemma faced by the government, advocated the use of volunteers to replace the striking workers. The volunteers, Kenworthy pointed out, might be called 'blacklegs' and 'scabs', but physical violence might be avoided by turning public opinion against the strikers.[16] What Kenworthy was proposing, in other words, was that the government should persuade those most likely to be affected by the strike, the middle classes, to form a strong opposition to the strikers. The government propaganda machine took the same view. It issued a statement to the press, announcing that the 'circumstances of the present crisis are such' that 'special measures' needed to be undertaken in order to 'secure the liberty of all peaceable citizens' and to 'protect them in the pursuit of their ordinary work'. To achieve this the Government appealed to the public for the establishment of 'Citizens' Guards'.[17]

Volunteering began to assume a war-like imagery and appeal. Volunteers gathering at Grosvenor House formed a spectacle, so *The Times* informed its readers, which recalled the early days of the war when 'men of all conditions of life leapt to the call of arms'. During the spectacle several public figures appealed to the unity and comradeship of the war. The Prime Minister, due to the sudden announcement of the strike, had to cancel an engagement at Carnarvon welcoming

12. 'A Survey of Revolutionary Feeling in the Year 1919', Directorate of Intelligence, Special Report No.13, PRO, Cab 24/96, CP462.
13. For the full discussion see, *Hansard*, 116/1514–5, 29 May 1919.
14. Churchill, W. MP, ibid., cl. 1517.
15. Colonel Wedgwood MP, ibid., cl. 1503.
16. Lieut. Commander Kenworthy MP, ibid., cl. 1501.
17. *The Times*, 27 September 1919.

soldiers from the Front who, according to the speech he was unable to make, 'so valiantly upheld the honour of their native land in the great struggle for human rights and freedom'. He called on the strikers to show similar virtues.[18] The National Free Church Council asked its local churches to 'preserve during the strike the atmosphere of mutual consideration, brotherhood, and sacrifices which linked all sections of the state during the war'.[19]

There was a huge response to the government's appeal for volunteers to operate the railways and enrol as special constables. Philip Bagwell pointed out that on no previous occasion had so many men and women whose names appeared on the pages of *Debrett's Peerage* offered their services for manual work during the strike.[20] *The Times* reported on the actions of the volunteer railwaymen, praising them for their 'pluck or devotion'. These, it noted, were 'exclusively young men who were on active service a year ago'. They did not wear a uniform; instead, they wore an armband to signify their volunteer status. *The Times* was very particular about their origins and background, describing them as what is:

> classed roughly as the public school type of man. Many were ex-officers, and nobody could have wished for a more cheerful, courteous and considerate body of public servants.[21]

These young, public school educated ex-officers were 'efficient in the work they performed', according to the reporter in *The Times*. What they might have lacked in manual skills, they made up for in 'trained minds' and the 'Englishman's splendid adaptability', and, moreover, were able to pick up 'what is called a skilled occupation in the labour world in a day'. For the rail passenger, there was no better reassurance than knowing that a 'squad of public schoolboys were stoking for dear life at the generating station'.[22] The public school education system was seen in this instance as not only providing a capable substitute for rail workers but also as displaying an exemplary brand of masculinity. Jonathan Rutherford has commented recently that the new ideal of manliness that emerged in the late nineteenth century relied on subordination to the national ideal and an enthusiasm for being 'normal'. Public schools began to cultivate the new brand of masculinity and to instil in their boys a readiness, courage, self-reliance and a willingness to seize opportunities, character and religion. According to Rutherford, 'the language of the public schools became the language of a national culture and its empire'.[23] As such, the hegemonic codes of

18. '"Prime Minister's Denunciation", An Anarchist Plot of Few', *The Times*, 29 September 1919.
19. *The Times*, 27 Sept 1919.
20. *Morning Post*, 04,06,07 October 1919, quoted in Bagwell, Philip, *The Railwaymen. The History of the National Union of Railwaymen* (London: 1963), p. 388.
21. 'Officer Drivers', *The Times*, 1 October 1919.
22. Ibid.
23. Rutherford, Jonathan, *Forever England. Reflections on Masculinity and Empire* (London: 1997), pp. 14–5.

masculinity advocated during the strike could be seen to be perpetuating the notion of manliness held prior to the war.[24]

The recollections of the volunteers offer an interesting insight into their sense of nationalism and duty. Chas Lake, who worked for the *Railway Magazine*, which was the official journal of the rail companies, wrote an article in the magazine about his experience as a volunteer engine-man on the Great Western Railway during the strike. He recalls 'jumping at the opportunity' to volunteer, and describes the solidarity amongst the middle classes during the strike.[25] He explains how the strikers 'hailed us with epithets' that were intended 'to express the disapproval of what we were doing', but that the 'hooting' of the strikers was 'more than made up for by hearty cheers by the passengers on the platform'. Of all his memories, the one that persists is of 'the shilling, which a beaming old lady handed me with her blessing on arrival at Paddington one evening'.[26] The fact that he was tipped seems to reinforce for him the strangeness of taking on a role very different to that prescribed by his own social status. This provides a particularly interesting insight into the status given to certain roles. Did Lake believe that social roles, and in particular male class roles, were a matter of choice rather than something that was inherited? One could argue that the whole idea of volunteering during the strike and taking on the role of train driver, porter or ticket inspector put these men into the realm of the unknown and allowed them to enter a world they could previously only have imagined – the world of what they perceived as their socially inferior male counterparts. Eric Hobsbawm has argued that the perceived dominance of the middle classes was based on a sense of the inferiority of the working classes. Such inferiority also implied an acceptance of their place in society; a sense that the workers ought to be content with their prescribed status and position.[27]

What is also significant is the way that public opinion was being manipulated in favour of the middle classes. The government and right-wing papers such as *The Times* portrayed the work of the railwaymen as unskilled and lacking any special abilities. The left-wing press and the NUR publications objected to these attacks on the workers and the implication that the volunteers could pick up the strikers' tasks with ease. The *Daily Herald* published its own criticisms of the situation, arguing that:

---

24. This is a notion which was also promoted during the war by the Non-Commissioned Officer system which was largely formed by public school educated recruits. Lord Haig declared in November 1914: 'Sent out young Oxford and Cambridge men as officers. They understand the crisis in which the British Empire is involved.' Towards the end of the war however, because of the number of casualties within the officers' ranks the promotion of soldiers to officers became common. See Winter, Denis, *Death's Men. Soldiers of the Great War* (London: 1978), pp. 63–4.
25. Lake, Chas, 'My Experience as a Volunteer Engine-Man on the Great Western Railway During the Strike', *The Railway Magazine*, 269 (November 1919), p. 299.
26. Ibid., p. 306.
27. Hobsbawm, Eric, *The Age of Capital 1848–1875* (London: 1995), p. 290.

> No trains ever seem to go where anybody wants them to, and even the Eton-cum-Oxford-cum Mayfair accents of the exquisite young man in the passionate socks, who struggles with the stiff doors of the Underground failed to console the flustered lady who pined to reach Paddington and was offered instead Mansion House or Charing Cross.[28]

A question that kept emerging in the left wing press was whether the establishment and the Northcliffe press in particular, were ignoring the contribution that the strikers had made to the war effort. The NUR argued that the establishment had used the workers at a time of need, only to ignore their needs once they became 'surplus labour' after the war. Reacting to this, the strikers also adopted the rhetoric of battle and warfare to support their cause, although this time the war was against capitalism. The strikers were promoted by their union as fighting a working-class battle against the 'entire forces of capitalism'. Unlike the government's attitude towards the strikers, however, theirs was a peaceful battle: 'Our cause is just. With folded arms we stand passive resisters; our only shield is the justice of our cause.'[29]

In using volunteers to keep the railways and other vital services functioning, the government was presenting the situation as one that affected the survival of the nation. It was also exploiting and manipulating class perceptions and stereotypes. The striking men were presented as selfish, greedy, and above all revolutionary, whereas the volunteers were heralded for their altruism and devotion to their country. Ross McKibbin has argued that in the years between World War I and II, working-class stereotypes were constantly hostile and often parodied by the press. In the years following the First World War, stereotypes became increasingly political and the working class came to be seen on the whole as a group of manual workers in well-organised and aggressive unions who were constantly bargaining with their employers and used the strike weapon as their final argument.[30] However, the male working-class stereotypes presented during the period of the strike were stereotypes that had their origins in the period prior to the war.

The New Man

In a book published the year before the war, entitled *The New Man* (1913), Philip Gibbs provides an impression of the changing image of men across the class system.[31] The concept of the 'New Man', developed in the period from the late

28. *Daily Herald*, 3 October 1919.
29. The Glasgow and District Railwaymen's Strike Bulletin, 30 September 1919, in MSS 127/NU/6/IN 16.
30. Ross McKibbin mentions the inter-war phrase 'the coals in the tab' as an example of the strength and hostility of the parodies and the stereotypes they were representing. McKibbin, Ross, *The Ideologies of Class. Social Relations in Britain 1880–1950* (Oxford: 1990), p. 271.
31. Rosa Bracco describes Gibbs as the ultimate middlebrow writer of the inter-war years. He wrote incessantly on contemporary social issues. All his analysis came back to the 'spirit of England', and the basic worth of the Empire. He was a strong advocate of the ills of a possible

nineteenth century to the years just before the First World War, has been compared with the rise of the 'New Woman',[32] who had her own perception of the new man as someone who was artistic and who complemented her own needs and abilities.[33] It soon became clear, however, that this perspective was unrealistic in that men already had many choices within a patriarchal society whereas women had only a few.[34] The idea of the new man proved to be an utopian concept which, according to Showalter, gave rise to an anxiety and crisis of masculinity during the late nineteenth and early twentieth centuries.[35] The boundaries between the sexes became rigid and clear cut, and sexual science proved the existence of innate, essential differences between the sexes, particularly in relation to their abilities, pathologies and desires.[36] Within this framework of gender polarities, men also found their roles demanding and difficult to sustain. There were demands to succeed financially at home and in the Empire, and 'the stresses of maintaining an external mask of confidence'[37] led to mental disorders such as neurasthenia.

The concept of a crisis in masculinity has given rise to several theoretical debates. According to R. Connell, the term 'crisis' presupposes a coherent system of some kind which is destroyed or restored by the outcome of the crisis. Masculinity does not represent a system in this sense, but needs to be seen rather in terms of a 'configuration of practice within a system of gender relations'. Instead of addressing a crisis in masculinity, one needs to address disruptions or transformations within a certain configuration: the 'crisis tendencies of gender orders'. For Connell, power

---

revolution and saw the war as a means of preventing revolution. See Bracco, Rosa Maria, *Merchants of Hope. British Middlebrow Writers and the First World War* (Oxford: 1992), p. 40.

32. See Showalter, Elaine, *The Female Malady. Women, Madness and English Culture, 1830–1980* (London: 1987), p. 38.

33. Lucy Bland offers a discussion of the concept of the New Woman and the New Man in relation to Karl Pearson's and Olive Shreiner's short-lived organisation at the turn of the twentieth century, the Men and Women's Club. See Bland, Lucy, *Banishing the Beast. English Feminism* and *Sexual Morality 1885–1914* (London: Penguin, 1995)

The concept of the New Man has been reinvented in the Western World in the late twentieth century as an ideological class icon. New Man is presented as a white, educated professional who is an involved and nurturing father in touch with his feelings and 'gentle' in his dealings with women. See Hondagneu-Sotelo, P. and Messner, M., 'Gender Displays and Men's Power', in Brod, H. and Kaufman, M. (eds), *Theorising Masculinities* (London: 1994), pp. 202–3. Also Segal, Lynn, *Slow Motion. Changing Masculinities, Changing Men* (London: 1990), pp. x–xiv.

34. Showalter, Elaine, *The Female Malady*, p. 57.

35. For a similar view, see Sinfield, Alan, *The Wilde Century. Effeminacy, Oscar Wilde and the Queer Moment* (Cassell: 1994), pp. 62–78.

36. Felski, Rita, 'Introduction', in Bland, Lucy and Doan, Laura (eds), *Sexology in Culture. Labelling Bodies and Desires* (Oxford: 1998). This collection of essays also stresses the constructive and empowering influences of sexological theories at the time for homosexual men and women and other sexual minorities.

37. Showalter, Elaine, *The Female Malady*, p. 9.

relations show the best visible evidence of 'crisis tendencies'.[38] Michael Roper and John Tosh have argued that masculinity is a tenuous concept because power itself is a continual process of contestation and transformation.[39] It is these power relations, their contestation and transformation, that are explored in Philip Gibbs' book, particularly the power relations that exist across different classes.[40]

Although Gibbs discusses the class system as a whole and the characteristics of the 'new man' in each class, what causes him greatest concern is working-class men. Whereas aristocratic men of that period were problematic, their shortcomings presented no major obstacle to society; in fact, they represented the 'pleasantest society in the world'.[41] The middle classes, particularly the lower middle classes, were equally unproblematic in that 'there is no distinctive type which may be labelled as middle class'. What defined the middle classes, according to Gibbs, was the suburbs. Ann Bermingham argues that the suburbs offered a model community, a fusion of notions of the city and nature.[42] In economic terms, the suburbs and their population were the main consideration for government policy at the time.[43] The suburb as a model community also offered a forum for normative masculinities, fencing off outside threats imposed by women, workers and homosexuals and establishing dominant forms of control through which these categories could be contained.[44]

---

38. Connell, R. W., 'The Social Organisation of Masculinity', in Whitehead, S. and Barrett, F. (eds), *The Masculinities Reader* (Oxford: 2001), p. 45.
39. Roper, M and Tosh, J, 'Historians and the Politics of Masculinity', in Roper, Michael and Tosh, John (eds) *Manful Assertions. Masculinities in Britain since 1800* (London: 1991), p. 18.
40. Several publications on masculinity and class examine the construction of masculinity within the working class and in relation to the role of women and the political and civil society. These masculinities were constructed in relation to notions of respectability and independence, which on the one hand related to the State's perception of respectability and the model family, and on the other hand depended on power relations between men and women.

    See, Walker, Pamela, '"I live but not yet I for Christ Liveth in Me". Man and Masculinity in the Salvation Army, 1865–90', in Roper, M. and Tosh, J. (eds) *Manful Assertions*.
41. Gibbs, Philip, *The New Man. A Portrait Study of the Latest Type* (London: 1913), p. 141.
42. Bermingham, Ann, *Landscape and Ideology: The English Rustic Tradition, 1740–1860* (Berkeley: 1987), p. 168.
43. Ross McKibbin argues that from the first half of 1920 onwards, Britain lived under a deflationary regime which put the safety of the financial institutions ahead of other interests. During this period the country was governed essentially in the perceived interests of those who felt themselves most likely to benefit from deflation, the professional and suburban middle classes and the holders of the government debt – which were often the same people. See McKibbin, Ross, *The Ideologies of Class*, p. 266.
44. Gibbs was not the only author to be preoccupied by the suburbs and its population. Masterman, Charles, *England After the War. A Study* (London: 1922), provides the reader with a fictitious 'Richford', a fortress where the middle classes live in order to hate the working classes. For a discussion of of the book's perspective on the consequences of the war on British society and notions of modernity, see Peters Corbett, David, *The Modernity of English Art, 1914–1930* (Manchester: 1997), pp. 62–4.

The suburbs have been associated with notions of uniformity, boredom and inactiveness, while the image of the man of the suburbs has been equated with someone who is de-masculinised and needs to re-establish his manliness. Michael Rosenthal has argued that after 1908 the Boy Scout movement came to be not only a response to widespread fears about physical and mental degeneration and their effects on the nation, race and masculinity,[45] but also a means by which boys and scout-masters from lower middle-class backgrounds could enhance their masculine status at a time when deskbound work and domesticity were perceived as feminising influences.[46] Men from both the lower and the upper middle classes feared comparisons with working-class men. For the working-class man, his manliness was bound up in the work that he did, which was largely manual, of a tangible nature and therefore had a certain value to it.[47] William Acton's assertion in 1857 that it 'seems necessary to give a man that consciousness of his dignity, of his character as head and ruler' was becoming increasingly difficult to sustain for middle-class men in a capitalist society where the means of production no longer defined masculine roles.[48]

Philip Gibbs, aware of the insecurities that middle-class and lower middle-class man faced, constructs a web of power relations between the working-class man and his lower middle-class counterpart. The city clerk is characterised by certain virtues which derive from the hegemonic conception of masculinity based on the public school ethos, such as uniformity, punctuality and endurance. He also has an 'admirable' brain, according to Gibbs. Despite a life of 'narrow experience' and 'daily drudgery', his brain is 'active and industrious and accurate', kept active by 'little things' such as 'sweet peas' and 'standard bread'.[49]

One could argue that Gibbs is being ironic in this depiction of the city clerk, but perhaps not, when we compare his description of the middle-class city clerk with

---

45. Max Nordau helped provide the basis for the spread of fears of degeneration in Europe and North America during the late nineteenth and early twentieth century. Nordau, Max, *Degeneration* (Lincoln: 1993, [1895]). For a discussion of the impact of Nordau's theory, see Pick, Daniel, *Faces of Degeneration* (Cambridge: 1989). For a discussion of Nordau's views in relation to the construction of masculinity in Europe during the early twentieth century, see Mosse, George, *The Image of Man. The Creation of Modern Masculinity* (Oxford: 1996).

46. See Rosenthal, Michael, *The Character Factory: Baden-Powell and the Origins of the Boy Scout Movement* (New York: 1986) for an in-depth discussion of the way in which the movement functioned in terms of inculcating masculine behaviour.

47. Joanna Bourke argues that between the 1870s and the First World War the masculinity of an individual could be construed in terms of the wages they earned for their labour, although after 1920 this became a 'fragile basis of masculinity' because many working-class men were at risk of being unemployed and their sons found themselves seated at desks performing menial and less obviously 'manly jobs'. See Bourke, Joanna, *Working-Class Cultures*, p. 44.

48. Acton, William *The Functions and Disorders of the Reproductive Organs in Youth, in Adult Age and Advanced Life*, quoted in Weeks, Jeffrey, *Sex, Politics and Society. The Regulation of Sexuality since 1800* (London: 1981), p. 39.

    On the worth of the middle-class man's work in relation to working-class men see also Sinfield, Alan, *The Wilde Century*, p. 64.

49. Gibbs, Philip, *The New Man*, p. 148.

the working-class man. Gibbs' initial image of the working-class man highlights his destructiveness, his arrogance and the miserable existence he leads:

> I have met him [the working-class man] when he has been on strike ... when he has been hurling 'kidney' stones – he picks them out of the roadways which were made by himself – at policemen ... I have seen him wreck fourteen tramcars in a big thoroughfare at mid-day when the police happened to be off guard. ... I have seen him in his pride and arrogance at a meeting when his delegates have issued an ultimatum to the masters and a threat to the Government. I have seen him scores of times, and in large numbers, broken on the wheel of life, out of work, feeding on charity, sleeping in miserable doss-houses.[50]

Gibbs sees the Education Act of 1870 as having contributed to the problems of the working-class man. The Act granted every citizen the right to an education, which gave him the opportunity to read 'light literature' and 'half penny weekly papers'. It also meant that he could read socialist propaganda which offered the possibility of planting revolutionary ideas in his brain.[51] Furthermore, he could read about the way in which 'those who have the luck' live: 'Everybody except the labouring classes seems to be buying motorcars, indulging in expensive hobbies.'[52] As a result, working-class man, 'stirred by the spirit of the age', the 'divine discontent', started to abandon the 'old ideas of duty and obedience'. Some even claimed that the working classes were becoming 'intellectualised beyond the nature of their work'. As Gibbs explains: 'It is impossible to do the work of a brute with the mind of a Polytechnic young man, or to do the work of a machine with a soul athirst for intelligent delight.'[53]

Although as Gibbs argues, 'the New Working Man has grown intellectually to the level of the middle-class man of the day', certain key differences also set the two classes apart. Working-class man, for one thing, was easily influenced: 'There are loud-mouthed fellows at the street corners who tell him about the tyranny of capital and the serfdom of labour, there are hundreds of little paper-covered pamphlets.' These elements made him 'think dangerously and [they] sow in his head the seeds of doubt and revolt'.[54] The New Working Man was no longer brutal, according to Gibbs, as he was beginning to realise that he held 'an even more formidable power' in his hands – the 'power of laziness'. This laziness, which Gibbs terms the 'gospel of the New Working Man', had 'handicapped the country against foreign competitors and [has] caused a stagnation among many great industries'.[55]

---

50. Ibid., p. 88. Gibbs is obviously referring to the civil unrest in the period just before the First World War during the industrial disputes.
51. Ibid., pp. 90–3.
52. Ibid., p. 92.
53. Ibid., p. 244.
54. Ibid., p. 96.
55. Ibid., p. 99.

Laziness was not the only new trait to distinguish working-class man: he also displayed a selfishness which was threatening the industrial progress of the nation. The 'terrors of race suicide do not alarm him', Gibbs writes: all that interested him was 'a certain John Jenkins in the present year of grace and his creature comforts, and his desire for an increase in wages, and his demand for a good time'.[56] Middle-class man, by contrast, had retained his 'sentiment of Imperialism', according to Gibbs, and 'applauds briskly when a young lady in tights waves a Union Jack in the limelight'. Gibbs presents imperialism and Britishness as converging on the character of the middle-class man, a shift which was also noted by others. 'Imperial Man' was characterised by his 'authority and the celebration of the will',[57] but he was also able to adapt to the demands of capitalism.

The rhetoric of the political establishment, the depiction of the strikers by the Prime Minister and the press as 'anarchists', along with Gibbs' writings, all represent what Judith Butler refers to as 'injurious speech'. Butler uses this term to include not only words and representations that cause harm, but the mode of address itself. She also indicates that while it may be demeaning to be called an injurious name, it is also possible to gain something from the experience: 'By being called a name, one is also, paradoxically, given a certain possibility for social existence.' In other words, the injurious address may produce an unexpected and enabling response.[58] The next section will examine this principle, and discuss the opportunities available to working-class men to re-assert themselves and prove that they could control their money and other aspects of their lives.

The Central Labour College

The National Council of Labour Colleges (NCLC) received a large proportion of its funding from the NUR. Its Annual Report for 1924 points out that 'one of the most noticeable features of the recent history of the working-class movement' was the 'growing recognition of the power of ideas'.[59] The NCLC was extremely alarmed about the activities of the 'Rothermeres of the Press',[60] which convinced the Labour movement 'that press control of working-class thinking is a danger

56. Ibid., p. 106.
57. Roper, M. and Tosh, J., *Manful Assertions*, p. 17.
58. Butler, Judith, *Excitable Speech. A Politics of the Performative* (London: 1997), p. 2. For a critical reading of Butler's notion of 'excitable speech', see Hatt, Michael, 'Race, Ritual and Responsibility: Performativity and the Southern Lynching', in Jones, A., and Stephenson, A. (eds), *Performing the Body/Performing the Text* (London: 1999).
59. The National Council of Labour Colleges, *History, Report and Directory* (London: 1924), p. 3.
60. The phrase refers to the power that Lord Rothermere was seen to possess through his papers, the *Daily Mail* and the *Daily Mirror*. After 1922, he also took over several newspapers owned by his brother Lord Northcliffe, although this didn't include *The Times*. Mowat, Charles, *Britain Between the Wars 1918–1940* (London: 1968), p. 244.

that cannot be over-estimated'. According to a leaflet published by the Central Labour College, education was the answer as it provided a shield for both capital and labour.[61] However, the education provided by the universities of the day was extremely limited. The NCLC argued that the teaching of social subjects was 'narrow', 'prejudiced and unscientific', and that the universities were blind to the 'central fact in capitalist society, the class struggle'.[62] It also held that the 'orthodox' education system was bound to be one that was circumscribed by the needs of the ruling classes.[63]

This view was reinforced by the fact that in 1908, students at Ruskin College, Oxford, founded an organisation called the Plebs League which acknowledged that education in the social sciences was, in a class society, a class matter. The following year, the students at Ruskin, led by the Plebs League, went on strike to declare their dissatisfaction over the way that the social sciences were being taught. This led to the foundation of the Central Labour College in 1911.[64] Having its base in London meant that the Central Labour College could offer something that Oxford could not: 'a working class environment for its working class education'. London, according to William Craik, 'made it possible for us to speak and work more effectively with the men and women outside the academic gate, with those who alone could overcome the enemy of the people'. In fact, Craik believed, the people had the need and the potential power to 'cast down the mighty from their seats'.[65] The transport industry was the biggest employer in London at the time, and the majority of its employees were railwaymen and dockers. It was natural, then, that the National Union of Railwaymen should become one of the two major funders of the Central Labour College.[66]

The purpose of the college was to help the workers in their 'industrial, political and co-op struggles', and the subjects on its curriculum were chosen with that end in view. The education was not intended as a 'selfish one'; nor was it aimed at providing the 'means for raising the men out of servitude'.[67] Its central aim was to empower a whole section of the population to rise above a certain stereotypical view of themselves imposed by the middle classes. The course subjects included History of Philosophy, Historical Method, Economics, Ethnology, Family and Social Life, Imperialism, Trade-Unions, Literature, Esperanto, Psychology and Public

61. 'To the Class that Holds the Future in its Hands', Leaflet published by the Central Labour College, MSS 127/LC/4/2/1/1.
62. The National Council of Labour Colleges, *History, Report and Directory*, p. 3.
63. Ibid.
64. This was based at 11 and 13 Pennywern Road, Earls Court. A full history of the funding and work of the college is provided by one of its former Principals, William Craik. See Craik, William, *The Central Labour College, 1909–29. A Chapter in the History of Adult Working Class Education* (London: 1964).
65. Ibid., pp. 97–100.
66. The ownership and control of the college subsequently passed to the NUR and the SWMF (South Wales Miners' Federation).
67. The National Council of Labour Colleges, *History, Report and Directory*, p. 7.

Speaking.[68] These subjects were seen as allowing 'a penetrating insight into the deepest foundations of society' revealing the process by which 'social structures arise and function'. Education, then, for the working classes, became a tool which they could use to overthrow these social structures and gain power in their own right.

The Plebs, a journal published by the Plebs League, was primarily aimed at informing the 'worker-students'. The National Council of Labour Colleges stressed the importance of publishing books which offered a different perspective to those used in mainstream education. The majority of their books were published collectively by the Plebs Textbook Committee rather than crediting individual authors. One that is of particular interest is the textbook on psychology. This source, entitled *An Outline of Psychology*, provides an insight into the way in which the personal and the political can coexist. More importantly, it provides a place for psychology to serve the working-class struggle rather than the inner world of the bourgeois individual.

Psychology was seen as a means of exploring 'man's place in nature' in the same way that Marxism was seen as providing knowledge of the 'economic and social man'.[69] However, psychology needed to be free of the 'taint of bourgeois ideology' if it was to 'realise the nature of its own aims'. Psychology also provided the tools to understand not only the minds of the working classes but also the 'working of our enemies' minds'. It was seen as 'confirming and supplementing Marxism in the theoretical, strategical and tactical fields', similarly to the way in which the 'Russian experiment [has] confirmed and supplemented Marxism in the field of practical endeavour.'[70] As such, psychology came to be a subject that was reclaimed from its bourgeois origins and provided a tool for both defence and attack.

The Plebs Textbook Committee saw the role of the 'capitalist press' as maintaining the 'dominion and the enforcement of passive acceptance' by employing the idea of suggestibility.[71] *An Outline of Psychology* highlighted the way that the press employed 'smart catch-phrases' to influence the 'popular mind'. The reporting of the strikes of 1919 provided a good example of the way in which the press sought to manipulate public opinion and spread damaging rumours. W. W. Craik, Principal of the Central Labour College, wrote about the press coverage of the 1919 NUR strike in an article in *The Plebs*: 'The ancient fetish of the public was, of course, again paraded in the foreground of the fight and the old ritual phrases were repeated ad lib

68. The Central College was a residential college. It comprised one lecture per week, which was followed by questions and discussion. During the same week, the students would meet the tutor in small groups for the purpose not only of revision, but also of developing critical self-expression. See The National Council of Labour Colleges, *History, Report and Directory*, p. 16.
69. Plebs Textbook Committee, *An Outline of Psychology* (London: 1921), pp. vii–viii.
70. Ibid.
71. Ibid., p. 121.

by the Fleet Street exorcists.'[72] The overall coverage represented, according to Craik, the dehumanisation of the railwaymen: they were portrayed as 'enemies of the social order' who were 'out to destroy the present fabric of Government'.[73] The portrayal of the strike itself by the press was according to Craik one of a 'wanton attack on the democratic government, civilisation, and the children's milk'. The press, Craik claimed, was using catch-phrases with which the 'public' rallied to the 'fight against the latest piece of 'frightfulness'.[74]

Propaganda affected those who were not class-conscious, according to the Plebs Textbook Committee.[75] Socialist propaganda needed to concentrate on the psychological complexes that unemployment and privation induced, if it was to be successful. The most powerful tool for the socialist, however, was 'autosuggestion'. The mechanism of 'autosuggestion' relied on the 'the sight of other persons engaged in any action, or the sound of the spoken words denoting that action'. Such actions were seen as a 'stimulus acting on [their] performance'.[76] The use of 'autosuggestion' according to the authors could result in Marxism becoming a 'revolutionary high-explosive'.[77] The authorities were aware of the possibilities that this could have for society, as the visual culture of the NUR strike demonstrates.

Banners and Revolution

This section will argue that the visual culture during the period of the strike and especially the union banners highlights the latent threat of Bolshevism and revolution for British society. For the strikers, the most enduring memories of this time were the marches and public meetings, in which union banners played an integral part. John Gorman describes 1919 as a boom year for banners. However, there was a marked difference between union banner imagery in the years immediately before, and the years immediately after the First World War. The banners used just after the war reflected the growing influence of syndicalist ideas and the Russian Revolution. They proclaimed that political and industrial action was needed to destroy capitalism. To read the slogans on the banners after the war, argues Gorman, is to

72. Craik, William, 'The Railway Strike', *The Plebs*, XI/10 (November, 1919), p. 164.
73. Ibid.
74. Ibid.
75. Plebs Textbook Committee, *An Outline of Psychology*, p. 119.
76. Ibid. This is inspired by the work of Baudoin, Charles, *Suggestion and Autosuggestion* (London: 1920). He was a member of the New Nancy School and his work was translated by Eden and Cedar Paul who contributed also to various Plebs textbooks. The actual mechanism of 'autosuggestion' was described as: 'The nervous mechanism underlying the imaginative representation is closely connected with the nervous mechanism upon which the performance of the action depends. When one mechanism is excited, excitement of the other mechanism readily follows. Imagination becomes action.' Ibid.
77. Ibid., p. 123.

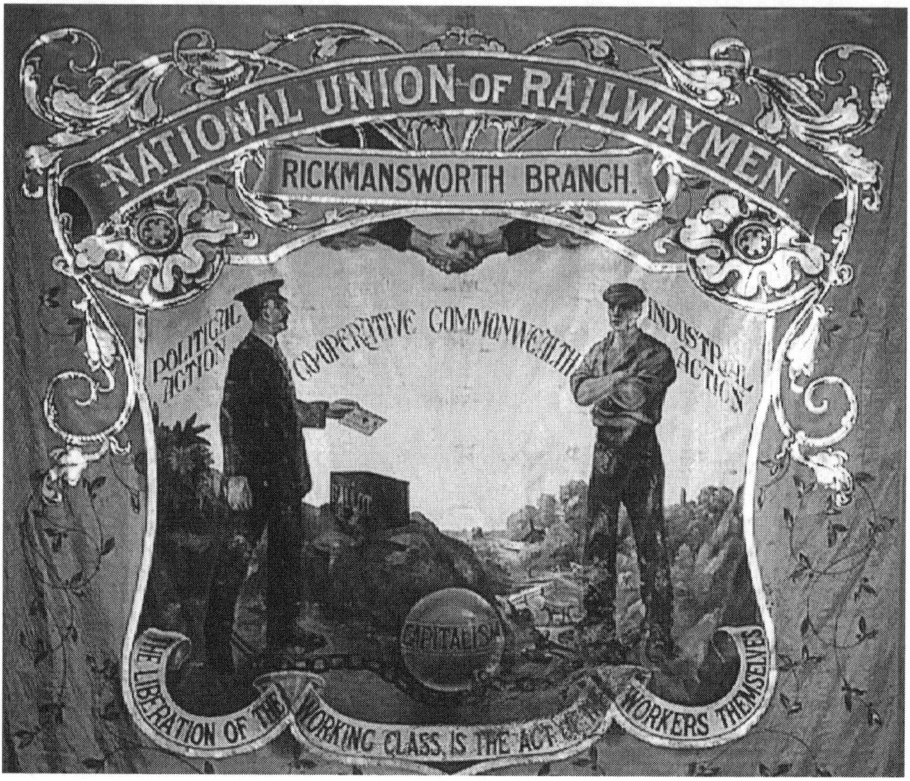

Figure 2.2 National Union of Railwaymen banner, Rickmansworth branch, no date

capture a flavour of the idealism and socialist aspirations of the unions at that time. Examples include 'Public Ownership', 'Nationalisation', 'State-Owned Cottages', 'Socialisation, Solidarity, Humanity', and 'The Wealth of the Workers'.[78]

The slogans of the NUR banners emulate this tradition of promoting political messages.[79] The Rickmansworth branch of the NUR *(Illustration 2.2)* devised a banner which showed two railway workers shackled by the huge ball and chain of capitalism, highlighting that freedom depended on political and industrial action. The slogan beneath this image declares that 'The Liberation of the Working Class is the Act of the Workers Themselves' and calls for 'Political

78. Gorman, John, *Banner Bright. An Illustrated History of the Banner of the British Trade Union Movement* (London: 1973), p. 46.

79. All information on the NUR banners is from the Labour History Museum, Manchester, where the majority of banners are kept. It is interesting to note that the banners where not catalogued until 1999. With the exception of John Gorman's book there has been no major work on the banners. I thank Phil Dunn for guiding me through the collection at the Labour History Museum and for his valuable information.

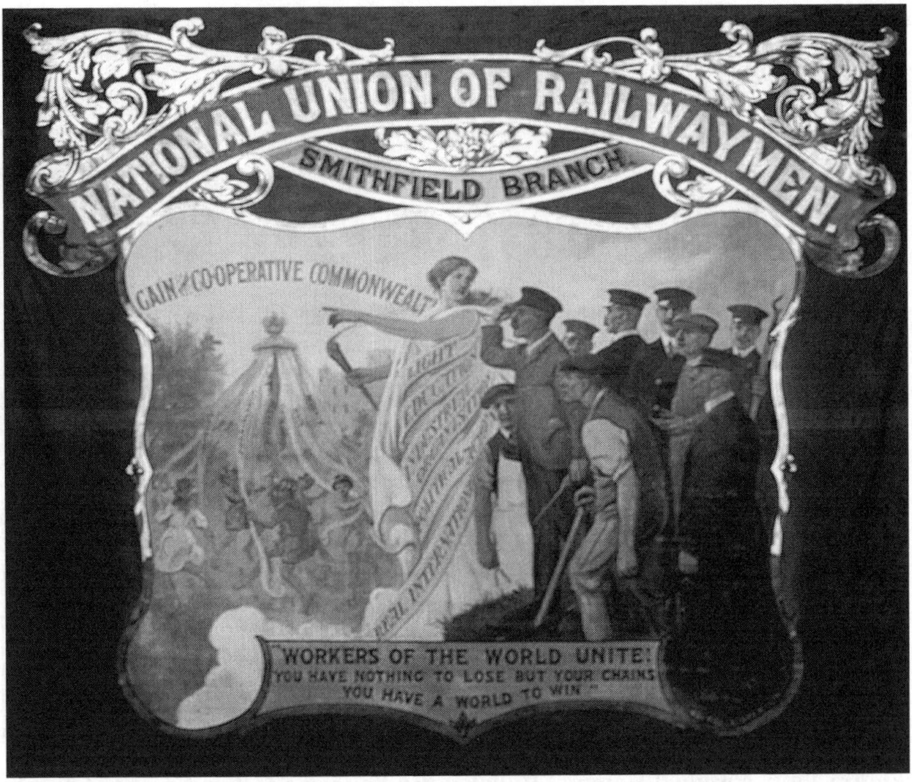

Figure 2.3 National Union of Railwaymen banner, Smithfield branch, no date

Action, Co-operative Commonwealth, Industrial Action'. The back of the banner proclaims that 'Unity is Strength', and asks for contributions to the Widows and Orphans Fund.

The wording on the banner for the Smithfield branch *(Illustration 2.3)* is more immediate: 'Workers of the World Unite! You have Nothing to Lose but Your Chains. You have a World to Win' referring to the *Communist Manifesto*.[80] The image is also more utopian than the Rickmansworth branch banner: in it, a female figure in the tradition of Walter Crane leads a group of workers and points towards a group of children who are playing around a maypole. The female figure is draped in a ribbon bearing the words, 'Real Intervention', 'Political Action', 'Industrial Organisation', 'Light', 'Education', and 'Co-operative Commonwealth'. The reverse side of the banner provides a less polemic view. It shows different aspects of the work of the railwayman at Smithfield station.

80. Marx, K. and Engels, F., *The Communist Manifesto* (London: 1933).

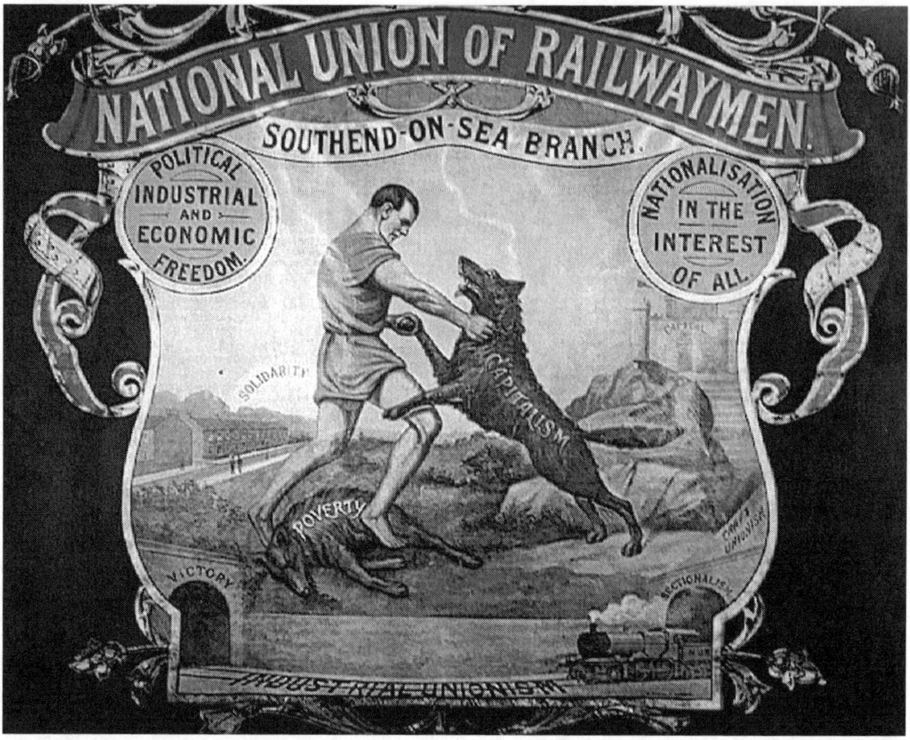

Figure 2.4 National Union of Railwaymen banner, Southend-on-Sea branch, no date

The Southend-on-Sea branch banner *(Illustration 2.4)* depicts a heroic male figure set against a semi-mythical, semi-contemporary landscape, and declares ‘Political, Industrial and Economic Freedom’ and ‘Nationalisation in the Interest of All’. The heroic male has just overcome the struggle of poverty and is fighting the wolf of capitalism. A. Williams argues that the style of the banners produced during this period was ‘cleaner and less cluttered’ and ‘more accessible to modern taste’[81] than the banners of the pre-war years. Most importantly, he argues, banner art ‘was no counter-culture’; its duty was to ‘communicate with the generality’ and to achieve this, it ‘employed the media of the commons’. For Williams, the imagery of the banner ‘moved with public art, most notably with the poster and advertisement art of the 1920s.[82]

The different influences on banner art before and after the First World War go further. After the war, the Labour Colleges, especially the Central Labour College with its NUR connections, played a big part in the imagery that appeared on the

81. Williams, A., ‘Introduction’, in Gorman, John, *Banner Bright*, p. 13.
82. Ibid.

NUR banners. As the analysis of the setting up of the Labour Colleges makes clear, 'smart catch-phrases' were a means of influencing the popular mind, and functioned as 'consciously formed thoughts'. Socialist propaganda, if it was to be successful, needed to concentrate on the psychological complexes brought about as a result of unemployment and privation, and autosuggestion played a significant part. The most important factor in socialist propaganda was the belief in the imminent breakdown of capitalism. Getting the common man to accept this belief and act on it depended on producing imagery that presented a realistic and at the same time dramatic picture of the economic environment of the day and the relationship of the worker to that environment. Any examination of the imagery and slogans of the NUR banners should take this on board.

The 'cleaner and less cluttered taste' of the pre-war banner cannot be attributed to a shift in modern taste alone. The banner provided a definite 'counter-culture' to the public monuments erected to commemorate the dead of the First World War, and it is only by looking at the banners as 'counter-culture' that we can understand their absence from the visual culture of the period. In the press coverage of the strike, there were no photographs of the banners held aloft by the strikers. However, their presence could not have been overlooked by the authorities, who kept a very watchful eye on the revolutionary tendencies of the returning working-class servicemen, particularly the strikers.

The advertising/propaganda posters produced by the Labour Research Department and circulated via the press provide a point of visual reference for the NUR strike. The majority of the posters showed only text and set out to explain the facts of the strike and the reasons behind it. The NUR poster *Is this Man an Anarchist?* (*Illustration 2.5*), is one exception, however, as it incorporates an illustration. This poster tries to refute Lloyd George's comments that the strike was an 'anarchist conspiracy' and the strikers were anarchists, and shows the imposing figure of the rail worker engaged in an innocent conversation with his family. In this way, the poster anchors the anarchic rail worker of government fears to the respectable institution of the family. Lisa Tickner, discussing the depiction of the suffrage campaign just before the First World War, has argued that suffrage imagery tried to hold up a mirror to potential converts and to suffragists themselves by focusing on a reassuring icon associated with womanliness. The iconography of the suffrage campaign was produced out of two elements: pro- and anti-suffrage arguments. In other words, suffrage propaganda was both informed by and cited this intertextuality.[83]

The NUR poster, as well as the NUR banners described above, uses the same kind of intertextuality as that of the suffrage movement to influence Britain's upper and middle classes. The message plays on the idea of the family as a unit incorporating wholesome values and ideals. The middle-class family was seen

83. Tickner, Lisa, *The Spectacle of Women. Imagery of the Suffrage Campaign 1907–14* (London: 1987), pp. 151–2.

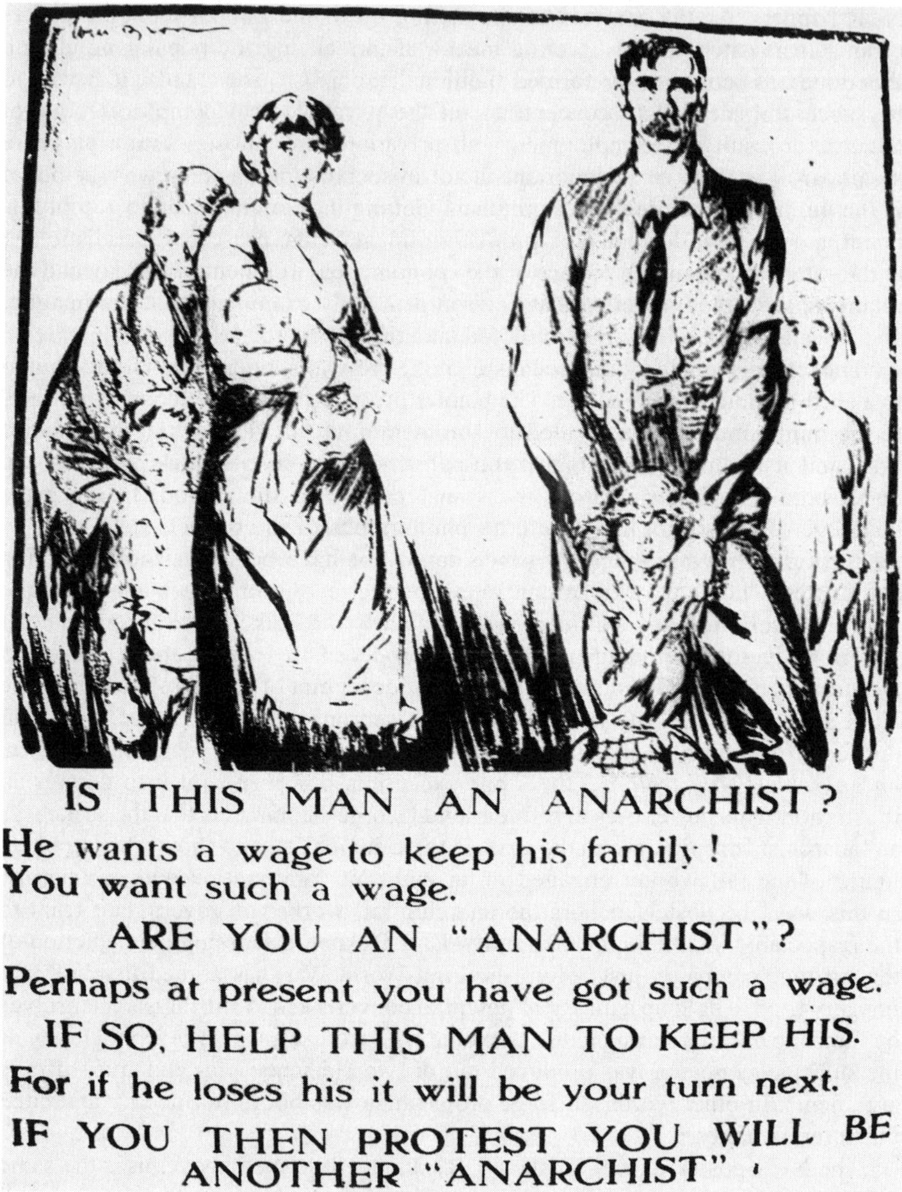

Figure 2.5 **Is this Man an Anarchist? Poster produced by the Labour Research Department. *Daily Herald*, 30/09/1919**

as a 'haven of domestic comfort and moral strength'.[84] Masculine self-respect depended not only on an exacting code of behaviour in public, but also on a properly ordered household and a commitment to family life.[85] Seen in this light, the poster can be interpreted as seeking the assimilation of the working-class man into the Victorian discourses of family values and codes. This need for assimilation presupposes notions of inclusion, exclusion and 'passing'. According to Sander Gilman, each class is defined economically, socially and erotically, and 'passing' refers to the desire to enter a new social class.[86] The NUR poster, when analysed within this framework, signifies a visual representation of the working-class man asking to pass as a middle-class man within the family, the bastion of morality and respectability. What is being signalled is the working-class man's dissatisfaction with his class status and the selfishness, laziness and immorality accorded to being working-class.

The poster can also be interpreted as promoting ideas that were outside the normalising discourse, such as the ideas advocated by the Central Labour College on the family. The home was seen as an economic institution which underwent 'profound changes' as a result of the capitalist industrial system, changes in food production and the changing role of women within the home. What is important is that:

> The capitalist system handicaps the worker who has a large family and practically places a premium on childlessness. ... These changes will exercise a profound influence on the house and on the conditions under which people will, or will not, consent to bear and rear children.[87]

The idea of conflicting psychological complexes provides an alternative interpretation for the poster. The *Plebs Textbook* describes the case of a class-conscious worker whose affection for his wife and children conflicts with his zeal for the revolutionary cause. Normal family instinct impels him to devote his leisure time to helping his wife in the home: 'This conduct will earn the approval of the bulk of the human herd,' states the *Plebs Textbook*, 'and will win the applause of such buttresses of capitalism as the organised churches.'[88] An opposite pull is exerted however by the 'revolutionary complex' which has multiple claims on his time. This complex

84. Davidoff, Leonore and Hall, Catherine, *Family Fortunes: Men and Women of the English Middle Class, 1780–1850* (London: 1987), p. 29.
85. Tosh, John, 'Domesticity and Manliness in the Victorian Middle Class. The Family of Edward Benson', Roper, M. and Tosh, J. (eds), *Manful Assertions*, p. 45. Tosh argues that in the late Victorian and Edwardian era, there was a growing separation between manliness and domesticity as a result of the ideas promoted by the 'New Imperialism'.
86. Gilman, Sander, *Making the Body Beautiful: A Cultural History of Aesthetic Surgery* (Princeton: 1999), pp. 22–3. See also Garber, Marjorie, *Symptoms of Culture* (London: 1999), chapter III. Garber discusses the implications of passing in relation to Jewish and homosexual men within western culture.
87. Plebs Textbook Committee, *An Outline of Psychology*, p. 116.
88. Ibid., p. 67.

is based on 'instinctive impulses, fortified by ideals of a better social order'. The revolutionary complex may bring the worker into: 'Courses which will involve privation and suffering for his nearest and dearest, unemployment for himself, and a great hardship for his wife and children.'[89]

Walter Benjamin, writing in the late 1920s in the aftermath of the mass Communist uprising suppression in the Ruhr region, has argued that the proletarian strike cannot be understood within the logic of 'positing', or the 'dialectic of performatives'. If one characterises the imposition of law as a performative act which posits conventions and legal conditions, then its dialectic, the proletarian strike, can be seen as 'deposing' or 'afformative'.[90] It is within these parameters that the visual culture of the strike can be understood as an afformative[91] act which provided a challenge to current beliefs and attitudes in relation to the working-class man, who became cast within a socio-political stereotype of selfishness, greed, revolutionary intent and employee bargaining.

It could be argued that the dialectical opposite for the NUR strike was provided by the performative acts of the unveiling of the First World War memorials and in this instance within the unveiling of memorials to the employees of the railway network.[92] The performative acts which took place within the official speeches, ritual and ceremonial of the unveilings imposed certain moral obligations upon those witnessing them.[93] The unveiling of the *London and North Western Railway Memorial* (LNWR) at London's Euston Station in 1921 will be discussed in relation to the gender performatives that were employed during the ceremony and in particular in relation to the manly, moral virtues required of the employees. The focal point of the unveiling was the awarding of military distinctions to those who had performed heroic acts, and who were seen as setting an example to others. How do these acts compare with the acts of the strikers two years prior to the memorial ceremony? The strikers stood accused of being selfish and revolutionary, and of acting in a way that could damage the country's fragile infrastructures. Their moral judgment was being held in question at a time when masculinity was characterised by courage, sacrifice

---

89. Ibid.

90. Benjamin Walter, 'Critique of Violence', in *Gesammelte Schriften*, Vol. II, p.193 quoted in Hamacher, Werner, 'Afformative, Strike. Benjamin's 'Critique of Violence', in Benjamin, Andrew and Osborne, Peter (eds), *Walter Benjamin's Philosophy. Destruction* and *Experience* (London: 2000).

91. The term afformative is used to denote an act that is antithetical to a performative act. Such an act works to 'depose' performative acts.

92. In railway stations all over the country, memorials were held to commemorate employees who had died during the war. In the mainline stations, the companies that formed the rail network established memorials to their employees. In London, the Paddington Station memorial for employees of the Great Western Railway is a sculpture by Charles Jagger of a soldier reading a letter.

93. Alex King has argued that the moral qualities of the dead were regarded as qualities that the living should emulate if they were genuinely to honour them. See King, Alex, *Memorials of the Great War*, p. 16.

and truth, virtues that were cultivated by the public school education system. Such hegemonic definitions of masculinity, reinforced by the memorials and the unveiling ceremonies were directly aimed at subordinating and controlling the returning serviceman.

The London and North Western Railway Memorial

> It will be some time before the strike is forgotten. Too many people suffered.[94]

The *LNWR Memorial* was unveiled on October 21, 1921, almost exactly two years after the NUR strike. The memories of the strike must still have been fresh in the minds of those present but if so, then this was not mentioned in any of the press coverage of the ceremony or referred to in the ceremony itself. Raymond Williams, commenting on the notion of 'selective tradition', has argued that the meanings of earlier historic episodes can be erased by subsequent hegemonic pressures.[95] Martin Jay takes Williams' theory a step further by arguing that 'digestive remembering' can only be premised on a certain forgetting, the forgetting of everything that resists incorporation into the system.[96] The unveiling of the *LNWR Memorial* served as a forum for erasing the revolutionary feeling that the NUR strike had inspired in the working-class men; the unveiling, in effect, created a 'hegemonic framing of memory'.[97] Frames also provide boundaries, which, according to Lynda Nead, raises important questions about 'who draws the lines, where they are drawn and for whom'.[98] Angus McLaren argues that during this period, the boundaries of masculinity were 'constructed and maintained by law, medicine, politics and popular ritual'.[99] This provides the basis of the argument in this section that the boundaries of masculinity were strictly defined and reinstated within the ritual of the unveiling of the *LNWR Memorial* and the iconography of the memorial.

Paul Connerton has argued that formalism and performativity play a key role in commemorative ceremonies.[100] This section will investigate their significance in relation to the working-class man. In commemorative rituals the human body is contained and regimented; the gestures and the language learned and internalised. Ritual, according to Roy Rappaport, signifies a participation 'in the construction

94. Lord Montagu of Beaulieu, 'On the Foot-plate', *The Nineteenth Century and After*, LXXXVI (November, 1919), p. 857.
95. Williams, Raymond, *Marxism and Literature* (Oxford: 1977), p. 117.
96. Jay, Martin, 'Against Consolation: Walter Benjamin and the Refusal to Mourn', in Winter, J. and Sivan, E. (eds), *War and Remembrance in the Twentieth Century* (Cambridge: 1999), p. 232.
97. Ashplant, T. G., *et al.*, *The Politics of War Memory*, p. 53.
98. Nead, Lynda, *The Female Nude. Art, Obscenity and Sexuality* (London: 1992), p. 33.
99. McLaren, Angus, *The Trials of Masculinity. Policing Sexual Boundaries, 1870–1930* (Chicago: 1997), p. 7.
100. Connerton, Paul, *How Societies Remember* (Cambridge: 1989), p. 61.

of a larger public order'.[101] He defines ritual as 'the performance of more or less invariant sequences of formal acts and utterances not encoded by the performer. As such, the form that is ritual is intrinsically reflexive in nature'.[102] In Rappaport's words, 'if the order of acts performed and utterances voiced by the actor is not encoded by him, his performance perforce conforms to that order'. This means that the participant subordinates him/herself to the order that the ritual encodes, simply by performing it. However, this is a two-way process which requires that on the one hand, 'the performer is incorporated into an order, [while] on the other, that very order is established'. More importantly, in performing a ritual, the 'performer accepts, and indicates to himself and others, that he accepts whatever is encoded in the ritual that he is performing'.[103]

The ritual of the unveiling of the *LNWR Memorial* provided a forum for redefining the working-class man and giving him a new status within society. During the ceremony, memories of war in the form of heroism, devotion to duty and self-sacrifice were not only recalled, but performatively imposed on the participants. In contrast, any memories of the strike were dismissed or erased from the ceremony. Forgetting was a political act in this instance. Eric Hobsbawm has argued that the 'politics of memory is an exercise in social engineering' and that what is preserved in popular memory is what has been 'selected, written, pictured and popularised'.[104]

The Euston Station memorial was unveiled by Field-Marshal Lord Haig, who delivered a 'striking address upon the fine work of railwaymen throughout the long period of hostilities'.[105] Lord Haig stressed the contribution of the railwaymen to the war effort, mentioning particularly their 'loyalty and unselfishness'. One needs to remember that these were the same men who two years earlier stood accused of being disloyal and selfish because of their demands for better pay. Lord Haig proceeded to congratulate the management of the LNWR on the 'generous way in which they have treated their men while serving with the colours, and since they returned' and on the way they had 'recognised the claims of the widows and dependants of the fallen'. His speech presented the LNWR as a caring and fair employer, which 'set a fine example in this matter to all employers'.[106] What was most important for Lord Haig, was the example set by the men who had died for those at the ceremony, and the need for the survivors to 'remember always' the 'burden these men bore so bravely'. Particularly poignant, for Lord Haig, was the 'unselfish co-operation' and

---

101. Rappaport, Roy, 'Concluding Comments on Ritual and Reflexivity', *Semiotica*, 30(1/2) (1980), p. 187.
102. Ibid.
103. The idea of obligation in performativity was developed first by Searle, J. R., *Speech Acts* (Cambridge: 1969).
104. Hobsbawm, Eric, 'Introduction: Inventing Traditions', in Hobsbawm, E. and Ranger, T. (eds), *The Invention of Tradition* (Cambridge: 2000), p. 13.
105. Lord Haig, 'Unveiling Speech', Euston Memorial, PRO, RAIL 2868.
106. Ibid.

'spirit of comradeship' that should be a guide and inspiration for Britain during the difficult times of reconstruction.[107]

The same rhetoric of self-sacrifice, courage and nationalism was also evident in the address given by the Chairman of the LNWR, Charles Lawrence, which emphasised the importance of learning from the 'conduct of these brave men'. Both employers and employees, Lawrence pointed out, should 'strive to act in a spirit of mutual sympathy', 'forbearance and absolute rectitude of purpose'.[108] The speeches by Lord Haig and Charles Lawrence provided a platform from which gender codes could re-insert the working-class men into the 'confines of a normative reproductive economy'.[109]

Lawrence's speech becomes more specific about the need for remembering and honouring the dead. However, he is talking about the relationship between employer and employee, rather than the need of the bereaved present at the ceremony. Jay Winter has argued that public commemoration after the First World War offered a focal point for the bereaved, translating their individual grief into acts of public mourning.[110] Lawrence's speech, however, provide no consolation for the bereaved, but represents an exercise in industrial relations, where the call for mutual sympathy, forbearance and magnanimity is represented by performatives rather than any real words of comfort.

At the opening ceremony of the Euston Memorial, Lord Haig represented the epitome of a certain masculine ideal, and as such set an example for others to follow. The Chairman of the LNWR stressed the manner in which the Field-Marshal's 'tenacity and determination of purpose' had guided the Army.[111] Most importantly, Lord Haig was the 'embodiment of public duty and of public service'.[112] This public service had manifested itself in a ferocious itinerary which entailed Lord Haig 'visiting all the great centres of industry, in order to 'plead the cause of his surviving officers and men'. As a consequence of this activity, Lord Haig was often perceived to be the embodiment of the dead servicemen; a messenger of the dead who delivered their messages throughout the nation. However, as well as visiting centres of industry, he also unveiled numerous memorials. Industrial relations and commemoration are thus conflated into a single act which sought to provide stability during an era of industrial strife.

Where did this need to continue the war rhetoric and to appeal to the dead as a way of improving industrial relations stem from? A closer look at the unveiling

---

107. Ibid.
108. Charles Lawrence, 'Unveiling Speech', Euston Memorial, PRO, RAIL 2868. Charles Lawrence was the brother of General Lawrence, who was Chief of Staff during the First World War.
109. Sherman, Daniel, 'Monuments, Mourning and Masculinity in France after World War I', *Gender & History*, 8/1 (1996), p. 84.
110. Winter, Jay, *Sites of Memory, Sites of Mourning. The Great War in European Cultural History* (Cambridge: 1995), p. 104.
111. Charles Lawrence, 'Unveiling Speech'.
112. Ibid.

provides some clues. In a letter to Charles Lawrence, the designer of the memorial, R. Wynn Owen, highlights his dissatisfaction at the lack of any guidelines to help the public understand the 'full significance' of the monument.[113] Wynn Owen had already provided the LNWR with his 'interpretation of the meanings of the architecture' of the memorial and had hoped it would be included in the unveiling ceremony speeches. He was particularly keen that Lord Haig should mention it in his speech, but instead of this, Lord Haig had requested information and statistics on the number of men who had joined, lost their lives, been awarded honours and, most importantly, whose dependants had been given financial allowances as well as pensions.[114] This material, Lord Haig used to promote good industrial relations and show how caring the LNWR was as an employer at this time of need. In his letter, Wynn Owen claims that he had given a copy of his interpretation to the LNWR publicity department for dissemination to the press, but that 'by some means no reference to it [had] appeared in any newspaper' and 'the press reports of the ceremony [had been] curtailed'. He was anxious that the meaning of his design should be made public, and suggested that November 11, 1921, a date almost three weeks after the unveiling, would be an appropriate day for his interpretation to be read. His reason for insisting on the matter was, he claimed, 'that the public could regard the monument with intelligence as to its meaning'.[115] However, in a reply to the letter, Charles Lawrence wrote that he thought that an 'explanation of the symbolism of the monument' was neither 'necessary' nor 'desirable'.[116]

Why was Wynn Owen's explanation thought to be unnecessary or undesirable? In his eyes, architecture was 'an expression of the living artistic spirit'. Like the human face, which, deprived of life, was devoid of expression, Wynn Owen believed that architectural structures, deprived of artistic spirit, lacked expression. In constructing the memorial, he had taken into consideration the Christian principles of justice and freedom for which the war had been fought, which he represented with a cross on each side of the obelisque. The four bronze figures on the monument represented the comrades of the fallen guarding their honour in a 'posture of reverence'.[117] What was important was that the memorial should be 'devoid of any element, which might mark it as an emblem of victory'. It was raised, Wynn Owen concluded, to the memory of the men who had 'heard the call'.[118]

The LNWR management, the government in the figure of Lord Haig and the architect of the memorial each projected their own interpretation onto the memorial. Moreover, each called on the memory of the dead: the artist, in order to promote his ideas and Christian beliefs, the management, in order to smooth industrial relations

113. Letter from R. Wynn Owen to C. Lawrence, PRO, RAIL 2868, 6 November 1921.

114. Statistics of the LNWR War Effort, PRO, RAIL 2868. This information was sent to Lord Haig together with the Chairman's speech on 4 October 1921.

115. Letter from R. Wynn Owen to C. Lawrence.

116. Ibid.

117. R. Wynn Owen, 'War Memorial in Euston Square. Interpretation of the Design', PRO, RAIL 2868.

118. Ibid.

within the company, and the government, in order to pave the way for an end to the revolutionary feeling and industrial unrest amongst the working classes.

However, a number of voices were still absent from the debates. The composition of the memorial committee provides one example. The committee for the LNWR memorial was largely made up of directors or managers of LNWR.[119] What it didn't include was any of the employees whose colleagues the memorial was meant to commemorate and who contributed a third of the memorial's total cost.[120] This group instead became participants in a spectacle organised by the management.

Another example of a voice that was absent from the debate is provided by the Roll of Honour.[121] This was presented to the nearest relative of each of the fallen as a 'personal memorial of his or her lost one'. The first page was illustrated with the flags of the Allied troops, and gave the name, railway grade and station, and naval or military rank of the 3,719 employees who had lost their life. This was followed by a full-page drawing of the memorial, which in turn was followed by the names of those men who had been awarded the Victoria Cross, together with a reproduction, in colour, of the Victoria Cross itself. The page also gave accounts of 'the gallant deeds for which the cross was awarded'.[122] Below are some examples of the 'heroic acts' and 'acts of bravery' that were acknowledged in the Roll of Honour.

Lance Corporal J. A. Christie, a parcels clerk at Euston Station, realising the difficult position that his unit found itself in, took a supply of bombs over the top, proceeding alone about fifty yards in the open along the communication trench, and bombed the enemy. He continued to do this alone in spite of very heavy opposition until his unit was in a safer position. Throughout 'he was subjected to heavy machine-gun fire and saved many lives'. By doing so, he showed the 'greatest coolness and total disregard for his own safety'.[123]

Private E. Sykes, labourer at the engineering section at the Western Front, despite heavy fire went forward and brought back four wounded – he made a fifth journey and remained out under conditions 'which appeared to be certain death', until he had bandaged all those who were too badly wounded to be moved. These 'gallant actions, performed under incessant machine-gun and rifle fire, showed an utter contempt of danger'.[124]

Coolness and disregard for one's own safety, conspicuous valour, and utter contempt for danger, here constitute the necessary ingredients for a heroic and

119. The members of the committee were: The Honorary A. H. Holland Hibbert, director and chairman of the committee, Colonel Lord Lambourne CVO, director, E.F.C. Trench, Chief Engineer, Mr F. Hare, Mr Hollywell, Mr Nash, all three of the General Manager's Department, and the architect Mr R. Wynn Owen.

120. The total cost was £12,500. The staff contributed £4,000.

121. The Roll of Honour was originated by F. Hare, of the General Manager's Department, Euston.

122. Pratt, Edwin, *War Record of the London and North Western Railway* (London: 1922), p. 69.

123. Ibid.

124. Ibid.

brave man. Each account strongly suggests a disregard for one's own life over the lives of others, and by implication, the nation. The three employees of the LNWR who were awarded the Victoria Cross set an example for those who survived, and yet after the Armistice the same men were portrayed as selfishly demanding higher wages and taking industrial action at a time when the nation was trying to reconstruct a ruined economy and tackle mass unemployment. It becomes clear that what the act of bestowing honours also symbolised, was an attempt to assimilate the working-class man into hegemonic codes of masculinity.

The Roll of Honour was meant to be 'treasured as a family heirloom'. Edwin Pratt has described it as an 'impressive contribution to the history of the Great War', since it showed how the 'personnel of one of our great railway companies served, suffered, and, also, won for themselves such conspicuous honour, when they went to the help of their country in her hour of direct need'.[125] Dying in this way became a sacrificial act that was meant to give significance to the person's death. Michael Rowlands has recently argued that a memorial becomes a monument and hence accommodates the grieving process of the bereaved when it acknowledges the importance of death by giving meaning to the sacrifice of the dead.[126] Did the memorial, Roll of Honour and the Victoria Cross achieve this?

It is important to look at the act of honouring as an act of assimilation rather than an acknowledgement of a sacrifice that has been made. Pierre Bourdieu has argued that to assign an essence, a competence, is to impose a right to be, that is an obligation of being so. It is to signify to someone what s/he is and how s/he should behave as a consequence. The code of honour, according to Bourdieu, is only a developed form of the expression that says of a man: 'he's a man's man'. To institute, to give a social definition, an identity, is also to impose *boundaries*.[127]

The unveiling ceremony imposed actual as well as artificial boundaries on those taking part. The LNWR nominated E. Sykes to perform the ceremonial act of placing the wreath. As such, he became the embodiment of the ideal working-class man: unselfish, patriotic and obedient, the personification of public duty and service. Other 'distinguished' employees, 'most of whom wore many war decorations, were drawn up in the form of a square around the memorial'.[128] *(Illustration 2.6)* They fenced off the memorial in imitation of the way that the bronze sentries on each of the four corners of the plinth, provided a kind of boundary to the memorial itself. Michael Rowlands argues that the 'visually empty repetition of the same image' in memorials 'signifies the absence of debt

125. Ibid.

126. Rowlands, Michael, 'Remembering to Forget: Sublimation as Sacrifice in War Memorials', in Forty, A. and Kuchler, S. (eds), *The Art of Forgetting* (Oxford: 1999), p. 137.

127. Bourdieu, Pierre, *Distinction: A Social Critique of the Judgment of Taste* (Cambridge Mass.: 1984), p. 120.

128. 'London and North Western Railway War Memorial', *The Railway Magazine*, 49 (Jul.–Dec 1921), p. 419.

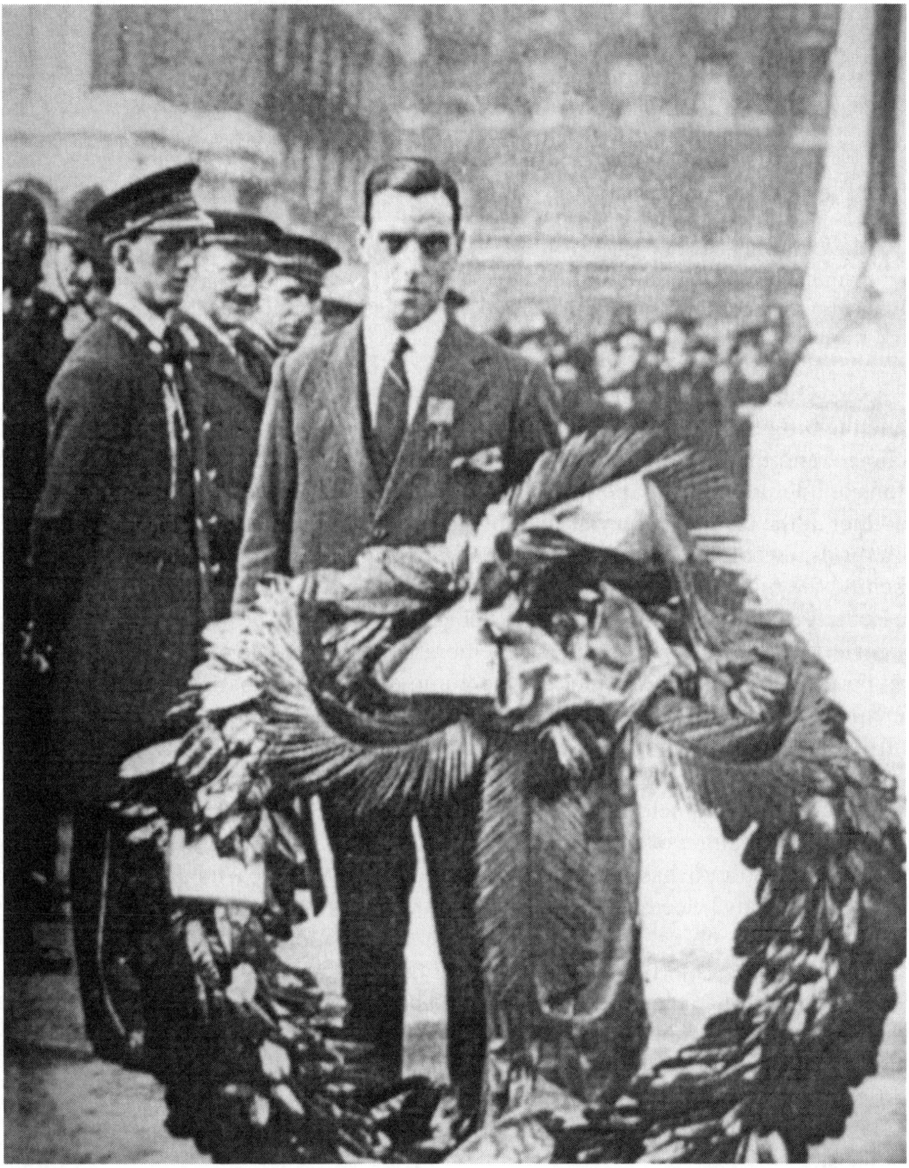

Figure 2.6 Ceremony of the Unveiling of the *LNWR Memorial*, Euston Station, London, sculpted by R. Wynn Owen (1921). *The Railway Gazette*, 28/10/1921, p. 641

by the living to the dead'.[129] The image of the soldier in uniform, represented by the four bronze sentries on the *LNWR Memorial,* was repeated in monuments across Britain. The questions they raised on individual and national identity will be explored in more detail in the next section.

The Picturesque Soldier

> Never has the soldier been more picturesque, more sculptural even, than he is today, with his helmet, his putteed or gaitered legs, and his rough overcoat, strapped and hung with weapons, haversacks, canteen tins, water bottles, and all the equipment of modern warfare.[130]

The exhibition on memorials held at the Victoria and Albert Museum in 1918 and the programme which accompanied it identified simplicity as the aesthetic of choice, and the figure of the soldier in uniform as the most representative image for commemoration of the First World War. E. Warren places the figure of the soldier at the centre of the war memorial, but also attributes to it certain aesthetic qualities, effectively distancing the soldier from the realities of war. The person behind the figure, as well as his equipment, uniform and the paraphernalia of war essential to fighting at the Front, have become strangely aestheticised.

The figure of the soldier in commemoration imagery has often been described as portraying 'the typical, indeed, the common victim or participant',[131] and the memorials of the First World War have been associated by some with a democratic, all-inclusive commemoration of the war. Yet, the simplicity of the figure of the soldier was problematic in resolving the grief of the bereaved relatives, more importantly, and something that is often ignored, it was problematic in resolving the grief and trauma of the ex-servicemen. Ashplant *et al.* believe that the image of the soldier hero has not been sufficiently analysed, particularly in relation to the 'subjective needs and desires that are mobilised by the official activities of commemoration'.[132] In the next section, the sculptural figures adopting the military stances of drill practice – standing to attention, at ease, reverse arms – will be examined in relation to the memories of ex-servicemen, particularly their recollection of the training that they underwent to discipline their bodies and spirit in accordance with military requirements. We will also discover the distinct differences between the memories of the soldiers being trained, and the officers who trained them and the implications of such distinction for the commemoration of the war.

---

129. Rowlands, Michael, 'Remembering to Forget: Sublimation as Sacrifice in War Memorials', p. 144.
130. Warren, E., *War Memorials* (London: 1919), no pagination
131. Penny, Nicholas, 'English Sculpture and the First World War', *Oxford Art Journal*, 4/2 (1981), p. 37.
132. Ashplant, T. G., *et al.*, 'The Politics of War Memory and Commemoration', p. 33.

Unconquerable Manhood

The *Gateshead Memorial*, in the form of a tomb containing a low relief bronze figure, provides a figurative representation of the absent body that the cenotaph was intended to symbolise in the repatriation and burial of the Unknown Soldier in Westminster Abbey. To what extent did the sculptural form of the soldier allow different interpretations of the war? For Alex King, the lack of any 'definite resolution' in figurative memorials of the First World War[133] gave viewers licence to interpret the memorials as they chose. Daniel Sherman, examining war commemoration in France, comments that the figure of the soldier, the *poilu*, became the most pervasive in French war memorials. Sherman argues that the figure of the *poilu* could 'conjoin national with local resonances' and was an important channel for grieving relatives and ex-servicemen.[134] Catherine Moriarty, on the other hand, believes that the public could not identify with the figurative sculpture of the First World War. This was because it provided a complete symbolic body in contrast with the absent, fragmented body of the war, stripping the dead of their personal identities and the circumstances of their death and replacing them with a public myth.[135]

This section will argue that only by examining another aspect of the commemoration of the war, namely, the notions of masculinity that were promoted by the figurative memorials, is it possible to explore the way that the public identified with the memorials. The relationship between masculinity and war commemoration has been studied in relation to Germany during the First World War, when the 'ideal manliness became symbolic of personal and national regeneration'. The 'common man was integrated into the camaraderie of the trenches as symbols of true masculinity'.[136] Looking at the example provided by France, Daniel Sherman argues that war commemoration not only reflected gender roles in French society, but also helped to construct these roles. France went on to develop a very specific aggressive and heroic masculinity during the war,[137] but Sherman does not see this as problematic in terms of the way the public were able to identify with the *poilu*.

Looking at the *Gateshead Memorial* from the point of analysis offered by Sherman or Mosse, the common soldier becomes a symbol of masculinity, standing guard over the cenotaph, where the bodies of his comrades are supposedly buried. The memorial committee for the Gateshead monument stressed the fact that it was dedicated to the devotion shown by 'all classes' during the war, and to their 'allegiance to the best traditions of our race'; it was

133. King, Alex, *Memorials of the Great War*, p. 141.
134. Sherman, Daniel, 'Art, Commerce, and the Production of Memory in France after World War I', in Gillis, John (ed.), *Commemorations* (Princeton: 1994), p. 202.
135. Moriarty, Catherine, 'The Absent Dead and Figurative First World War Memorials', *Transactions of the Ancient Monument Society*, 39 (1995), p. 38.
136. Mosse, George, *Fallen Soldiers. Reshaping the Memory of the World Wars* (Oxford: 1990), p. 54.
137. Sherman, Daniel, 'Monuments, Mourning and Masculinity', p. 92.

there to 'enshrine the names and deeds of those who fell in the Great War'.[138] The soldier guards the 'Room of Remembrance', in the centre of which stands a stone lectern bearing the inscription, 'Their Bodies are Buried in Peace but their Name Liveth for Evermore'. Above the lectern on which the Book of Remembrance sits is an 'Everburning Lamp, emblematic of our undying memory'.[139] The stone portal is inscribed with the Latin phrase '*Mors Janua Vitae*' (Death is the Gate of Life), which uses what Paul Fussell has described as 'high diction'[140] and carries a certain exclusivity in its own right. The figure of the soldier, by being incorporated within the aesthetic language and symbolism of the cenotaph and inscriptions, becomes part of the hegemonic masculinity characterised by self-sacrifice, devotion to duty, and defence of the qualities of the race – ideals which the memorial committee identified as central to the memorial. These ideals are in turn bestowed upon the soldier himself, who is described by the memorial committee as a 'warrior nine feet high, depicting our 'Manhood', in an attitude of 'Defence: strong, motionless and unconquerable.'[141]

What is important is the way in which masculinity is contained within the figure of the soldier, especially in his posture of alert defensiveness that represents 'unconquerable manhood'. Commenting on the construction of masculinities within the military establishment, David Morgan argues that of all the sites where masculinities are constructed, those associated with 'war and the military are some of the most direct'.[142] The memorial achieves the construction of definite masculine roles by placing the soldier in the military position of attention.

The war and the post-Armistice civil discontent and unrest, however, revealed a number of discontinuities. The public school ethos with its characteristics of fortitude, endurance, self-sacrifice and discipline that the readers of the *Daily Telegraph* insisted were an antidote to the civil unrest,[143] revealed discontinuities in the ways in which such masculinities were perceived and promoted as unproblematic and universalising. The imposition of the public school ethos was seen as problematic by several commentators writing in the liberal journal *The Nineteenth Century and After*, who identified the pressures on men to conform to a highly idealistic notion of masculinity.[144] Many of the journal's middle-class contributors held public

138. Gateshead War Memorial Committee, *Gateshead and the Great War. A Retrospective and a Reminder*, IWM, Ephemera, Memorials, Box C, May 14, 1922, p. 24.

139. Ibid., p. 11.

140. Fussell, Paul, *The Great War and Modern Memory* (Oxford: 1975), p. 21.

141. Gateshead War Memorial Committee, *Gateshead and the Great War*, p. 11.

142. Morgan, David, 'Theatres of War: Combat, the Military and Masculinities', p. 165.

143. Courtney, W. L., *Is it a New World? A series of Articles and Letters contributed by Correspondents to the Daily Telegraph, August–September, 1920* (London: 1920).

144. For the period of the First World War, see Bourke, Joanna, *Dismembering the Male. Men's Bodies, Britain and the Great War* (London: 1996); Showalter, Elaine, *The Female Malady. Women, Madness and English Culture, 1830–1980* (London: 1987); Caesar, Adrian, *Taking it Like A Man. Suffering, Sexuality and the War Poets* (Manchester: 1993).

school education to blame for these pressures. Wilfrid Ewart[145] argued that the post-Armistice problems that the country was facing were due to the public school education of the middle-class man and in particular the 'hero-worship' that these schools inspired, which in many instances was very difficult to emulate.[146] Those who did not conform to the mould, especially those considered weak or 'sensitive', soon 'lagged behind'.[147] Ewart sees the public school system as producing insular men who held 'uncompromising aspirations' and who were clinging to 'bygone times'. Most alarmingly, 'by the masses, even his manliness was suspect'.[148]

T. H. Procter, an ex-combatant himself, saw the war as providing a further rift for hegemonic masculinities. For Procter, the 'marked loss of idealism' and 'general feeling of disillusionment' that permeated the post-war years were due to the fact that men were trained to kill.[149] During the war, the Army had trained men so that they would be strong enough to kill the enemy; the wounded were taken care of, not necessarily to save them pain but to 'patch them up and send them back to kill more Germans'. The 'business of killing' had the additional outcome of making men aware of their own mortality.[150]

Death and the destructiveness of war seem to be the only elements to have left their mark on the returning soldier. Procter lists a whole series of effects that he describes as 'superficial'. He claims that comradeship, seen as the 'general fusion of the classes' and promoted as 'the most precious thing of all', showed very little evidence of having a 'permanent influence in national life' and that it was remarkable how quickly the 'heroes of the trenches became once more "the lower classes"'.[151]

The hold that the war had over the returning soldier during the subsequent civil unrest of 1919, was, however, overwhelming. Procter repeatedly refers to feelings of disillusionment and discouragement. Life in the trenches, with its long hours of

---

145. Wilfrid Ewart was among those who Rosa Bracco defined as middlebrow writers of the inter-war years. See Bracco, Rosa, *Merchants of Hope*, p. 50.
146. Ewart, Wilfrid, 'The Young Men of England', *The Nineteenth Century*, DXIII (November 1919), p. 799.
147. Ibid., p. 800.
148. Ibid., p. 804. Ewart does not elaborate this further, but one may assume that he is referring to middle-class man being seen as unmanly by working-class men. See Sinfield, Alan, *The Wilde Century*; McLaren, Angus, *The Trials of Masculinity*.
149. Procter, T. H., 'The Motives of the Soldier', *International Journal of Ethics*, XXXI (Oct 1920), p. 44.

    This was a view shared by others, especially those based in the psychoanalytic profession, including the famous psychoanalyst W. H. R. Rivers whose work with shell-shocked soldiers will be examined in more detail in Chapter 3, and Freud's follower Ernest Jones. See Jones, Ernest, 'War and Individual Psychology', *Sociological Review* (London, 1915); Rivers, W. H. R., 'War Neurosis and Military Training', *Mental Hygiene,* II/4 (1918); Joanna Bourke has also examined the effects of killing on combatants in twentieth century warfare. See Bourke, Joanna, *An Intimate History of Killing. Face-to-Face Killing in Twentieth Century Warfare* (London: 1999).
150. Procter, T. H., 'The Motives of the Soldier', p. 44.
151. Ibid., p. 45.

inactivity and sudden bursts of activity and excitement, made readjusting to civilian life a very difficult task. 'We have lost habits of industry', Procter comments, before continuing: 'We have degenerated in mind and soul.'[152] The men were emotionally drained: 'we have exhausted our capacity to feel,'[153] Procter concludes.

Mass impulses, shouting and rushing forward with a crowd were the only way of arousing the returning soldier, according to Procter. Independent thought was discouraged in the Army. As a result, the returning soldier suffered from a 'loss of power to judge' for himself and was 'left with a horrible numbness of mind and soul'. Procter's argument, particularly his claims about the inability of the servicemen to be excited and their incapacity to feel, needs to be examined in relation to the Army's perception of the individual, and the function of military training to reduce the capacity for fear. Fear was also a feature in the commemoration of the war, and the following sections will attempt to examine this more closely.

Fear, Attention and Discipline

Joanna Bourke has argued that the chief function of military training was to 'convert civilians into effective combatants'. Men needed to be taught more than the mechanics of using a rifle. Military training had to 'imbibe military traits' such as 'toughness, alertness, loyalty and discipline'.[154] Discipline in particular was seen as a means of controlling fear. Major J. F. C. Fuller[155] recognised the importance of using psychological tactics to suppress individuals and crowds. He wrote:

> Once won men may be slaughtered, they may be annihilated, but they will not be conquered.[156]

For Fuller, instincts and habits provide a means of conquering men.[157] The strongest instinct is self-preservation. Fuller explains how during peace, we 'must decide how fear and fatigue, those enemies of man's mind and body, affect him; how the instinct of self-preservation may be controlled and disciplined'.[158]

Theories on crowd control,[159] combined with theories on human instincts, provided a solution to the unpredictability of fear and fatigue. The Army is the ultimate

152. Ibid., p. 47.
153. Ibid.
154. Bourke, Joanna, *An Intimate History of Killing*, p. 72.
155. According to Joanna Bourke, Fuller was the most prescient military philosopher of the twentieth century. See Bourke, Joanna, *An Intimate History of Killing*, p. 85; On Fuller's work with the Tank Corps during the First World War and his involvement with Aleister Crowley, see Wright, Patrick, *Tank. The Progress of a Monstrous War Machine* (London: 2000).
156. Fuller, J. F. C., *Training Soldiers for War* (London: 1914), p. v.
157. McDougall, William, *An Introduction to Social Psychology* (London: 1908).
158. Fuller, J. F. C., *Training Soldiers for War*, p. 16.
159. Fears of the crowds, their perceived uncontrollable powers and unreasoning behaviour gave rise to a number of publications. Theories of crowd psychology and control became

example of crowd organisation and control. The exaltation and intensification of emotion that is characteristic of all crowds is what enables men in the army to face danger. The army embodies traditional sentiments, especially admiration for certain moral qualities: courage, endurance, trustworthiness, and cheerful obedience. These sentiments are then addressed in training and impressed on every recruit, especially new members, by way of mass suggestion: 'a continuous bombardment of military impressions which form the sentiments, change the emotions and control the instincts of the soldier.'[160] Uniformity of character and spirit is the desired outcome.

The official military training manuals provided a guide to controlling non-desirable instincts and establishing uniformity within the different ranks. The *Training and Manoeuvre Regulations* manual states that the function of training is 'to develop the mental, moral and physical qualities as highly as possible in each individual', and to provide the ability to 'move rapidly in formed bodies without confusion'. The training must be based on 'uniformity of action'[161] and instil in each trainee the 'fighting spirit' which provides the 'will to advance at any cost in order to close with the enemy and kill him'. Discipline, 'the ingrained habit of obedience', is paramount, since it controls and directs the fighting spirit.[162] Discipline also makes organisation effective, while uniformity is at the heart of effective organisation: 'Only if it is uniformly organised in every part can a force be relied on by its commander to carry out the same orders in the same way.'[163]

Discipline is achieved by means of a process called the 'close order drill'. The purpose of the trainer, according to the *Platoon Training* manual, is to 'control firmly the will of the soldier'. The manual states that close order drill is the first and quickest method of teaching discipline and controlling the will of the soldier.[164] The drill begins with the soldier being taught to stand to attention. Attention is in fact the purpose for which drill was invented: 'It secures the whole attention of the man to his commander.' The soldier demonstrates attention by maintaining

---

prominent at the beginning of the twentieth century with the publication in 1896 of Gustave Le Bon's book *The Crowd. A Study of the Popular Mind.* Robert Nye argues that such theories flourished, following the violence that erupted in the Paris Commune, and provided the backbone for the work by Le Bon. The theories, according to Nye, were based on the assumption that the violence of the crowd was a consequence of the industrialisation and rapid urbanisation that took place during the nineteenth century. The 'alienation and social disorganisation characteristic of these processes encouraged collective violence. The crowd theorists tried to find ways in which crowds could be controlled. In Britain a number of books appeared following the publication of Le Bon's book, most notable of which were Martin Conway's *The Crowd in Peace and War* and William McDougall's *The Group Mind.*

See Nye, Robert, *The Origins of Crowd Psychology. Gustave Le Bon and the Crisis of Mass Democracy in the Third Republic* (London: 1975), pp. 123–147.

160. Ibid., p. 14.
161. War Office, *Training and Manoeuvre Regulations* (London: 1913), p. 9.
162. War Office, *Platoon Training* (London: 1918), p. 20.
163. Ibid., p. 2.
164. Ibid., p. 22.

absolute silence, his body held rigid as he waits for the word of command.[165] If drill movements are added, 'the instant, unhesitating and exact obedience of orders' is also achieved.[166]

Major R. F. Legge suggests that when men ask why they need to go through this procedure, they should be told that 'this is the first lesson in self-control'. There is something in the steadiness, rigidity and silence of standing to attention that Major Legge finds extremely appealing. He describes an incident, reported by an officer, when a hundred men of the Gordon Highlanders regiment stood to attention in the hot Indian sun, which encapsulates his fascination:

> They stood to attention in the hot Indian sun, in marching order, for over one hour. He said they simply fascinated him, his eyes kept turning away from the gorgeous spectacle surrounding him, back to those silent Highlanders, who, with their officer standing in front, looked as though they had been hewn out of rock. He said he never saw a move from them the whole time.[167]

The method of instruction in training was also important. Simplicity was vital: formal orders needed to be 'firm' and 'simple'.[168] J. F. C. Fuller argues that 'we must inculcate the idea of simplicity from the very first'. The reason for this was that the simpler the teaching, the easier it was to suggest and to repeat, the quicker it could be assimilated and the more likely it was to be remembered. The simpler the picture, argued Fuller, the more precise was the mental picture in the mind of the mass, for the 'mass does not reason'.[169]

The ultimate outcome of military discipline was to 'turn a crowd of men into an army'.[170] In doing so, discipline turns men into the parts of a machine. General Sir Ian Hamilton provides a mechanical parable to illustrate this. He compares the production of a battalion with that of a locomotive. In the case of the battalion, raw lads are enlisted, dressed in uniform and formed into small squads. The squads are formed into sections and are roughly knocked into shape. The sections are formed into platoons and companies and drilled. The battalion is held together by discipline: a many-headed mob has become a battalion – one word from the Colonel, and the battalion will spit fire; another word, and it will advance to conquer. In the case of the locomotive, ore is brought to the surface. Metal is run off into ingots of uniform size. Parts of the machine are roughly knocked into shape. The various parts are grouped and perfected. The finished parts are assembled. The machine is held together by clamps, rivets and steel framework: a heap of rubbish has become a locomotive. At the driver's touch, it will 'belch forth steam and advance to the conquest of space'.[171]

165. Ibid., p. 23.
166. War Office, *Field Artillery Training* (London: 1914), p. 24.
167. Legge, R. F. (Major), *Mainly About Discipline* (London: 1914), p. 20.
168. War Office, *Platoon Training*, p. 22.
169. Fuller, J. F. C., *Training Soldiers for War*, p. 37.
170. Anon., *What Every Soldier Ought to Know* (Oxford: 1915), p. 4.
171. Hamilton, Ian, *The Soul and Body of an Army* (London: 1921), p. 26.

The observations on training provide an insight not only into the direct relationship between fear and ways of controlling its presence within the troops, but also into the ways in which the individual whom the military authorities hold in very low esteem, a 'heap of rubbish' as General Sir Ian Hamilton puts it, can surrender himself to the command of the superior officer. In surrendering himself, however, another process is introduced: the transformation of the individual into a mass and a spectacle. Guy Debord argues that the spectacle 'erases the dividing line between self and the world', and the self is 'eventually overwhelmed'.[172] The individual as a spectacle is available for inspection, admiration and aestheticisation. In the figure of the 'picturesque soldier', the individual is erased and becomes part of the spectacle. Susan Stewart argues that the art of public space is 'an eternalised parade', a 'fixing of the symbols of public life'.[173] As an eternalised parade, it seeks a 'seamless presentation'.[174] The connection between the seamless presentation and the figure of the soldier in the public commemoration of the war becomes one with the soldier in the spectacle of military training, and represents what Michel Foucault describes as the 'body of the condemned'. The body is entangled within power relations and these 'invest it, mark it, train it, torture it, force it to carry out tasks, to perform ceremonies' and most importantly, to 'emit signs'.[175] These signs are articulated at the 'level of the individual's body and gestures'.[176] Foucault argues that the soldier was someone who 'could be recognised from afar' because he 'bore certain signs' such as courage, strength and valour, all of which belonged to a 'bodily rhetoric of honour'.[177] For Foucault, however, such bodily discipline forms a 'policy of coercions that act upon the body' in order to manipulate its elements, its gestures, its behaviour'.[178] What were the implications of this manipulation for the returning soldiers?

The rigorous training that the ex-servicemen had undergone made it impossible for them to identify in a positive way with the 'picturesque soldier' standing to attention. Moreover, it was the officers who had given the training and the orders to the soldiers. Second Lieutenant Donald Hankey presents the officer as having a 'good deal of prestige' and, 'by virtue of his immunity from manual work and competition, his superior dress and standard of living, [appearing] to be a higher sort of being altogether'.[179] The officer was in a position of superiority compared with the soldiers he trained and inspected. As Dennis Winter argues, all an officer needed was 'authority'. This was reflected in the training he received. The course

172. Debord, Guy, *The Society of Spectacle* (New York: 1994), p. 153.

173. Stewart, Susan, *On Longing. Narratives of the Miniature, the Gigantic, the Souvenir, the Collection* (London: 1993), p. 90.

174. Ibid., p. 85.

175. Foucault, Michel, *Discipline and Punish. The Birth of the Prison* (London: 1991), p. 25.

176. Ibid., p. 27.

177. Ibid., p. 135.

178. Ibid., p. 138.

179. Hankey, Donald, *A Student in Arms* (London: 1917), p. 45.

for prospective officers lasted one month, with a 'final selection made in games of rugby or soccer according to the respectability of the violence displayed and quickness of reaction generally'.[180] Once trained, the officers were wrapped in an aura of dignity by the 'dress and the physical separation which traditionally went with his position'.[181] In this way, the officers, who traditionally were selected from the 'gentlemen' class, took on those 'appurtenances of distinction which marked the authority of a civilian gentleman'.[182] The uniform represented 'one such trademark': while the other ranks wore the 'shabby garb of the artisan', the officer 'equipped himself at his own expense in the khaki equivalent of hunting dress'.[183] Dressed in the uniform of the gentleman, the 'circumstances of the officers' daily living were approximated as closely as possible to those of the country house'.[184] The officers' superiority was reinforced by the way they saw the other ranks: Officer Chapman describes the subaltern as an unknown 'shadowy creature' with 'bowed head' and 'humped shoulders'.[185]

The figure of the soldier, as depicted on the *LNWR Memorial* and the majority of the commemorative sculpture of the First World War, with his head bowed, is the unknown shadowy figure on which the officer class looked down from his position of authority and relative comfort. We cannot therefore see this figure as 'picturesque', and need to consider it within the parameters of the distinction and division of the officer and subaltern, a division that relied to a great extent on the codes of masculinity contained within the public school ethos.

The lower ranks viewed the training and in particular the drill positions with contempt. F. Noakes recalls that 'with rifles we marched, counter-marched, wheeled right and left, inclined and formed squads and about turned until we were streaming with sweat and weak in the knees with exhaustion'.[186] V. Garratt's recollections of drill practice form a similar picture. Garratt remembers the training ground and the training instructors as trying to 'knock-out' of recruits 'whatever decent elements of manhood stood in the way of military efficiency'.[187] Two competing masculinities emerge in this context: the working-class masculinity that Garratt felt was knocked out of him on entering the training grounds, and the masculinity imposed by the military training. This training, according to Garratt, was designed to 'wring all the finer qualities and sensibilities' out of the recruits: its aim was to

180. Winter, Denis, *Death's Men*, p. 66.

181. Ibid., p. 67.

182. Ibid.

183. Ibid.

184. Ibid. See also Simpson, Keith, 'The British Soldier on the Western Front', in Liddle, Peter (ed.), *Home Fires and Foreign Fields. British Social and Military Experience in the First World War* (London: 1985). For a view on the paternalistic nature of officer/soldier relations, see Sheffield, Gary, *Officer-Man Relations, Morale and Discipline in the British Army 1902–22*, Unpublished PhD Thesis (University of London: 1994).

185. Officer Chapman, quoted in Winter, Denis, *Death's Men*, p. 50.

186. Noakes, F., *The Distant Drum* (London: 1952), quoted in ibid., p. 39

187. Garratt, V. W., *A Man in the Street* (London: 1939), p. 152.

'pour in the blood-lust and the mechanical desire to kill'.[188] Garratt recalls that the instructors used ridicule and insult to strike at 'the most vulnerable part of a man's nature'. The experience of standing to attention was therefore not only physically exhausting, but also designed to humiliate and demean the soldier. Joan Scott has argued that experience interrogates the process by which subjects are created.[189] As such, the experience of the soldiers who underwent training drill underpins their subjectivity, which in turn refuses identification with the figure of the 'picturesque soldier'.

Silence, Stillness and Discipline

Silence was another important factor in the goal of disciplining the soldier. 'Next to steadiness in the ranks, comes *silence* on the parade ground', according to Major Legge.[190] The absence of silence showed a severe lack of discipline. Order and absolute precision were other elements of drill practice, with order taking on a particularly fundamental role. J. F. C. Fuller describes it as a way of reducing 'the motions to and from combat formations to a habit' and consequently, as helping to build morale.[191]

Stillness and silence were not only crucial to military training; they also played a major part in the Armistice Day celebrations. On that date, even the weather, in its 'utter stillness', provided the perfect background to the ceremony.[192] *The Times* reported that the 'indescribable' stillness was 'thrilling in its intensity', and combined with the silence, made a 'remarkable impression upon the mind of the people'.[193] The military ritual of guarding the Unknown Warrior along the procession in London provided an added intensity:

> The stillness that held these Guardsmen and their heads bowed, their arms reversed ... established an invisible veil between that hollowed spot and the turbulent flood of London.[194]

The soldiers provided a barrier between the crowds and the spectacle of the coffin of the Unknown Soldier that was transferred from Victoria Station to Westminster Abbey. Susan Stewart has argued that between the spectators and the parade there is always a 'perfectly uniform line'. This line according to Stewart is designed not so much in order to perfect the parades 'spatial closure', but in order to 'protect the parade from the interruptions of inversion of speech', providing it with 'integrity and

188. Ibid.
189. Scott, Joan, 'The Evidence of Experience', in Abelove, H., Barale, M. and Halperin, D. (eds), *The Lesbian and Gay Studies Reader* (London: 1993), p. 426.
190. Legge, R. F. (Major), *Mainly About Discipline*, p. 20.
191. Fuller, J. F. C., *Training Soldiers for War*, p. 104.
192. *The Times*, 12 November 1920.
193. Ibid.
194. Ibid.

an aura of completeness'.[195] The coffin of the Unknown Soldier was duly set down in Westminster Abbey. Four sentries were positioned at each corner of the coffin. This, along with the soldiers bordering the route of the procession, provided protection from 'interruptions', and curtailed any possibilities of the public being able to inscribe freely on the body of the Unknown Soldier. The silence was punctuated by military commands from the officers. The orderliness and slowness of the procession as it made its way through the streets of London, gave the ceremony a sense of 'majesty' and 'pathos'. The crowds were later described by *The Times* as 'so symmetrical that they might almost be ranked'.[196]

The same military ceremonial and 'fencing' off of the crowds, was also apparent at the unveiling of the Cenotaph later in the day. Four 'tall Guardsmen' stood at ease at the four corners of the Cenotaph. At a quarter before noon, the orchestra played the Last Post, and the four Guardsmen, 'with the elaborate movements of ceremonial drill, reversed their rifles, crossed their hands on the butts and stood with lowered heads'. So the four Guardsmen 'stayed, like images of military mourning', *The Times* noted, maintaining this attitude of respect 'without the visible tremor of a nerve'.[197]

One of the most frequent symbols of the commemoration of the First World War was the image of the soldier obeying the instruction 'reverse arms!'[198] Guy Debord has argued that the language of the spectacle is composed of signs from the dominant positions of society.[199] The visual culture of post-Armistice Britain borrowed a number of images from military drill positions used in military training for the visual culture of the commemoration of the war. What is significant is that it was the soldiers and not the officers who had been party to this training, and the non-commissioned officers in many cases were those who had delivered the training. This is not to argue that post-Armistice society was a military society, but that military discourse permeated the language used to describe and inscribe the commemoration of the First World War in what Michel Foucault described as 'politics being the continuation of military models and as a technique of internal peace and order'.[200] Paramount in this model is the adoption of certain tactics that 'make it possible to understand the army as a principle for maintaining the absence of warfare in societies'. This according to Foucault results in a 'permanent coercion not to the general will but to automatic docility'.[201]

A similar crowd demarcation and ceremonial had also been evident at the unveiling of the *LNWR Memorial*, discussed in the previous section *(Illustration 2.7).*

195. Stewart, Susan, *On Longing*, p. 85.
196. *The Times*, 12 November 1920.
197. *The Times*, 21 July 1919.
198. It is also important to note that after the permanent Cenotaph was erected, there were suggestions that it should be altered to include life-size, realistic bronze statues of sentries at each corner. However, the design remained unchanged and was later adopted by other memorials. Lutyens to Sir Alfred Mond, PRO WORK 20/39, 29 July 1919 .
199. Debord, Guy, *The Society of Spectacle*, p. 13.
200. Foucault, Michel, *Discipline and Punish*, p. 168.
201. Ibid., p. 169.

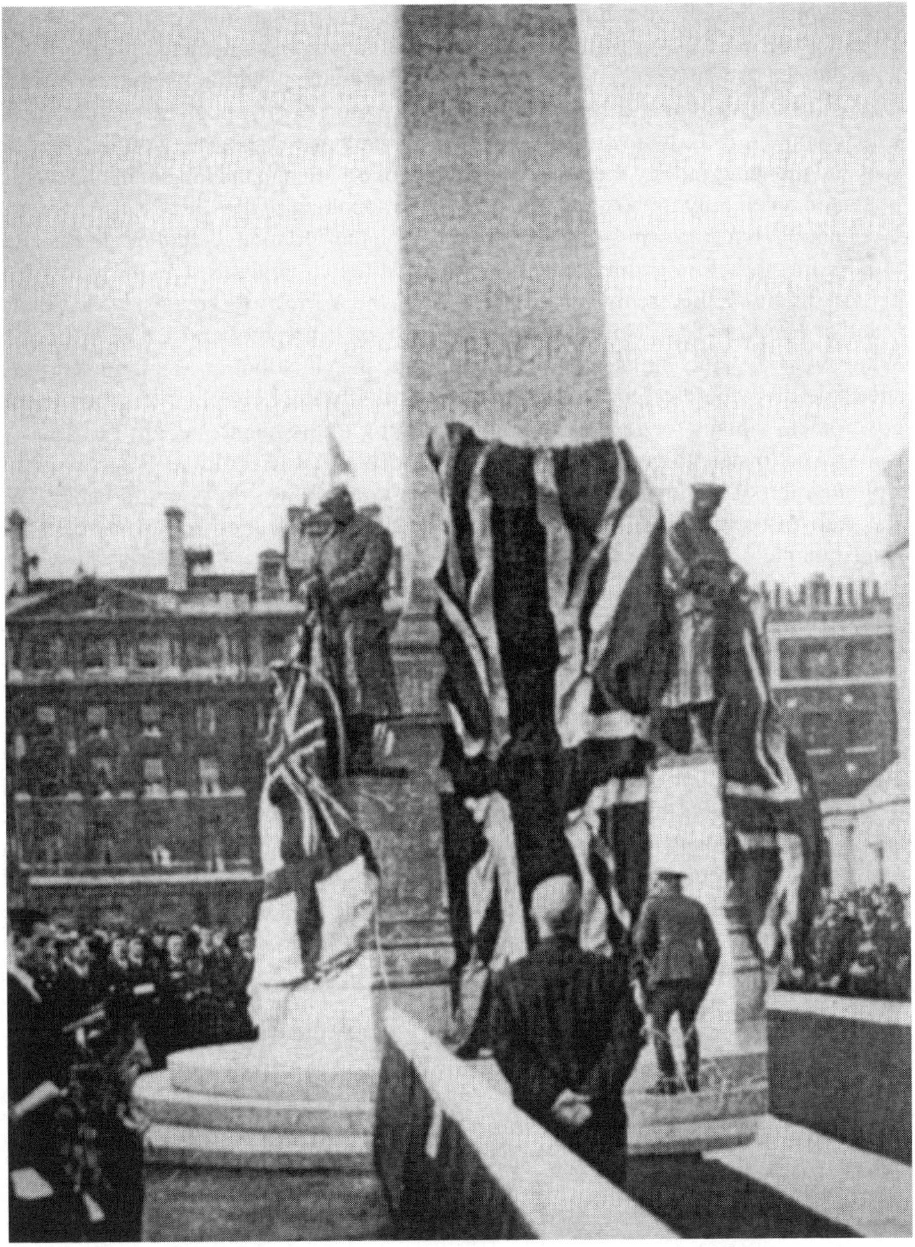

Figure 2.7 Ceremony of the Unveiling of the *LNWR Memorial*, Euston Station, London, sculpted by R. Wynn Owen (1921). *The Railway Gazette*, 28/10/1921, p. 641

'Distinguished' employees formed a line around the memorial in a ceremony that was carefully orchestrated by company officials. Lord Haig was instructed to step down from the platform and proceed to the memorial, where he would find a marked spot at the foot of the memorial on which to stand. Once there, Lord Haig was to pull a cord which would unveil the monument. It was stressed that be must stand on this precise spot and that after pulling the cord, he should move a 'step to the left so that he would be standing centrally to the memorial during the sounding of the Last Post'.[202]

The *L&NWR Railway Gazette* commented on the ceremony's 'complete absence of pageantry', before adding that, 'it is true that the church was represented by her highest dignitary, the Archbishop of Canterbury, the Army by its greatest leader, Field Marshal Haig, and the Company by its Chairman, Directors and Chief Officers'. What the magazine omits to point out is that the unveiling was organised as a spectacle that would offer the maximum opportunity for Lord Haig to promote the government's plans for reconstruction. According to the magazine, all the officials were asked to stand together 'for a common sincere tribute'.[203] Lady Haig asked for a photograph of the unveiling and a framed photograph was duly sent to her.[204] The spectacle of the unveiling and its memory, perfectly framed, could now live on the Haigs' mantelpiece.

'Silence' is 'more eloquent than words' the Chairman of LNWR declared in his speech at the unveiling of the *London and North Western Railway Memorial*. The commemoration of the First World War, through the highly regimented unveiling ceremonies, the naming of the dead, and the bestowal of honours such as the Victoria Cross, provided acceptable ways of being a man. Boundaries imposed throughout the unveiling ceremonies not only defined norms of masculinity but also offered protection: protection of middle- and upper-class masculinities from the threat imposed by the working-class servicemen. Susan Stewart has argued that the hero, which honours such as the Victoria Cross recognise, needs to be seen as 'larger than life', a 'giant', who is 'inaccessible to lived experience'.[205] The ex-servicemen had to move beyond the lived experience of the war. The next chapter will examine the possibilities that the commemoration of the war offered to help them come to terms with the trauma they had faced.

202. 'Instructions for Unveiling – Lord Haig', PRO, RAIL 2868.
203. 'War Memorial at Euston', *The L&NW Railway Gazette*, Cutting in PRO, RAIL 2868.
204. Letter to Lady Haig from LNWR, n.d., PRO, RAIL 2868.
205. Stewart, Susan, *On Longing*, p. 91.

Chapter 3

Abjection, Idealisation, Trauma and Acting-Out of Masculinities in the Inter-War Years

The *Machine Gun Corps Memorial (Illustration 3.1)*, also known as the *Boy David Memorial*, at Hyde Park Corner, London, was sculpted by Francis Derwent Wood RA. It takes the form of a male youth cast in bronze, and the inscription on the pedestal reads, 'Saul has slain his thousands but David his tens of thousands'.[1] On the back of the pedestal is a brief history of the Machine Gun Corps and the places where it served, including the number of men who served in the corps, the number of dead and the number of wounded. The bronze figure is lean and muscular. His left hand holds a sword, while his right hand gracefully touches his waist. His right leg is slightly bent, giving the whole figure a semblance of lightness. On each side of the pedestal, encircled by two wreaths, a machine gun waits poised and ready to fire. A helmet and backpack rest at the foot of each gun.

The figure of the *Boy David* provides a departure from the iconography of the First World War memorials, particularly the figure of the soldier in uniform that was so common to these memorials. Its classical nude form is stripped of the modern instruments and uniform of war, which have instead been placed on the pedestal. The statue displays what Charles ffoulkes, the curator of the Imperial War Museum at the time the memorial was unveiled, called the 'most beautiful representation of the human form that we have in London'.[2] Recent commentators have observed the impossibility of any association being made between the 'common soldier'[3] and the *Boy David* because of the classical form of the latter and the fact that it is a male nude. Other critics have contrasted the figure with the 'realistic', fully equipped figures of Charles Jagger's *Royal Artillery Memorial (Illustration 3.2)*, which stands opposite the *Boy David Memorial*[4] in Hyde Park.

1. *Holy Bible*, I Samuel, 18.v.7.
2. ffoulkes, Charles, *Arms and the Tower* (London: 1939), p. 144.
3. Penny, Nicholas, 'English Sculpture and the First World War', *Oxford Art Journal*, 4/2 (1981), p. 39.
4. Richard Cork has argued that 'anodyne figures of naked heroes' like the 'muscular youth' of the *Boy David Memorial*, were 'disgracefully irrelevant'. See Cork, Richard, *A Bitter Truth: Avant Garde Art and the Great War* (New Haven and London: 1994), p. 281.

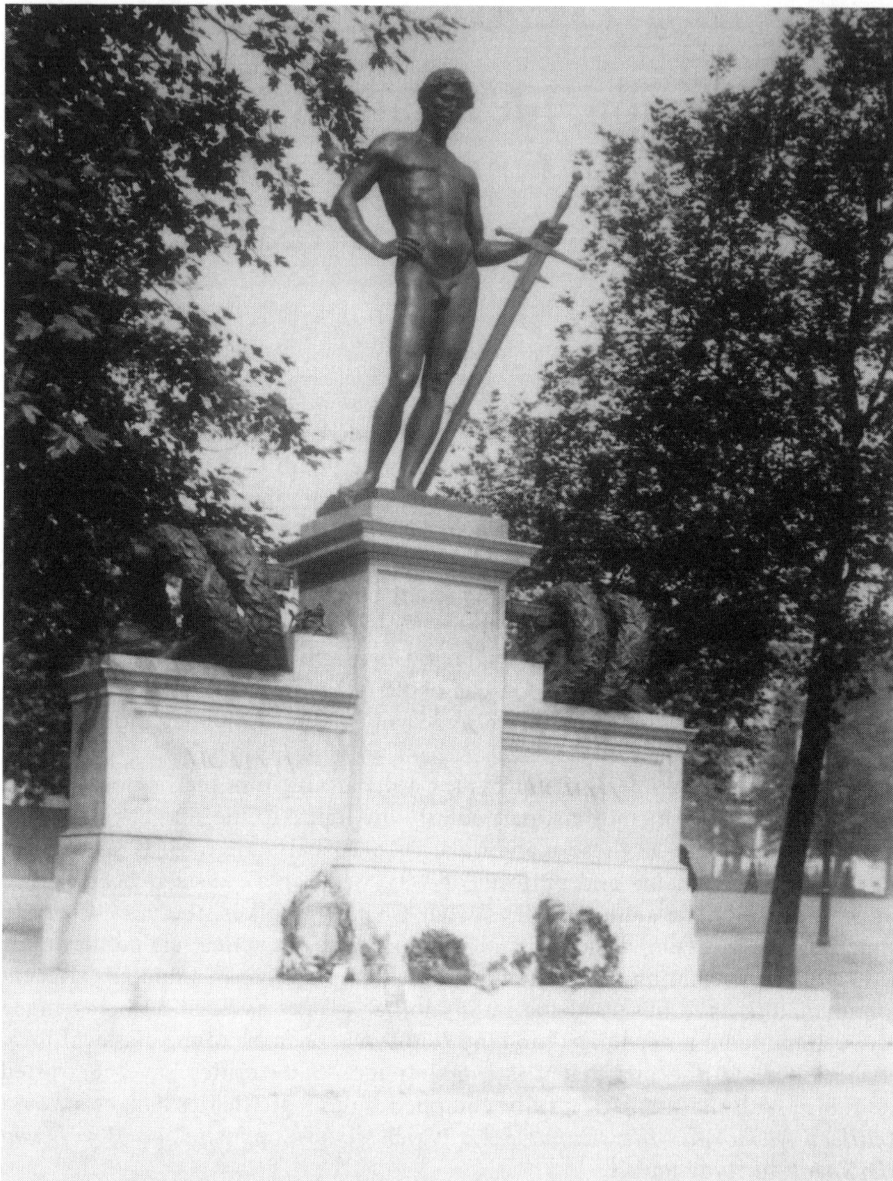

Figure 3.1 ***Machine Gun Corps Memorial*** **(1925), Hyde Park Corner, London, Francis Derwent Wood**

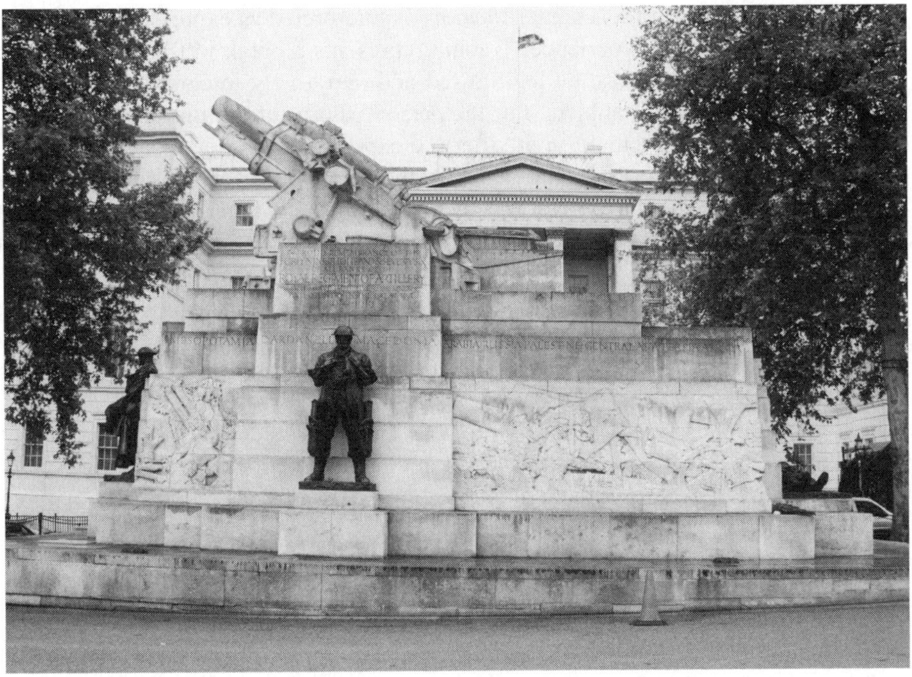

Figure 3.2 *Royal Artillery Memorial* (1925), Hyde Park Corner, London, Charles Jagger

Can the naked body of the *Boy David* provide a point of identification and reference for the returning servicemen in a way that the uniformed body, as discussed in the previous chapter, could not? This chapter examines the subject of trauma in relation to the memory of war, not only as it applied to those on the battlefield but also how it affected non-combatant troops, and the sculptor himself. What possibilities did the commemoration of the First World War offer as a means of expression for the combatants and their personal traumas? Could the expression of such private memories in relation to the public commemoration of the war be understood within a 'hegemonic process of ideological domination and resistance'[5] for and against normalising masculinities?

Penelope Curtis describes the figure as a 'languid naked youth' which stands in contrast with the 'energetic and realistic depiction' of Jagger's gunners. See Curtis, Penelope, *Sculpture 1900–1945* (Oxford: 1999), p. 54. On the work of Derwent Wood, see Beattie, Susan, *The New Sculpture* (New Haven and London: 1983).

For an approach that takes into account some of the concerns of this chapter, see Crellin, Sarah, 'Hollow Men: Francis Derwent Wood's Masks and Memorials, 1915–1925', *The Sculpture Journal*, Vol. 6 (2001).

5. Ashplant, T. G., Dawson, G. and Roper, M., 'The Politics of War Memory and Commemoration. Contexts, Structures and Dynamics', in Ashplant, T. G., Dawson, G. and Roper, M. (eds), *The*

For the purposes of this chapter memory is interpreted as expressing a narrative rather than replicating experience. Trauma represents a break in this narrative and traumatic memories need to be legitimised and narratively integrated so that they lose their hold over their subject. For the person who went through the experience, these memories either remain vivid after the experience, or they resist integration. The memories cannot become narratives in their own right for two reasons: either the traumatised events have been mechanically re-enacted as a drama rather than synthetically narrated by the memorising agent who 'masters' them, or they remain 'outside' the subject.[6]

This chapter examines trauma in relation to the body and bodily traumatic memories in order to question the possibilities that commemorative representations of the body allowed for such memories to be resolved and integrated within the self. Could the *Boy David* offer a point of transference for the bereaved, and if so, which masculinities was it trying to project? The body is central to the process of transference, as it is the site of destruction and reconstruction as well as the core of idealisation. Moreover, traumatic memories are assumed to have a somatic nature;[7] they are 'full of fleeting images, the percussion of blows, sounds, and movements of the body'.[8]

The body, this chapter will argue, provided not only a site of destruction and disgust, but also a form for *esprit de corps* and desire. This dichotomy is problematic, however, and points to the ways in which the 'mourning of survivors complicates politics', particularly the politics of masculinity.[9] Dominick LaCapra, drawing on Freud's theory of mourning, distinguishes between two memorial positions in relation to trauma: acting-out (melancholia), and working through (mourning).[10] Acting-out is based on tragic identification and the constitution of one's self as a surrogate victim. It relies on over-identification and repetition: keeping the wounds open results in re-traumatisation. Working through, on the other hand, involves self-reflexivity, a determination of responsibility, and some element of distance. A goal rather than an end, working through is a process of evolution that is never fully accomplished and is therefore never free of some element of acting-out.[11]

Politics of War Memory and Commemoration (London: 2001), p. 13.

6. Bal, Mieke, 'Introduction', Bal, M., Crewe, J. and Spitzer, L. (eds), *Acts of Memory. Cultural Recall in the Present* (New England: 1999), p. viii.
7. Coombes, Annie E., 'The Art of Memory', *Third Text* (Summer, 2000), p. 50.
8. Cuthbertson, Roberta, 'Embodied Memory, Transcendence and Telling: Recounting Trauma, Re-Establishing Self', *New Literary History*, 26, 1995, p. 174, cited in Coombes, Annie E., 'Art of Memory', p. 50.
9. Ashplant, T. G., *et al.*, 'The Politics of War Memory and Commemoration. Contexts, Structures and Dynamics', p. 34.
10. Freud, S., 'Mourning and Melancholia', 1917 [1915] in Strachey, J., *The Standard Edition of the Complete Psychological Works of Sigmund Freud*, Vol. 14 (London: 1991).
11. LaCapra, Dominick, *Representing the Holocaust. History, Theory, Trauma* (Ithaca: 1994), p. 198.

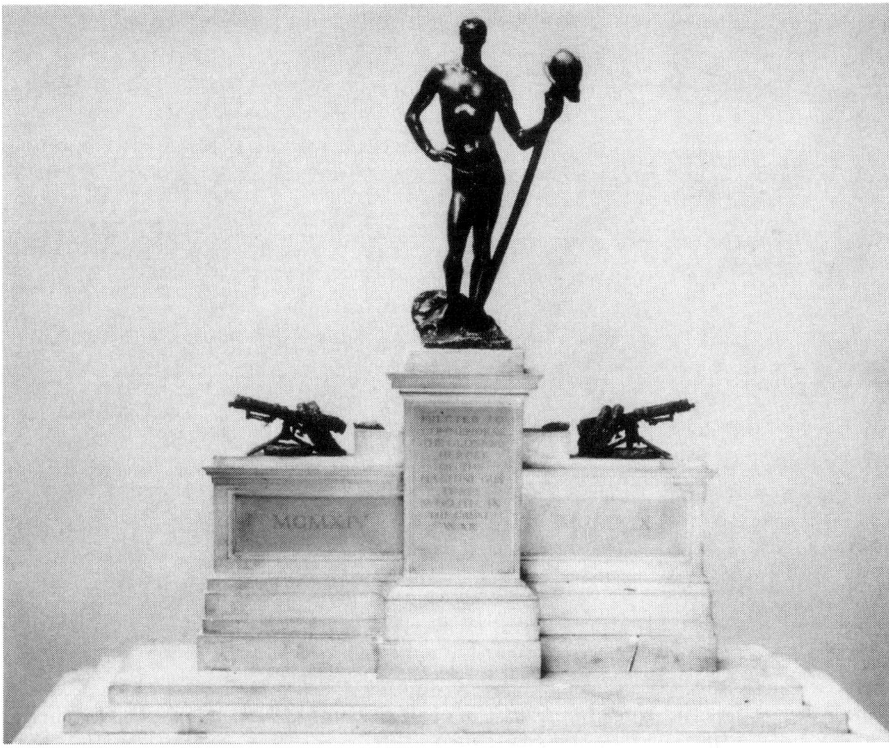

Figure 3.3 Initial Model for the *Machine Gun Corps Memorial*, Francis Derwent Wood, no date

Several instances of acting-out will be examined in this chapter. The men who witnessed the dismembering of the male body, regardless of whether it belonged to the enemy, their comrades, or was their own body, re-enact the trauma of that encounter. The acting-out and the effectiveness of the commemoration of the war will be discussed in relation to the writings of Lt. Col. Graham Seton Hutchison and the facial masks created by the sculptor Francis Derwent Wood. Seen within a framework of disgust and desire, the *Boy David* can become a forum for various interpretations, without necessarily offering a resolution.

Controversy

The *Boy David Memorial* generated two controversies. The first controversy derived from the fact that the initial model submitted to the memorial committee of the Machine Gun Corps had to be altered because the figure of the *Boy David* was considered unacceptable. In the original model *(Illustration 3.3)*, the body is thin and emaciated, and the handle of the sword is obscured by the helmet. The

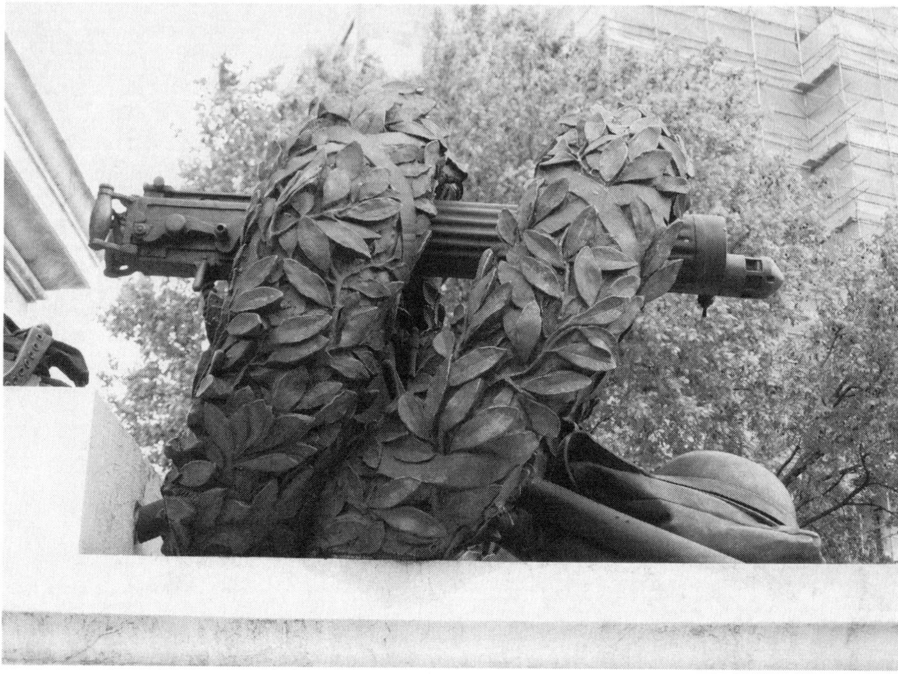

Figure 3.4 Detail, *Machine Gun Corps Memorial* (1925), Hyde Park Corner, London, Francis Derwent Wood

wreaths on the machine guns appear at the back of the guns as compared to the actual memorial *(Illustration 3.4)*. The backpack and helmet are absent from underneath the machine guns. On seeing this version of the memorial, the First Commissioner, Lord Crawford, relayed his annoyance to the Secretary of the Department of Works, M. Conolley. According to the First Commissioner, he could 'foresee that the model will be hotly criticised by members of the committee' and believed that the model had 'unquestionably certain shortcomings' which were 'so obvious in character'.[12] Although we will never know what problems the First Commissioner saw in the figure of the *Boy David*, it is easy to deduce that the statue was always going to be problematic. This highlights the perception of what was an acceptable 'male body' during the period of reconstruction following the First World War and the complications that a body that did not conform to acceptable norms of masculinity could instigate in a culture where homoeroticism could provide a challenge to such norms and uncover their shifting and fragile basis.

The second major controversy came after the unveiling, when the inscription 'Saul has Slain …' was seen by some to be promoting and favouring aggression and

12. Letter from the First Commissioner Lord Crawford to M. Connolly, Secretary, PRO, WORK 20/146, 20 December 1921.

war rather than reconciliation. The International Arbitration League[13] sent a letter of complaint to the Commissioner of Works, pointing out that the inscription gave an entirely false interpretation of national feeling, and was 'an insult to the brave dead whose memory is commemorated'.[14] The response from the Department of Works explained that the 'artist embodied in his design a statue of David as a symbol of the important part which a small weapon played in the Great War', and that the inscription was therefore not one to which the Commissioner could take exception.[15] The matter was subsequently discussed during Parliamentary Question Time by Locker-Lampson MP (Conservative), who argued that without the inscription, 'the statue would not be identified by everyone'.[16] Colonel Phillips, a member of the Machine Gun Corps Memorial Committee, had written in a letter to Sir Lionel Earle at the Department of Works, that 'any alteration in the inscription would unanimously be opposed'. Colonel Phillips, like Locker-Lampson, believed that 'the statue of David as a symbol of the Machine Gun Corps [was] rather meaningless'.[17] It becomes clear that it was not the inscription that was at the centre of the controversy, but the statue itself.

These objections also reveal the triangular relationship between the figure of David, the inscription and the machine guns. In order to unravel the relationship between the three parts of the memorial, one needs to examine the connection between the sculptural establishment and the notions of masculinity promoted within it, and at the same time consider the notions of masculinity being promoted within the military establishment. The sculptor, who was usually male, was seen as needing to be in control and able to dominate the material.[18] Clay was favoured over stone because of its obedience and malleability.[19] Sculpture was seen as virile,[20] and the sculptor, like the climber, needed strength to master each peak.[21] Sculpture was seen as a comrade/mistress who would accompany the sculptor to the grave.[22] A similar

13. The International Arbitration League was founded by Sir Randall Cremer (who had been awarded the Nobel Prize for Peace in 1903) following the Franco-Prussian War of 1870 and in order to maintain Britain's neutrality. Initially it was formed as the Workmen's Peace Association. Cremer was elected a Liberal MP in 1885. See Evans, Howard, *Sir Randal Cremer. His Life and Work* (London: 1909).
14. Letter from F. Maddison, Secretary, International Arbitration League to Viscount Peel, First Commissioner of Works, PRO, WORK 20/146, 26 July 1925.
15. Letter from the Private Secretary of the First Commissioner, to F. Maddison Secretary, International Arbitration League, PRO, WORK 20/146, 26 July 1925.
16. Parliamentary Debate, PRO, WORK 20/146, 4 August 1925.
17. Letter from Colonel Phillips to Sir Lionel Earle, Department of Works, PRO, WORK 20/146, 25 August 1925.
18. Parkes, Kineton, *Sculpture of Today* (London: 1921), p. 26.
19. Toft, Albert, *Modelling and Sculpture. A Full Account of the Various Methods and Processes Employed in These Arts* (London: 1911), p. 33.
20. Royal Society of British Sculptors, *Modern British Sculpture* (London: 1921).
21. Bayes, Gilbert, *Modelling for Sculpture. A Book for the Beginner* (Harrow: 1930), p. 39.
22. Jagger, C. S., *Modelling and Sculpture in the Making* (London: 1933), p. 9.

rhetoric runs through the military establishment, although the relationship between sculptor and clay is replaced by the relationship between man and machine. Man becomes an accessory to the machine, which is presented in anthropomorphic terms. The combatant had to compete with the efficiency of the machine, and in order to do so, needed to be a 'manly man', distinguished by courage and self-sacrifice. The reward was comradeship.

The memories of the machine-gunners of the First World War, however, reveal the extent to which they had lost any control over their lives.[23] The machine gun and the standards of cleanliness and hygiene that they were expected to maintain, were out of their control. The boundaries of their bodies no longer existed; the inside had become the outside, and was no longer contained within the boundaries of the self. This experience has the effect of blurring and confusing the senses. Corpses become not only a visual but also a physical reality. More importantly, they become the embodiment of lack of containment. Corpses have to be disposed of, or just ignored. These experiences form the traumatic memories that this chapter will attempt to address in relation to the form of the memorial.

Parallel to these memories lie other memories of comradeship and the male body as a source of visual, but most importantly, tactile, comfort and pleasure. Are these memories represented in the form of the memorial, and if they are, how are they represented? What is the relationship between the traumatic memories of the returning soldiers and the experiences of comfort and reassurance they derived from living in a community of men?

The Man Constructed – The Gun, Gunner and the Ideal Man

> War today is more bloody and more destructive than any war of other days, because of the enormously increased perfection of weapons of attack and defence.[24]

Freud's observation on the destructiveness of new weapons was a view shared by many critics. Mechanisation was one of the main characteristics of the First World War. Guns had become more sophisticated, and bullets could travel with much higher speeds, resulting in greater devastation when they entered the human body. It was the introduction of the machine gun, however – the 'Maxim' and later the 'Vicker' – that brought the greatest devastation. From the beginning of the First World War, the

---

23. Recent studies on the commemoration of the First World War take no account of the memories of the men whom the monuments are supposed to represent. One could argue that this constitutes a major drawback. See King, Alex, *Memorials of the Great War. The Symbolism and Politics of Remembrance* (Oxford: 1998), and Moriarty, Catherine, 'The Absent Dead and Figurative First World War Memorials', *Transactions of the Ancient Monument Society*, 39 (1995), pp. 7–40.

24. Freud, S., 'Thoughts for the Time on War and Death' (1915), in Strachey, J., *The Standard Edition of the Complete Psychological Works of Sigmund Freud*, Vol. 14 (London: 1991), p. 278.

Germans adopted machine guns in large numbers. The result was highly damaging for the Allied forces. John Ellis, commenting on the social history of the machine gun, argues that in Britain, the military and political authorities were divided when it came to the production of large numbers of machine guns. The military supported a training programme that was still mainly concerned with field tactics used in the Boer War.[25] The political establishment, on the other hand, realised the importance of the machine gun from the early stages of the war. The Ministry of Munitions rallied the press to promote the use of the machine gun, stressing that the Germans held a stronger position over the British due to the heavy weapons they employed on the battlefield.[26]

The *Illustrated London News* devoted an entire page to the machine gun *(Illustration 3.5)*. The photographs show the relationship between man and machine, and the important role that the machine gun was to take by the end of the war. The gun and its constituent parts are numbered and named in the middle section of the page. The techniques employed in its production and praise for the 'perfection' of the machine are shown in the bottom third of the page in a section subtitled, 'A sign of perfect construction', reassuring readers that new standardised techniques of production could produce a perfect machine. In the top third of the page, man and machine come together. The first two pictures depict man as the inventor/demonstrator, in charge of the machine, while in the third picture, with man sitting behind the machine gun, the gun becomes an extension of his own self. As Walter Benjamin noted, the relationship between the human body and the new technologies of war was becoming more comprehensive: 'In order to deploy energies of such proportion, fitting one's sword-arm no longer suffices,' he wrote, 'for this is a mobilisation that requires extension to the deepest marrow, life's finest nerve.'[27] The machine gun then is portrayed not merely as an extension of the body, but as something emanating from 'the deepest reaches of the self'.[28] The machine gun proved that man was no longer master of the battlefield, but servant to the machine.[29] The machine gun's special features proved the inefficiency of man in an era when efficiency was both a necessity and a national goal.[30] Due to its fixed platform, the gunfire could be concentrated over a wide area, which meant that only a few men needed to be engaged in operating the gun. Its fixed platform provided 'less scope for the errors introduced into infantry fire by the

25. Ellis, John, *The Social History of the Machine Gun* (Baltimore: 1986), p. 117.
26. Ministry of Munitions, reported in *Illustrated London News*, 3 July 1915.
27. Benjamin, Walter, 'Theories of German Fascism', quoted in Burstein, Jessica, 'Warship Segments: Lewis, Prosthesis, Fascism', *Modernism/Modernity*, 4/2 (1997), p. 149.
28. Burstein, Jessica, 'Warship Segments', p. 149.
29. The man/machine debate was a debate that ran for a number of years prior to the First World War, and one which the war exemplified rather than dampened. See Pick, Daniel, *War Machine. The Rationalisation of Slaughter in the Modern Age* (New Haven and London: 1993), pp. 170–2.
30. See Searle, Geoffrey, *Eugenics and Politics in Britain, 1900–1914* (Leyden: 1976).

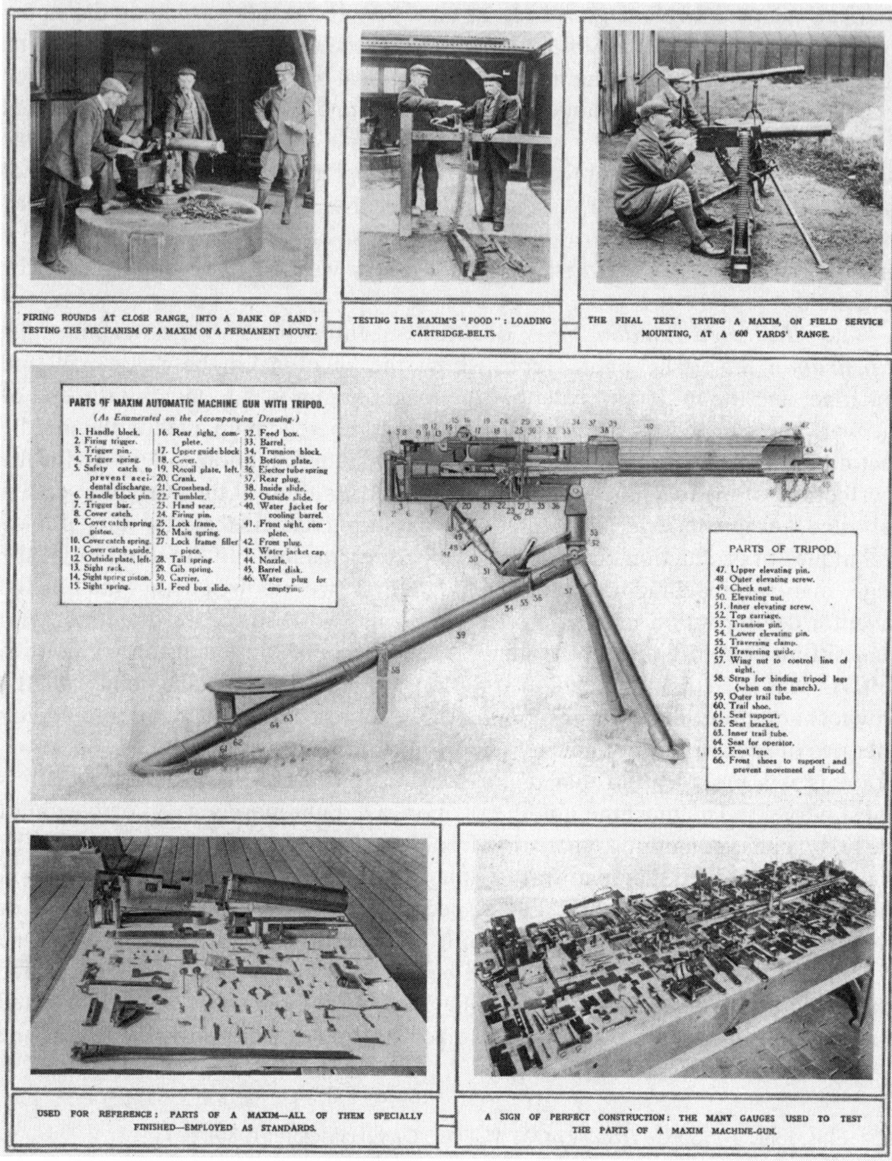

Figure 3.5 The Machine Gun. ***Illustrated London News*, 01/07/1915**

human element'.[31] At a time when large numbers of men were being immobilised because of shattered nerves, the machine gun also meant that these 'nerves and excitement' could 'to a large extent' be eliminated.[32] Individual temperaments were also suppressed, since in 'the excitement of battle there are few men who fire with anything approaching the steadiness of a fairly good shot on the rifle range'. The outcome was this: as 'the firing tends to become excited, the bullets go high'.[33] This use of sexualised anthropomorphic terminology to describe the machine gun runs through the operating manuals and reinforces the idea of the gun as a prosthesis and extension of the human body. Despite being a prosthesis, however, it is clear that it is the gun and not the soldier who is in control; the soldier is the one who ultimately is being manipulated through the perceived efficiency of the machine gun.

The notion of the gun being in control presents a contradiction when it comes to what was required of the gunner. The expectation was that he should be a 'manly man'[34] possessing a good physique, willpower and determination, initiative, and a mechanical turn of mind.[35] Lieut. Col. Hutchison argues that even the shape of the man's head, the prominence of the forebrain, and the general physical structure of the man acted as 'a guide as to his suitability'. Strong legs, lungs and stomach muscles were paramount. The development of the back muscles was also very important because it is the back and shoulders that 'bear the burden' of the gun's weight.[36]

A further element in the composition of the manliness of the gunner, according to Hutchison, was the male homosocial environment in which the gunner worked. Comradeship, which 'passes the love of women', was for Lieut. Col. Hutchison the 'intangible which locks men together'. This bonding was best achieved in the playing field, and he urged officers to 'participate with their men in every form of manly exercise'.[37] Hutchison argues that self-sacrifice as the cause of an ideal could only 'be found in that very homely and intimate relationship of comradeship'.[38] Self-

31. Longstaff, F. V. and Atteridge, A., *The Book of the Machine Gun* (London: 1917), p. 179
32. Ibid.
33. Ibid.
34. Hutchison, Graham Seton, *Footslogger. An Autobiography* (London: 1931), p. 142.
35. Bostock J., *The Machine Gunners' Handbook. Including the Maxim, Lewis, and Colt Automatic Machine Guns* (London: 1916), p. 1.
36. Hutchison, G. S., *Footslogger*, p. 142.
37. Ibid. Hutchison's ideas are very much embedded within the promotion of physical culture in the late nineteenth century. These ideas which came out of fears of degeneration and national decline were embedded in public school education and organisations such as the Boy Scout movement and Cadet Corps. For a further discussion of the devolpment and purpose of these organisations and the importance of physical education see, Mangan, J. A., *Athleticism in the Victorian and Edwardian Public School: the Emergence and Consolidation of an Educational Ideology* (Cambridge: 1981) and Mangan, J. A. and Walvin, J. (eds), *Manliness and Morality. Middle Class Masculinity in Britain and America* (Manchester: 1987).
38. Ibid., p. 221. The phrase that Hutchison uses is a biblical reference and comes from David upon learning of Jonathan's death.

sacrifice would ultimately bring death, but as Hutchison quotes, 'How beautiful to die in perfection!'[39]

For Hutchison, who fought for four years on the Western Front and whose memoirs repeatedly draw attention to the carnage of war, the assertion that there is beauty in dying seems rather unexpected. As Trudi Tate has argued, 'two sights are figured repeatedly in the soldiers' narratives of the Great War: corpses and bodies in pieces'.[40] Tate questions what such representations mean conceptually, historically and within the context of the memoirs.[41] This chapter will go on to discuss some of the ways in which the narratives of the machine-gunners' memoirs, with their constant references to corpses and bodies in pieces, converge on the memorial of the *Boy David.*

The Symbiosis of Gun and Gunner

The lean, strong figure of David with his washboard stomach, strong chest and muscular thighs, embodies the ideal man to carry and operate the machine gun in battle. It is only when the memories of the machine gunners are juxtaposed with the figure of David that a different reading emerges. Their memories tell a very different story of the coexistence of man and machine than that offered by the hegemonic memories and narratives of the military authorities.

A memory that features often in the diaries and memoirs of the First World War combatants is the recollection of the sheer weight of the machine gun. S. B. Abbot remembers how powerless he felt, in recalling an incident when, carrying the gun along the trenches with his companion, he suddenly fell in the mud and 'hysterical with weakness', could not lift his end of the gun.[42] Cleaning the gun was a routine that had to be performed daily and which further enslaved the gunner. P. G. Ackrell describes the procedure:

> The guns were thoroughly cleaned and stripped down. The barrel was pulled through, and hot water and a cleansing rod was used. The rod was pushed through the barrel several times with a piece of flannelette … Sometimes a double pull through was used with a piece of gauze wire in one of the loops. After this the barrel was slightly greased – also the remainder of the parts were oiled slightly.[43]

The anthropomorphic and highly sexualised language used to describe the gun provides a contrast with the lack of hygiene among the combatants themselves, and a constant reminder of the unequal symbiosis between the gun and the man operating it. The entries in the diary of S. Bradbury provide an example of this. Bradbury

39. Ibid., p. 222
40. Tate, Trudi, *Modernism, History and the First World War* (Manchester: 1998), p. 64.
41. Ibid., p. 65.
42. Abbot, S. B., IWM, 78/36/1, no pagination.
43. Ackrell, P. G., *My Life in the Machine Gun Corps* (Devon: 1966), p. 7.

makes almost daily reference to the cleaning of the gun, while entries describing his personal wash and bathing routines are few and far between.[44] Nevertheless, the bathing ritual is described in great detail, when it *does* take place,[45] and the relish with which it is portrayed seems to epitomise the reverence with which the cleansing ritual was held during the First World War. Cleansing became a way of containing the horrors of the battlefield. Cleaning the gun provided a way of erasing the horrific injuries it caused. Mary Douglas has argued that 'dirt offends against order'. For Douglas, eliminating dirt is not a negative movement, but a positive effort to organise the environment'[46] and, most importantly, for a 'pattern to be maintained'. Maintaining a pattern involves 'no distinction between primitives and moderns',[47] but in 'primitive culture the rule of patterning works with greater force'. Douglas's insight reveals the intensity of the need for pattern in the lives of servicemen.

Another element that becomes evident in the memoirs and the description of the bathing ritual is the high visibility given to the naked body during the war. The naked male body, like the gun, was a site of inspection and rejection,[48] idealisation and destruction, admiration and comfort. Unlike the gun, however, it was more easily disfigured and destroyed. Shown in its nakedness, the male body provided for the combatants a reminder that they were alive. In this respect, the statue of *Boy David* and its nudity provide an affirmation of the wholesome male body, especially as it was one of the very few memorials of the First World War to show the male body in its naked form. There are two problems, however, with this analogy: one is the coexistence of the nude body and the machine gun; the other is the idealisation of the body in the form of an allegorical ideal male figure.

The relationship of the figure to the gun is an ambivalent one. The guns are the bearers of gallantry, exemplified in the two wreaths encircling each gun. David is there to show off his killing capabilities – a 'killer of tens of thousands'. The memorial of the Machine Gun Corps is unique in acknowledging the fact that war is about killing as well as being killed. The inventor of the machine gun, Hiram Maxim, described it as the most efficient 'killing machine'.[49] The combatants needed to compete with such an efficient killer if they were to be the bearers of gallantry. The military authorities' aim was to create these efficient killers. Heroism and conquest became fused within military discourse. According to the *Field Service Regulations* handbook of 1920, it was the 'bold offensive spirit' and the 'national determination to conquer' that provided the most important aspects for the training of the soldier.[50]

44. Bradbury, S., IWM 81/35/1, p. 15.
45. Ibid., p. 35
46. Douglas, Mary, *Purity and Danger. An Analysis of Concepts of Pollution and Taboo* (London: 2002) p. 2.
47. Ibid., p. 41.
48. Bourke, Joanna, *Dismembering the Male. Men's Bodies, Britain and the Great War* (London:1996), chapter 4.
49. Quoted in Ellis, John, *The Social History of the Machine Gun*, p. 1.
50. War Office, *Field Service Regulations. Vol II. Operations* (London: 1920), p. 13.

Within military discourse, conquering and the offensive spirit were somehow cleansed of their association with killing. It was the training of the combatants that was to provide the real basis for the efficient killer. Bayonet training was one of the most important aspects of the training. Joanna Bourke has argued that bayonet training remained central to military training despite an awareness that modern technologies and rapid-fire rifles had greatly limited its usefulness.[51] The reason that this element was retained, Bourke identifies as being due to the capacity of the bayonet to force combatants to 'leave their trenches and engage with the enemy, whereas bombs, grenades and bullets encouraged men to cower from the enemy'.[52] In other words, while the technologies of war inspired fear, the use of the antiquated bayonet contributed towards the creation of a 'bold offensive spirit' and 'determination to conquer'.[53]

The offensive capabilities of the bayonet are encapsulated in the 1915 War Office manual on Bayonet Training.[54] In order to gain 'efficiency with the bayonet', the manual advocates that men should be put through a rigorous training which includes instruction on the most efficient way to hold the rifle, and an emphasis on the need for speed, energy and for the attack to be 'pushed well home'.[55] A 'spirit of aggression and alertness' was paramount.[56] The instructor needed to ensure speed in the 'delivery of the point and the withdrawal' and in particular, 'a good point before a quick withdrawal'. The point, in this instance, meant the wound that the bayonet was inflicting on the enemy's body, while 'withdrawal' meant the removal of the bayonet from the body. 'Considerable force' was required to withdraw the bayonet, the manual notes, especially 'should it meet a bone'. Getting the men to pierce discs on dummies tested the accuracy of targeting the aim. The manual states that: 'counting the number of discs carried will always add a competitive interest and for the actual competitions, marks can be allotted for the number of discs carried.'[57]

Should a bayonet attack fail, then the manual recommends that the attacker 'employ any method', such as using the rifle's butt or issuing a 'forward jab', which meant jabbing the bayonet at the opponent's face.[58] Nowhere in the manual does the word 'wound' appear. The process of wounding and ultimately killing another person is described in the most abstract terms. Elaine Scarry, commenting on the language used in war, has argued that although the main purpose of war is to injure, it usually 'disappears from view by simply being

51. Bourke, Joanna, *An Intimate History of Killing. Face-to-Face Killing in Twentieth Century Warfare* (London: 1999), p. 89.
52. Ibid., p. 92.
53. War Office, *Field Service Regulations Vol. II, Operations*, p. 13.
54. War Office, *Bayonet Fighting. Instruction with Service Rifle and Bayonet* (London: 1915), p. 1.
55. Ibid.
56. Ibid., p. 2.
57. Ibid., p. 8.
58. Ibid., p. 6.

omitted'[59] or being given an 'active redescription'.[60] The procedure appears to produce no blood or mess. The rifle and bayonet are major components of the memorials of the First World War and transform the male figures into soldiers. As in the training manual, however, the bayonet and rifle are abstracted from the messiness of killing and become instead a sign of heroism. Moreover, as Scarry argues, 'although a weapon is an extension of the human body' because of its collective designation as 'arms', the human body is also an extension of the weapon itself.[61]

In the *Boy David Memorial* it is a sword,[62] the heroic predecessor of the bayonet, which gives him the capacity to kill. The machine gun, the bearer of gallantry, which bears two wreaths, provides a further means of killing. The relationship of the human figure to the technologies of war in the memorial becomes more ambivalent. On the one hand, the memorial emphasises the frailty of men. The human figure can be seen as subservient to the machine, echoing the fear that the technologies of war inspired. On the other hand, the memorial can be seen as overcoming the frailty of men, with the sword symbolising the containment of fear. What is significant is that the wreaths signalling the sense of gallantry encircle the machine guns, rather than the man himself.

The relationship of the figure to the machine guns, if read in this way, goes some way towards explaining the opposition of the International Arbitration League to the inscription, and the need to alter the position of the wreaths in order to make the guns more prominent. The ideal male nude needed a reason for his existence. He needed to be empowered with the capacity to kill by the thousands, and to die in a self-sacrificial act. The figure of David is steeped in religion. While the uniformed figure of many memorials with its associated memories of training, inspection and control was unable to unite the working-class and middle-class ex-servicemen returning from the Front, the statue of David, with its biblical connotations, was able to offer a point of unity in his technical competence and his ability to overcome a much more powerful enemy.

The wholeness of the nude body represented in David provides a unified and wholesome memory of the body in perfection. The question remains, however, could the idealised body of David provide a point of identification and reference

59. Scarry, Elaine, *The Body in Pain. The Making and the Unmaking of the World* (Oxford: 1985), p. 64.
60. Ibid., p. 66.
61. Ibid., p. 67.
62. Charles ffoulkes although agreeing with the representation of the figure of David disagreed with the choice of sword by the sculptor. Before being appointed curator at the IWM, ffoulkes was Keeper of Arms in the Tower of London, and it is within his expertise on armoury that he argued against the use of the sword that he describes as a 'Swiss two-hand sword'. Instead he suggested to the sculptor, Francis Derwent Wood, to place a sling in the hands of David. See ffoulkes, Charles, *Arms and the Tower*, p. 144.

for the traumatic memories of the servicemen?[63] And what impact would such traumatic events have on the accepted codes of masculinity?

The Abjected Inside

The memoirs of combatants are filled with descriptions of horrific wounds, death, mutilation, bodies invaded by disease and parasites, and bodies attacked by rats, the weather and the military machine. Their memories are often 'too hideous and ghastly' to describe, but this does not prevent them from attempting to do so.[64] Dori Laub, referring to Holocaust survivors, has discussed the idea of 'testimony' for survivors of traumatic events and the need to 'tell their stories'. This imperative to tell is seen by Laub as an all-consuming life task, leading to the reconciliation of two worlds.[65] The memoirs of the servicemen need to be seen within these parameters, and this chapter raises the question of whether this 'imperative to tell' the traumatic experiences can be projected onto the memorial, and whether they bear any relationship to the *Boy David Memorial.*

Corpses, scattered body parts, and the smell of decomposing bodies were all part of daily life in the trenches. P. G. Ackrell recalls his daily duties as a runner and the route he had to take along a trench that had been dug through the graves of soldiers: 'Protruding from the sides were portions of feet and various parts of the human body.'[66] H. R. Butt observes in his diary that the ground was 'covered with shells and quite a few bodies', and with 'men lying with heads and feet and parts of their bodies showing through the mud'.[67]

The sight of body parts was not confined to a few passing moments. Part of everyday routine was eating one's meals 'with dead German boots staring you in the face out of the parapet', or using the dead bodies to 'step on in the trenches to get out of the mud'.[68] 'What ghastly sights there are to be seen here!' recalls Captain D. H. Pegler, before proceeding to describe these ghastly sights in detail.[69] The constant presence of the dead led to the combatants becoming saturated with images of death and destruction and sometimes unable to 'take any more notice of a dead person now than we do of a rat'.[70]

Julia Kristeva's analysis of the corpse in relation to subjectivity and abjection offers an insight into the combatants' refusal to look at the corpses. The corpse,

63. On possibilities of identification of the viewer in relation to sculpture see Potts, Alex, 'Male Phantasy and Modern Sculpture', *Oxford Art Journal*, 15/2 (1992): 38–48.
64. Atkins, A. L., IWM, P267 and Bradbury, S., IWM, 81/35/1, are two of these examples.
65. Laub, Dori, 'Truth and Testimony: The Process and Struggle', Caruth, C. (ed.), *Trauma. Explorations in Memory* (Baltimore: 1995), p. 63.
66. Ackrell, P. G., *My Life in the Machine Gun Corps*, p. 31.
67. Butt, H. R., IWM, 97/26/1, p. 14.
68. Ibid.
69. Pegler, Captain D. H., IWM, 82/7/1, Entry 15 September 1916.
70. Butt, H. R., IWM, 97/26/1, p. 17.

'the most sickening of wastes',[71] marks the threshold between the subject that the person was, and the object he will become, which threatens to contaminate or dissolve the subject.[72] It breaks down the distinction between being and non-being, and destroys the 'I'. In some memoir passages, however, the corpse becomes a source of fascination. A part of the enemy's body could also become a sort of curiosity, as A. J. Abraham recalls: 'I noticed a human nose sticking out of the ground. The eye sockets were full of earth but his wax like nose projected and a sergeant from another unit, also spotted it and started to poke it into grotesque shapes with the tip of his walking stick.'[73] Kristeva argues that the corpse marks the border that confirms the living person as alive, and is therefore both a source of strength and affirmation for the person witnessing it.[74] In particular, Trudi Tate observes, 'the act of looking at the corpse is an attempt to turn the abject into an object; to reassert the boundaries of the living body'.[75] A similar scene to the one described by Abraham appears in Henry Barbusse's war memoir *Under Fire* (1916). Commenting on the scene that Barbusse depicts, Tate argues that the body, by being presented as 'grotesque and comical', becomes 'inoffensive'.[76] By incorporating the dead body into their memoirs, Barbusse and all the other servicemen 'comfort the material body rather than an abstract idea of the glorious dead'.[77] For them, commemoration of the war is an impossibility.

Other forms of narrative which the *Boy David Memorial* goes some way to addressing, recall the act of killing. Killing Germans could provide excitement in some cases. Major T. H. Westmacott remembers that one of the officers in his unit took out a patrol in order to 'collar any Boche that happens to pass'. Major Westmacott himself was not included in the patrol: 'I am not allowed to go myself, because I command the squadron. Wouldn't it be fun!'[78] Joanna Bourke has commented that

71. Kristeva, Julia, *Powers of Horror. An Essay on Abjection* (New York: 1982), p. 3. Julia Kristeva argues that the abject is what makes impossible the identity of both the subject and object. The abject indicates the subject's vulnerability and its dependence on the object. The abject is part of the subject although it is figured as an impossible object. The abject is the marker of erogenous zones. The subject must expel all abjects (tears, saliva, faeces, urine) in order to establish a clean and proper body. However, this constitutes an impossibility in that these abjects can not be expelled as they form the basis of corporeal existence. This impossibility also indicates the unstable positioning of identities in relation to bodily boundaries and the possibility of turning into the viscera of the body out of which the subject was formed. See Grosz, Elizabeth, in Wright, Elizabeth (ed.), *Feminism and Psychoanalysis. A Critical Dictionary* (Oxford: 1992), pp. 197–8.
72. Ibid.
73. Abraham, A. J., IWM, P191, p. 91.
74. Kristeva, Julia, *Powers of Horror*, p. 4.
75. Tate, Trudi, *Modernism, History and the First World War*, p. 74.
76. Ibid.
77. Ibid., p. 75.
78. Westmacott, Major T. H., IWM, 87/13/1, Letter to his wife, 3 September 1915.

although they would rarely admit this, killing offered some combatants an 'orgasmic joy'.[79]

It was not only the sight of human destruction that remained ever present for the soldiers; the lifeless, mutilated bodies had to be touched and carried.[80] Touching the bodies provided H. R. Butt with a tactile memory of the dead. The forces of nature accentuated the stiffness and coldness of the dead male body. Freezing weather made the dead bodies go completely rigid; they were 'like a rock', as S. B. Abbot remembers. Their stiffness and their awkwardness constitute a tactile memory of death and destruction, which invades the living body and has to be cleansed from it. Mere sight was not to be trusted in distinguishing the dead from the living; touch was needed to confirm what sight could not. S. B. Abbot remembers the way that when the area became 'paved with bodies' and every shell hole had 'its one or two occupants in such an attitude', he and his comrades had to 'speak to some and touch them before we were convinced that they were dead. Sitting, lying, or even reading, it was only the stone-like feel of their limbs that proved that they had gone west'.[81]

The visual and physical contact with the dead and mutilated could be heightened, depending on one's relationship with the person – especially if the battlefield provided one's first encounter of this experience. A. L. Atkins remembers how his 'chum', was 'caught' by a German sniper, 'straight through the head and the side of his face'. He goes on to say that he 'won't attempt to describe him. The sight was too ghastly', adding that, 'although I have seen hundreds of dead since, I don't think I shall ever forget my first experience of the front line'.[82] In some instances, the disfigured bodies had to be identified. S. Bradbury remembers how one morning after roll call they had to inspect 'four long lines of dead', many of them 'horribly disfigured. One 'poor chap', Bradbury continues, 'had the whole of his face blown away'. The sight was too 'terrible to look at'.[83] Such sights were made even more horrible by 'flies crawling all over them'.[84]

The sensation of being wounded is often described as one of 'surprise'. S. B. Abbot remembers that although apprehensiveness, anger, and 'even fear' went through his mind, it was the feeling of surprise that remained with him.[85] His first shock was seeing the blood streaming from the wound and the ugliness of the ripped flesh, exposing the elbow bone. It is not the fear of death, but the ugliness of the torn flesh and the revelation of the abjected inside of the body that provides the source of surprise. Abbot goes on to describe another incident when his unit was due to relieve a trench that had just been mortared. On entering the trench they were faced with a 'frightful mess from the explosion', the 'walls were splashed with the brains of the

79. Bourke, Joanna, *An Intimate History of Killing*, p. 371.
80. Butt, H. R., IWM, 97/26/1, p. 37.
81. Abbot, S. B., IWM 78/36/1, no pagination
82. Atkins, A. L., IWM, P267, p. 14.
83. Bradbury, S., IWM, 81/35/1, p. 34.
84. Ibid., p. 114.
85. Abbot, S. B., IWM 78/36/1, no pagination.

unfortunate ones' and the 'trench was still slippery with blood'.[86] The slimy inside becomes a threatening, repulsive outside.[87]

Vision and touch were not the only senses to face an assault. P. G. Ackrell remembers that the smell of decomposing flesh was an equally frightful reminder of the scattered body parts that formed part of the landscape. For Ackrell, the 'stench was sometimes unbearable', especially in 'summertime and very hot weather'.[88] Smell was a reminder not only of the body's decomposition from the inside, but also of an external threat. Gas attacks were a common occurrence at the front line. The effects of gas attacks, loss of vision, speech and movement, accompanied by vomiting, tears and intense sweating, blurred the boundaries between outside and inside. The abjected bodily fluids provided a way of cleansing the body of the intruding gas. It is symbolic that in the absence of gas masks, combatants used 'pieces of rag soaked in urine'[89] to protect themselves.

Amongst all this destruction, death and mutilation, the spectacle of the male body with or without uniform is one that recurs frequently in the memories of the combatants. A. L. Atkins describes the sight of men in uniform as 'impressive': 'We used to mount guard in sun helmets, drill suits and full pack and it was an impressive sight to see all the men in line with bayonets and brass work gleaming in the sun.'[90] Atkins' observations reveal the significance of not only the uniform, but also the clean gun with its bayonet and shining brass work constituting a prosthesis to the male body. By contrast, mud, with its slippery and glutinous qualities acting as a strong reminder of the inside of the body, takes away the cleanliness of the gun and the body, and implies decay, degeneration and disgust.

The body was not only invaded and torn up by objects; the memories of the combatants include the sensation of the body being invaded by other living organisms: lice, scabies and rats. The inquisitive eye of the military establishment, which needed to inspect the men for fitness and disease, was a further invasion into one's privacy and sense of self. Inspecting for lice was one intrusion. The inspection parade was called 'Arms Up, Trousers Down'. It meant the men parading up and down before the military doctor, pausing in front of him, dropping their trousers and raising their arms.[91] The raising of the arms, signifying defeat during combat, exposes the defeat of the combatants in front of the military establishment, and the vulnerability of their manhood. Trudi Tate has argued that the inspecting eye of the military machine cast the 'subject in an anxious, powerless position'.[92]

---

86. Ibid.
87. See Tweweleit, Klaus, *Male Fantasies II. Male Bodies: Psychoanalysing the White Terror* (Oxford: 1989).
88. Ackrell, P. G., *My Life in the Machine Gun Corps*, p. 31.
89. Ibid., p. 35.
90. Atkins, A. L., IWM P267, p. 7.
91. Beater, O. L., IWM 86/65/1, no pagination.
92. Tate, Trudi, *Modernism, History and the First World War*, p. 101. Tate draws on Lacan's concept of the gaze as a source of anxiety and powerlessness.

This anxious, powerless position also provides a blow to perceived codes of masculinity, which position the male viewer as the source of the gaze rather than the recipient.[93] The actual writing of the memoir constitutes another anomaly to these codes. Laura Marcus has argued that there is a distinction between autobiography and memoirs. According to Marcus, the distinction lies between those 'human beings who are capable of self-reflection [autobiography] and those who are not [memoir]'[94] More importantly, the distinction is bound up with 'issues of power and powerlessness',[95] and memoirs are more often associated with female authors. The experience of pain, the sight of the corpse, the mud, and the inquisitive gaze of the military establishment all led to a collapse of the borders around which accepted codes of the masculine self were constructed, and which the commemoration of war attempted so hard to restore with its insistence on honour, sacrifice and heroism.

Trauma and Class

> In the dream I would find myself alone in a battered trench on a hot sunny day. No sound or shot or shell could be heard. This in itself was sinister and I realised that my company had withdrawn and I had been forgotten. Without instructions I could not leave my post, although I was aware of stealthy enemy movements all around me. No enemy ever appeared and I would awake in a state of great agitation.[96]

The dream described above was a recurrent one that visited A. J. Abraham intermittently until the 1930s.[97] The writer Edmund Blunden was another former soldier to be plagued by recurrent dreams. His book *The Bonadventure* (1922), describes a trip that he made across the Atlantic to South America and preceded his famous war memoir *The Undertones of War* (1928). In *The Bonadventure* he writes that once the ship entered the tropics, an ordeal began which gave rise to 'wild and vivid dreams'.[98] In one dream, he was walking along a weedy river which he knew to be 'the innocent shallow stream I once met and knew in Kent'. As the dream progressed, the stream grew more and more foul with 'weeds and grotesque in stagnation' and then all of a sudden was teeming with 'tremendous fish': 'These fish lay watching, stretched from one bank to the other; their number, my loneliness,

93. Laura Mulvey has developed this idea in relation to film spectatorship and the male gaze that renders the female actor powerless. See Mulvey, Laura, *Visual and Other Pleasures* (London: 1989).
94. Marcus, Laura, *Auto/biographical Discourses. Theory, Criticism, Practice* (Manchester: 1994), p. 21.
95. Ibid., p. 151.
96. Abraham, A. J., IWM, P191, p. 2.
97. Ibid., p. 1.
98. Blunden, Edmund, *The Bonadventure. A Random Journal of an Atlantic Holiday* (London: 1922), p. 40. It is interesting to note that this book is relatively unknown in comparison with *The Undertones of War* (1928), which contains none of the dreams described in *The Bonadventure*.

their immensity, my fixity conspired to frighten me unspeakably.'[99] The scene changes quickly to Paddington Station. Blunden is racing with his friend 'C' to catch the train. Suddenly, 'C' is in his grave and Blunden is in a trap outside his old home: 'A stranger stands in the road, cuts his throat; I look on, smile, and shudder, for he races after the trap with his knife'.[100] There was no escaping the dreams. Although Blunden awoke several times during the night, once he fell asleep he returned to the same haunting images. What made the dreams worse was a 'persistent force about them'. They took him back to his experiences at the Front, and: 'I woke up alive, having again suffered more from fear and the atmosphere of it – in projection – in a few seconds, than I was ever conscious of suffering in a day of the actual war.'[101]

Stagnation, decay and stickiness, blood and decapitation, and waking in a state of great agitation and fear haunted the men after their return, yet few went on to describe these dreams in their memoirs. To a large extent the dreams remain private, defying communication. The actuality of war is, however, evident in all memoirs. A number of psychiatrists who treated shell-shocked servicemen recorded accounts of the dreams described by their patients. The narratives furnished by the case studies offer a glimpse of the suffering and intensity of the experiences of war.

A number was assigned to each case study and each case presents the trauma that instigated the shock, the symptoms, treatment and outcomes.[102] Case 176 suffered from restless sleep and unpleasant dreams of the battlefield. He wept a lot, claiming that the sight of the dead frightened him.[103] Case 181, who suffered from functional aphonia, had the taste of blood constantly in his mouth and the smell of corpses in his nostrils. His symptoms would worsen towards nightfall and became especially bad whenever he had anything to do with the wounded.[104] Case 334 saw his best friend being torn to pieces by a shell and when the body was removed, lost consciousness. He had no memory of the period from when he went to help remove the torn body of his friend until his arrival at the hospital. Some memories of that period would later return, but the majority of that time was lost to him.[105]

In the dreams of the ex-servicemen, disembodied heads and mutilated bodies featured with disturbing regularity. Case 341 had a recurring dream of being called by a woman to see her husband's body, which was about to be buried. The body had no legs and the face was hidden by a stone slab. On moving the stone, the body came alive and the head 'spoke to me, imploring me to see that it was not buried'. The burial party arrived and he found himself about to be buried with the legless body, at which point he woke up. The legless body appeared in other dreams, but its face

99. Ibid.
100. Ibid., p. 41.
101. Ibid., p. 42.
102. Southard, Elmer, *Shell shock and other Neuropsychiatric Problems: Presented in Five Hundred and Eighty-Nine Case Histories from the War Literature 1914–18* (Boston: 1919). The collection includes cases from the major participant countries in the war.
103. Ibid., p. 238.
104. Ibid., p. 245.
105. Ibid., p. 712.

would change.[106] Case 343 describes a soldier and his comrade who were out in the cold and trying to warm their hands. The comrade placed his hand against the man's cheek and said, 'That hand is cold'. At that moment he was shot dead. The memory of this incident reappeared not only in his dreams, but whenever it was quiet: closing his eyes, he could feel the cold hand against his face.[107]

W. H. R. Rivers, Medical Officer at the Craiglockart War Hospital in Edinburgh,[108] where soldiers and officers suffering from shell shock were treated, argued that there were two main factors in the aetiology of shell shock: congenital or acquired tendencies towards nervous or mental instability, and the conditions at the Front including the exhaustion and emotional shock that the combatants had faced. The military training played a major part in both factors, as well in the specific form that the neurosis took.[109]

Rivers identified two important groups among those suffering from shell shock. In one group, the disorder found expression in a definite physical form, such as paralysis, mutism or convulsive seizures. Sufferers in this category were prone to suggestion. Rivers identified this group as suffering from hysteria, with the symptoms being more common amongst soldiers than officers. In the other group, the symptoms were less pronounced. The men suffered from lack of physical and mental energy, sleep disorders, depression, irritability and gaps in memory. This set of symptoms was more likely to apply to officers, and this group of patients was described as suffering from neurasthenia.[110] The distinction between the two groups had class implications, as the majority of these officers belonged to the middle and upper classes and had been through the public school system, whereas the majority of the soldiers came from the working classes.[111] The significance of these distinctions will be examined in more detail later in this chapter, along with their impact on the visual culture of the commemoration of the First World War.

Rivers saw shell shock as the result of a conflict between the instinct of self-preservation and certain standards of thought and conduct. From infancy, parental influence was directed at the suppression of fear. However, Rivers claimed that there was little in the 'ordinary life of the modern civilised man' that was likely to 'set up any conflict between the instinct of self-preservation and acquired social standards'.[112]

---

106. Ibid., p. 470.
107. Ibid., p. 474.
108. See Slobodin, Richard, *Rivers* (London: 1997), for a biography of Rivers. Rivers was a distinguished physiologist, psychologist and anthropologist. His work at Craiglockart Hospital became popularised in Pat Barker's *Regeneration Trilogy* and the film based on this, *Regeneration* (Norstar Entertainment).
109. Rivers, W. H. R., 'War Neurosis and Military Training', *Mental Hygiene*, II/4 (1918), pp. 513–14. See also Rivers, W. H. R., 'The Repression of War Experience', *Lancet*, 2 (February 1918) and his major psychoanalytical work, Rivers, W. H. R., *Conflict and Dream* (London: 1923).
110. Ibid., pp. 514–15.
111. Winter, Denis, *Death's Men. Soldiers of the Great War* (London: 1978), pp. 63–4.
112. Rivers, W. H. R., 'War Neurosis and Military Training', p. 516.

The object of military training was to equip the soldier to meet the 'special assaults on the instinct of self-preservation'. The physical symptoms 'incapacitate the soldier from further participation in warfare', resulting in the removal of 'all immediate necessity for conflict between instinct and duty'. The neurasthenic symptoms of the officers, on the other hand, represent a case of conflict not having been resolved.[113]

Rivers argued that the reason for the difference in the way that the two groups reacted could be found in the difference between their education and social background. The officers were more educated than the soldiers and their 'mental life more complex and varied'. By implication, the officers were less likely to be 'content with the crude solution of the conflict between instinct and duty' which was manifested in 'such disabilities as dumbness or the helplessness of a limb'. However, although the officers might have demonstrated physical characteristics such as temporary mutism and paralysis in the early stages of shell shock, they were not satisfied with 'these solutions of their conflict' and their disabilities quickly disappeared, to be replaced by 'symptoms directly dependent on anxiety'.[114] It is these anxieties that were exemplified in the commemoration of the First World War and led to the acting-out of masculinities in the inter-war period.

Rivers, examining in more detail the public school background of the officers, argued that games and contests were very important in repressing not only expressions of fear but also the emotions themselves.[115] According to Rivers, the simpler mental training that the soldier received in school in comparison with the officer made him 'more easily content than the officer', leading to the 'crude solution of the motive' that resulted in some form of physical disability.[116] The education system, particularly the public school ethos, was a major preoccupation of reconstruction debates. Public schools, it was claimed, promoted exemplary codes of masculine behaviour such as courage, endurance and self-sacrifice, which could help rebuild the country after the war. The fact that the symptoms displayed by the officers being treated for shell shock manifested themselves in ways that were not visible to others meant that the middle and upper classes were once again displaying the qualities of stoicism and self-sacrifice that their education had instilled in them. By contrast, the selfishness of the working classes, whose educational background did not lend itself to such qualities, was evident in the visibility of their shell shock symptoms, which commanded visual attention.

The difference in symptoms was distinguished not only by the educational background of the two groups, but also by the military training they received. The aim of military training was to adapt the soldier to act as a component of a whole unit. Habit through drill, and power of suggestion were used to create the perfect soldier, while for the officer, sublimation and repression were an essential part of their training, providing them with the capacity to cope with the stresses of warfare.

113. Ibid.
114. Ibid., p. 517.
115. Ibid.
116. Ibid.

Rivers argues that the officer is 'driven by his position to repress the expression of emotion far more persistently than the private soldier'. The soldier, on the other hand, has to 'think only or chiefly of himself'.[117] The egoistical image of the working-class man is evoked once again.

Rivers was not the only medical officer to suggest that class distinctions contributed to the different symptoms of shell shock. The official medical history of the war argued: 'Any soldier above the rank of corporal seemed possessed by too much dignity to become hysterical.'[118] This image of the working-class man was also promoted by the War Office Committee of Enquiry into Shell Shock, whose findings were published in 1922.[119] Ted Bogacz has analysed the proceedings of the Committee and notes that its make-up was overwhelmingly middle- and upper-class. With the exception of one member, all were a product of the public school system. Bogacz points out that the members were 'extremely class conscious', and that this was evident in their discussion of the lower orders and other ranks, particularly when they were apportioning blame. Any blame was attached to the men rather than the atrocious conditions at the Front.[120] Jay Winter has argued that the only way to understand the significance of the discourse of shell shock 'is to identify its socially ascribed class character'. Shell shock was part of the language of the officer corps and, as such, was a 'code to describe the shock of the ruling elite, whose sons and apprentices, being groomed for power, were slaughtered in France'.[121]

The categorisation of shell shock symptoms according to class distinctions had certain implications for the definitions of masculinity at the time. It had particular implications for the way that the *Boy David Memorial* was seen by establishment figures, and helps to explain why there was such emphasis on the figure of the uniformed soldier in memorials of the First World War.

The medical images of the hysterical shell-shocked combatants also provide an explanation for the way in which the body is presented in hysterical disorders. The photographs published by Elmer Southard to illustrate the case studies of shell shock show the subjects before and after treatment *(Illustration 3.6)*. The perceived indexical and hence 'true nature' of photography[122] is used to document the physical change that takes place in the body of the shell-shocked soldier. John Tagg has claimed that the 'knowledge of truth of which photography became the

117. Ibid., p. 525.

118. MacPherson, W. G., Herringham W. P., Elliott, T. R. (eds), *History of the Great War, Medical Services. Diseases of the War* (London: 1923), p. 18, quoted in Bogacz, Ted, 'War Neurosis and Cultural Change in England, 1914–22: The Work of the War Office Committee of Enquiry into "Shell-Shock"', *Journal of Contemporary History*, 24/2 (1989), p. 232.

119. Bogacz, Ted, 'War Neurosis and Cultural Change in England', p. 232.

120. Ibid., pp. 239–41.

121. Winter, Jay, 'Shell-Shock and the Cultural History of the Great War', *Journal of Contemporary History*, 35/1 (2000), p. 10.

122. See Evans, Jessica, 'Introduction. Cultures of the Visual', in Evans, Jessica, and Hall, Stuart (eds), *Visual Culture. The Reader* (London: 1999), p. 13.

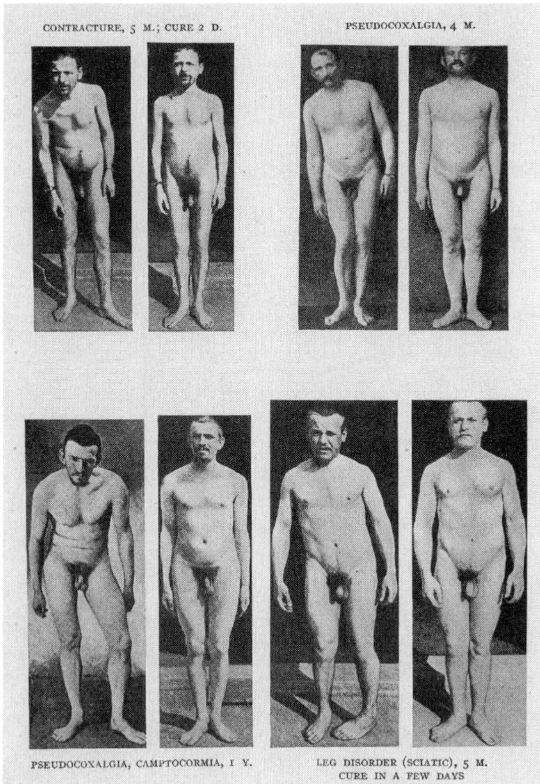

Figure 3.6 Cases of shell shock (hysteric symptoms) before and after treatment. Southard Elmer, *Shell Shock and Other Neuropsychiatric Problems: Presented in Five Hundred and Eighty-Nine Case Histories from the War Literature 1914–18* (Boston, 1919), p. 784

guardian was inseparable from the power and control which they engendered'.[123] This power is represented in the healthy images of the body. The patient is shown standing to attention, to prove that he has regained his health. It is significant that this health is demonstrated by a military position which epitomises the obedience and control that were the desired outcomes of military training. The body of the patient has been transformed by what the military authorities termed the 'first lesson in self-control'.[124] The position of standing to attention is expected to erase the somatic memories of the traumatic event that gave rise to the body's dislocation.

Juliet Mitchell argues that the person displaying symptoms of hysteria, regressing to the experience of his own body, distorts and contorts his face and body. To an onlooker, the body can appear either disabled or 'mad'. It is the feelings that make

123. Tagg, John, *The Burden of Representation* (London: 1987), p. 65.
124. Legge, R. F. (Major), *Mainly About Discipline* (London: 1914), p. 20.

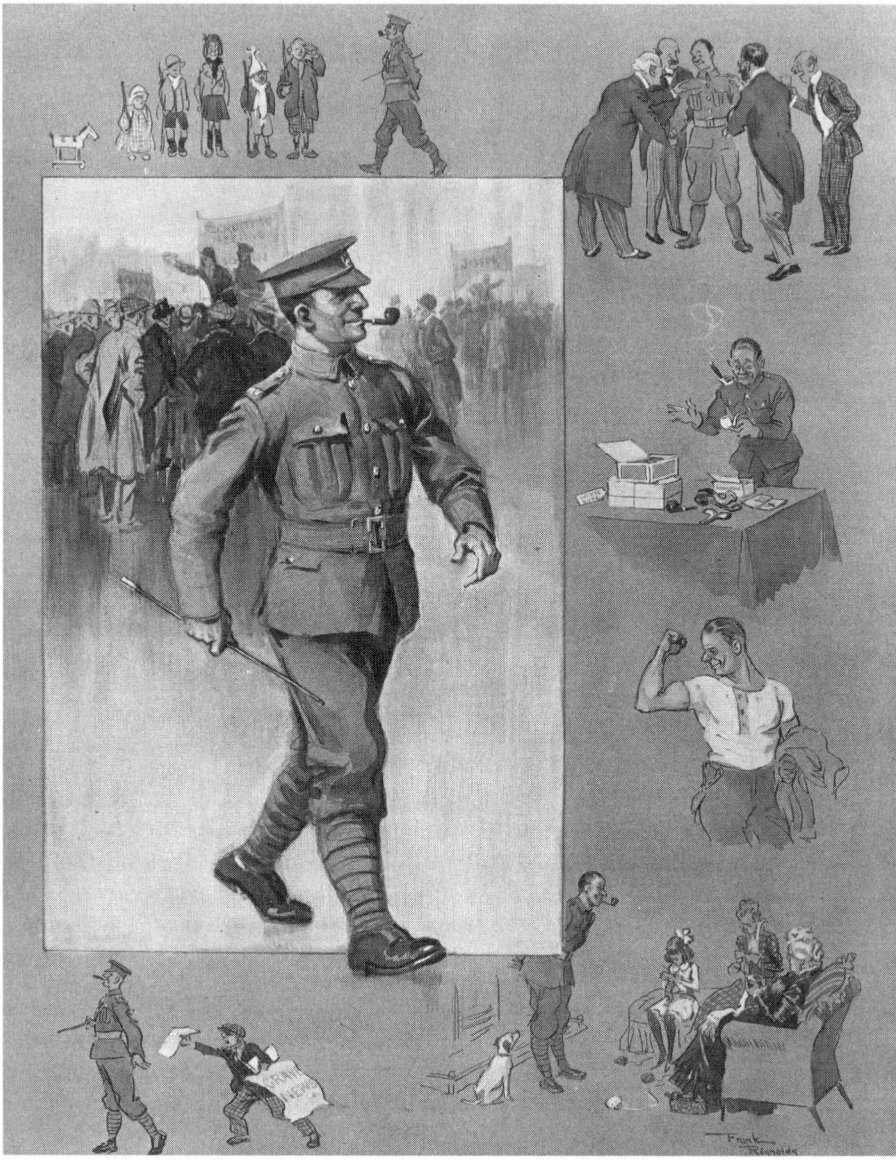

Figure 3.7 The Man Who has Answered the Call and the Man Who has Not. *Illustrated London News*, 20/11/1915

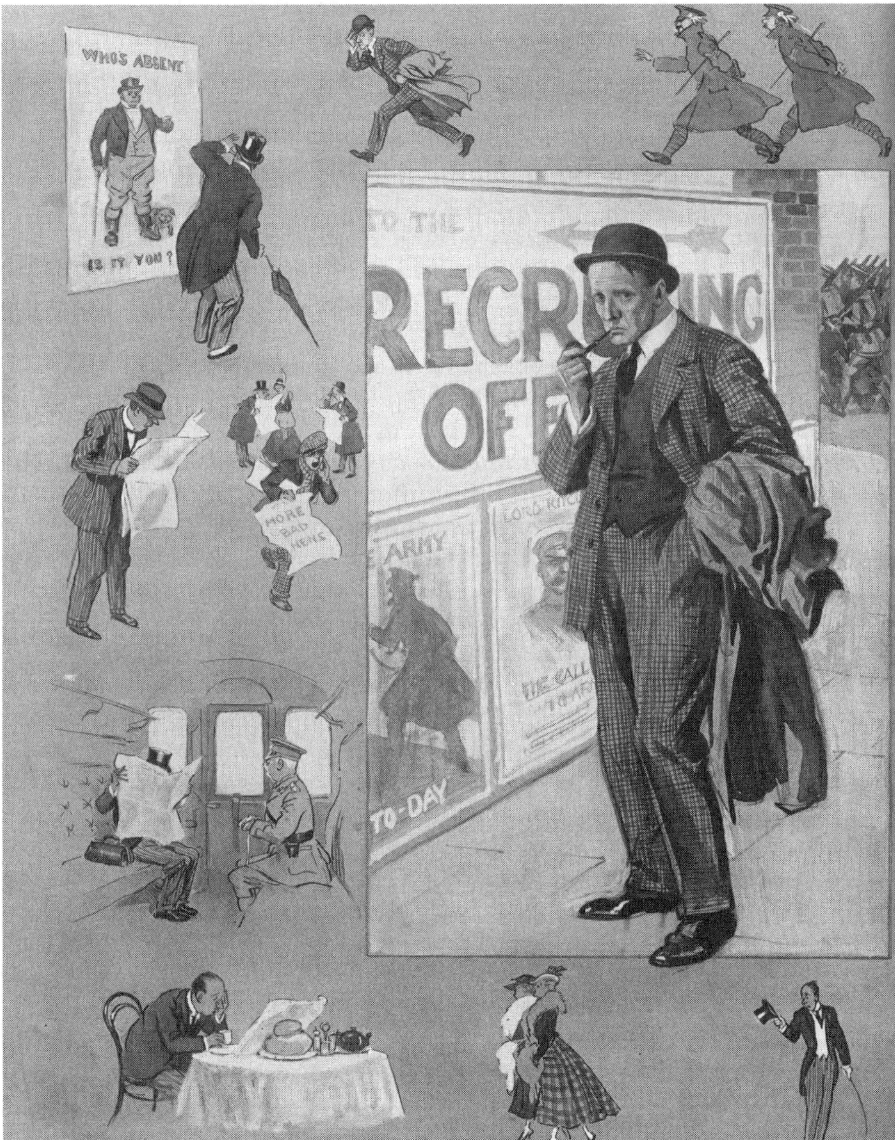

Figure 3.8 The Man Who has Answered the Call and the Man Who has Not. ***Illustrated London News*, 20/11/1915**

the body contort and the face scrunch up in emotional pain. Although a characteristic of hysteria is amnesia, argues Mitchell, this amnesia usually affects events and ideas rather than feelings. Feelings are remembered in the body, in a way that Melanie Klein has called 'memories in feelings'.[125]

In Southard's photographs, the picture of the patient before treatment shows a body that has become dislocated and no longer conforms to the ideal symmetrical presentation of the healthy body. It is hunched and cannot stand straight, and represents a departure from the perceived ideal image of masculinity. Judith Butler has argued that the gendered self is structured by repeated acts, which take on the form of particular gestures and postures. These acts seek to 'approximate to the ideal of a substantial ground of identity'.[126] The hysterical body is unable to carry out these acts and therefore cannot achieve the ideal masculinity.

The recruitment campaign for the First World War[127] offers an example of the way in which prescribed masculine roles were used to boost the number of soldiers. The double page spread in the *Illustrated London News (ILN) (Illustration 3.7 and 3.8)* published in November 1915, a year after the start of the war, was aimed at increasing the numbers of volunteers enlisting in the forces. The number of recruits had fallen, following the initial enthusiasm, and the government was keen to rectify the situation through the press. The two images featured in the *ILN* article depict binaries of sociability which focus on posture. The man who has answered the call is shown in full uniform, standing upright and confident in a manner not dissimilar to that of the rehabilitated shell-shocked servicemen. The man who has not answered the call is hunched and wears civilian clothes that look creased and unkempt in comparison with the pristine uniform of the volunteer. The images accompanying these two themes also contribute towards an understanding of the acceptable hegemonic masculinities that were based on work, physical strength and the family. The uniform, David Morgan argues, 'absorbs individualities into a generalised and timeless masculinity'.[128] The man who enlisted provides the timeless and generalised masculinity of the war years. It is this masculinity that the post-war commemoration tries to emulate in the form of the 'picturesque soldier'. They both rely on the uniform, but more importantly on posture, gestures and bodily memory to present a timeless version of masculinity.

The shell-shocked body, which shares with the body of the man who does not enlist an air of defencelessness, provides a threat to the masculine ideal because it reveals the instability of the masculine identity. According to Judith Butler, any discontinuities in the gender acts which prescribe our identities

125. Mitchell, Juliet, *Mad Men and Medusas. Reclaiming Hysteria and the Effects of Sibling Relations on the Human Condition* (London: 2000), pp. 212–13.

126. Butler, Judith, *Gender Trouble: Feminism and the Subversion of Identity* (London: 1990), p. 141.

127. For a discussion of propaganda during the war see Reeves, Nicholas, *The Power of Film Propaganda. Myth or Reality?* (London: 1999).

128. Morgan, David, 'Theatres of War: Combat, the Military and Masculinities', in Brod, H. and Kaufman, M. (eds), *Theorising Masculinities* (London: 1994), p. 166.

'reveal the temporal and contingent groundlessness of the ground'.[129] Moreover, the hysterical body has no clearly defined borders. The asymetricality of the body and its exaggerated, uncontrolled gestures defy the fixity of borders and turn the person into a 'carnivalesque' figure which, according to Susan Stewart, overturns and challenges hierarchies.[130]

The importance of erasing such images from the memory of the war is illustrated by a film produced at Netley Psychiatric Hospital and Seale Hayne Rehabilitation Farm, one of the main hospitals to treat shell-shocked patients after the First World War. The film shows soldiers rather than officers who have been diagnosed as suffering from hysterical symptoms.[131] As in the photos by Elmer Southard discussed previously, the soldiers are shown before and after treatment. Where the film and the photos differ, however, is in their ability to show the real impact of these symptoms on the lives of the men. To a great extent, the hysterical symptoms that these men display involve uncontrollable bodily movements, and the severity of their symptoms cannot be captured in a photograph. The moving image is shocking even today in its portrayal of a mental condition that deforms the body and demonstrates its fragility. The film also highlights the impact that the symptoms must have had on visual culture at the time. This goes some way towards explaining the need to reform the hysterical body, to rehabilitate it, but most importantly, to erase it from the memory of the war.

The film shows the possibilities of rehabilitation. Each patient is introduced with a short narrative title that gives the name and type of hysterical symptoms and in some cases the event that led to the shock. This is followed by details of the length of treatment and its outcomes. Private Pudmore is introduced as suffering from hysterical 'shuffling gait' after being buried alive following a shell explosion. He suffered complete paraplegia for ten months, but six weeks after being admitted to the hospital, began to show signs of improvement. The film sequence attempts to capture this improvement. Private Pudmore is seen getting out of his wheelchair, and walking a short distance. He leans close to the wall, touching it constantly for support *(Illustration 3.9)*. His body shakes uncontrollably, making it very difficult for him to walk in a straight line.

The film moves to Private Willis, who suffered 'hysterical pseudo-spastic gait' following spinal concussion after being buried in a shell explosion. His extensive, uncontrollable movements mean that like Private Pudmore, he walks with great difficulty. Private Williams is then shown walking very slowly towards the camera. He suffered hysterical 'slippery ice gait', after spinal concussion from a shell explosion, when he was also buried alive. His face is tense with the effort of walking in an imaginary straight line. Like Private Willis and Private Pudmore,

129. Butler, Judith, *Gender Trouble*, p. 141.

130. Stewart, Susan, *On Longing. Narratives of the Miniature, the Gigantic, the Souvenir, the Collection* (London: 1993), p. 107.

131. The film is approximately fifteen minutes in length. *War Neuroses. Netley 1917, Seale Hayne, 1917–18*. Wellcome Trust Film Unit, Wellcome Trust.

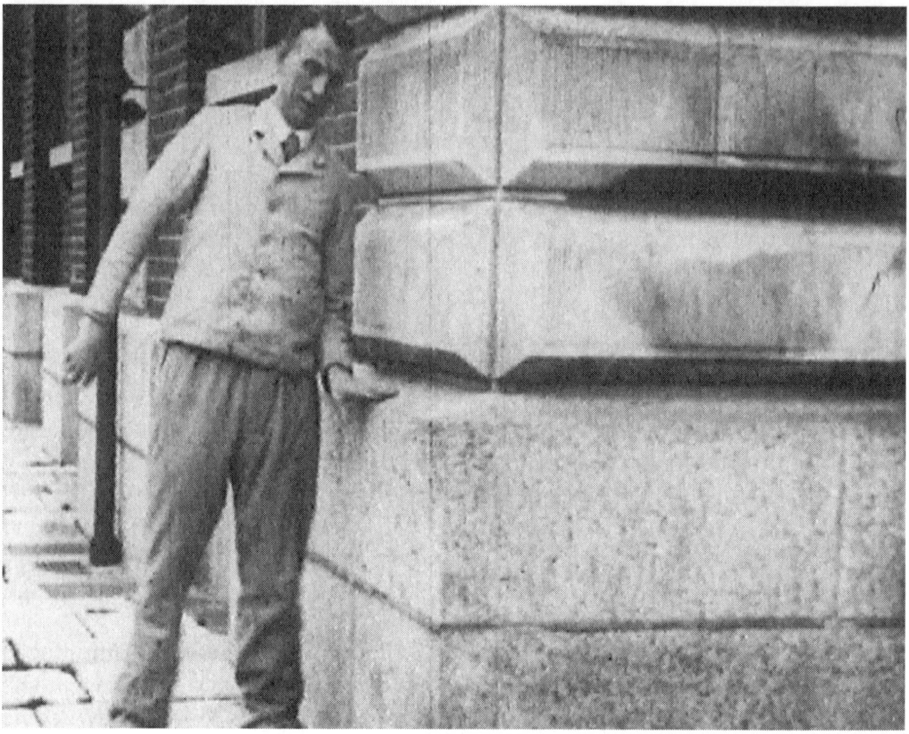

Figure 3.9 Private Pudmore at Netley Psychiatric Hospital, Film Still. *War Neuroses. Netley 1917, Seale Hayne, 1917–8.* Wellcome Trust Film Unit

he appears to have forgotten the cultural postural conditioning that would enable him to walk upright. This amnesia is a physical amnesia. The body has forgotten certain culturally specific postures that define and inscribe it as a socially acceptable masculine body.

Once each of the servicemen has been paraded in front of the cameraman they are shown standing to attention next to one another. Each man then walks towards the camera and away from the frame. Each has been cured. The physical memory of the upright position and the ability to walk in a straight line have been reinstated. The camera further testifies to their rehabilitation in a scene showing a group of servicemen in uniform performing drill exercises in the hospital grounds. The men start by standing to attention and then go on to perform synchronised gymnastic movements.[132] The hysterical body and its uncontrolled movements have been reintegrated into the military discipline of drill exercises.

132. Joanna Bourke has argued that during the war there was an attempt to control men physically and mentally. This could be described as a form of state surveillance, which

The imperative need to discipline the male body can also be linked to the shell-shocked hysterical body of the working-class male whose uncontrollable, undisciplined movements can be compared to the fear of the crowds and the way in which they needed to be contained and controlled. The commemoration of the war offered the opportunity to establish this control: first, in the orderly, perfectly formed and contained ritual crowds who attended the unveiling ceremonies and secondly, in the stillness of the commemorative figure of the soldier in drill military positions. The hysterical body like the crowd, was just too fearful in its unpredictability and capacity for disobedience.

The last part of the film is broken down into two scenes. In the first, the men after being treated are shown working on a farm and performing a useful role within the community. In effect, the rehabilitated soldier has been transformed into the exemplary citizen who will work selflessly and die for his country. In the final scene, the rehabilitated soldiers are shown re-enacting a battle in the grounds of Seale Hayne Farm. The clip is introduced by the title: 'Battle of Seale Hayne – Directed, photographed and acted by convalescent war neurosis patients.' The patients are kitted out in full combat uniform, complete with rifles and are being inspected by an officer. They proceed to march to the imagined battle, where they are shot, wounded and carried away by stretcher-bearers. The re-enactment of the battle makes them relive the traumatic events that they experienced and that led to their hysterical somatic symptoms.

The scenes in the film raise questions about the way that the body was viewed by the patient and the representation of the body in commemoration. Juliet Mitchell argues that in extreme pleasure or pain, the body normally goes missing. If something can be acknowledged as missing, then it can be re-presented. However, for the body to feel safe enough to vanish and return, that is, to re-present itself, it needs first to feel sufficiently secure.[133] The security felt by the returning soldier was not sufficient for the body to be re-presented, as has already been discussed. The soldier in the memorials of the First World War was depicted in various military drill positions, in particular, standing to attention, with its connotations of discipline and the mastering of fear. This depiction was extremely problematic for the shell-shocked soldier for whom standing to attention had become bound up with the trauma of his experiences.

There is one particular scene in the film which raises interesting comparisons with the *Boy David Memorial*. In most scenes, the patients are seen walking around the grounds of the hospital, fully dressed. However, in one scene, a patient who is described as suffering from 'hysterical pseudohypertrophic muscular paralysis' stands naked in an empty room. His shoulders are held stiffly back and his whole

led to pseudo-scientific methods of disciplining the body in post war society – the Bruce Sutherland System of military drill being one example. Bourke, Joanna, *Dismembering the Male*, p. 171.

133. Mitchell, Juliet, *Mad Men and Medusas*, pp. 210–12.

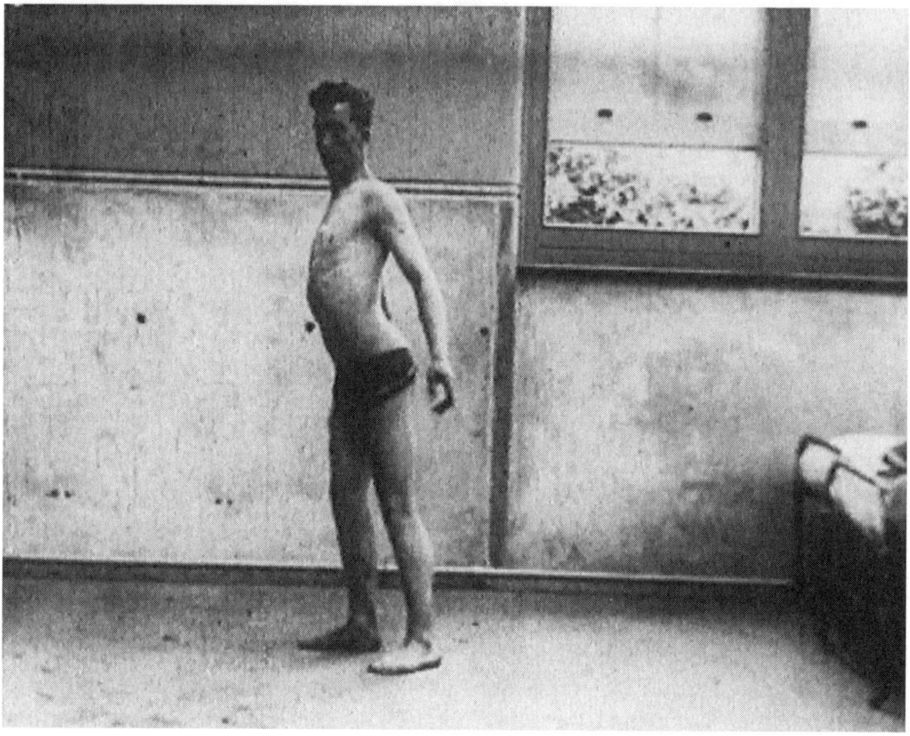

Figure 3.10 Patient at Netley Hospital. Film Still. *War Neuroses. Netley 1917, Seale Hayne, 1917–8.* Wellcome Trust Film Unit

demeanour is one of rigid self-consciousness (*Illustration 3.10*).[134] This posture is symptomatic of hysteria but also shares a remarkable similarity with the posture of the *Boy David* (*Illustration 3.11*). In both, the leg is slightly bent and the spine angular. In both there is a sense of movement that is being contained. Although the posture of the *Boy David* is informed by the classical and renaissance tradition in sculpture, it is impossible to ignore the associations with the body of the hysterical soldier. The symptoms of the hysteric, which are highly visible in the shivers, the numb paralysed body and the uncontrolled movements, have all been described as infantile and by implication unmanly. Juliet Mitchell argues that the 'infant is the preverbal baby, unable to explain himself, reacting in his body'. Likewise, the 'formation of femininity is seen to take place in the earliest infantile period'.[135] Some might equate the infantile movements and postures of the hysteric with feminine

134. He subsequently falls to the floor and tries to stand up again, but is unable to do so. A week later he is shown at the rooftop of the hospital in uniform, performing the same exercise. This time he is able to get up.

135. Mitchell, Juliet, *Mad Men and Medusas*, p. 160.

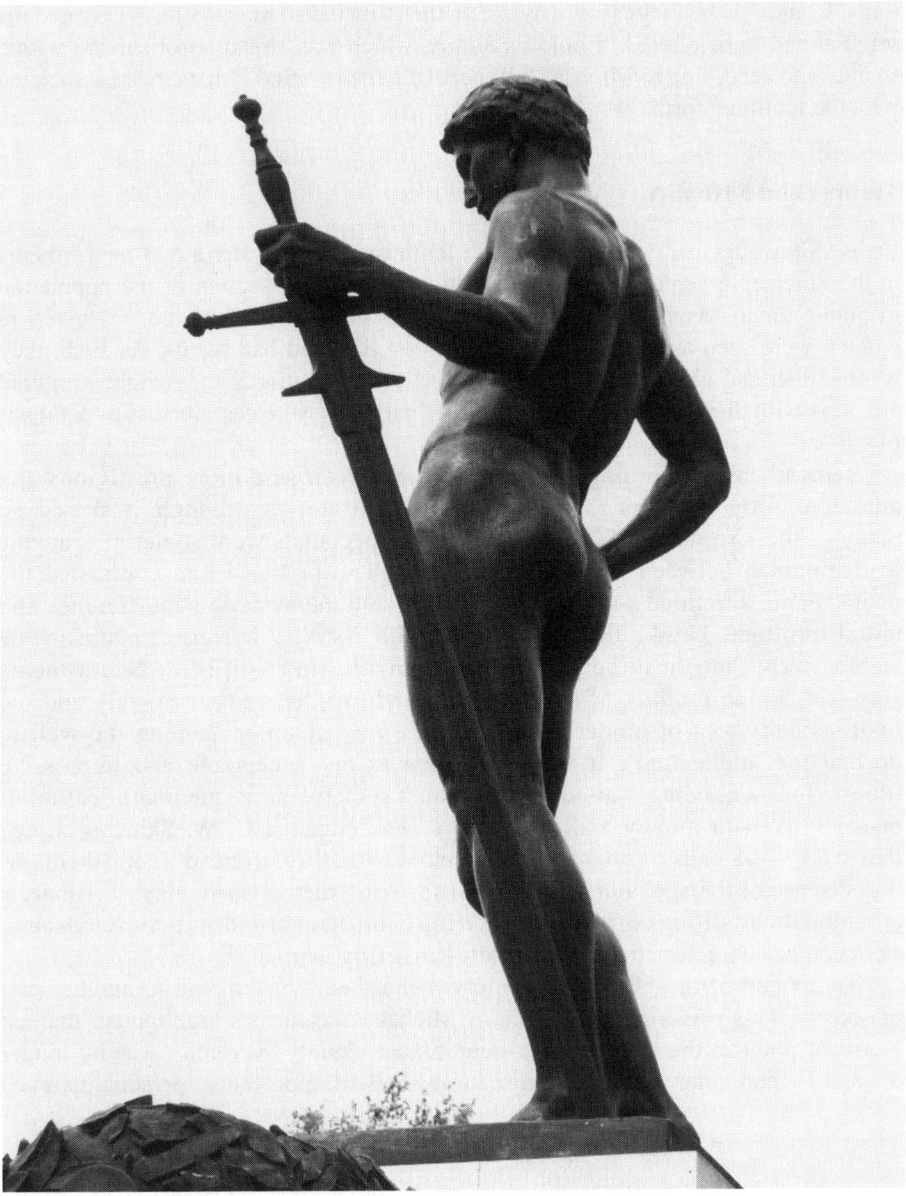

Figure 3.11 Figure of *Boy David*, Machine Gun Corps Memorial (1925), detail. Francis Derwent Wood

traits. Could this be the reason why the statue attracted so much controversy and the original had to be altered? Could its nudity, which was already problematic within society and according to Michael Hatt needed to be justified,[136] have been associated with the feminine form?

Trauma and Sexuality

Elaine Showalter has written about the feminisation of hysteria and neurasthenia in the nineteenth century. Women constituted the largest section of the population in public lunatic asylums and other private institutions of that time.[137] Hysterical women were seen as the products of poor heredity and bad habits. As such, they were selfish and absorbed in a 'morbid self-contemplation', and sought to attract attention with their symptoms. Symptoms of paralysis were described as a 'paralysis of will'.[138]

Neurasthenia, according to Showalter, was seen as a more prestigious and attractive form of female nervousness than hysteria, although it shared so many of the symptoms of hysteria that even specialists were sometimes unable to distinguish between the two. The medical profession often contrasted the neurasthenic's 'refined and unselfish nature' with the hysteric's indifference and moral turpitude. Unlike the 'disagreeable and disliked' hysterics, neurasthenic women were thought to be co-operative, ladylike and well-bred. Neurasthenia was seen as the product of modernity, an industrialised urban society and the luxuries and vices of modern life, and was very common 'among the well to do and the intellectual'. It was even seen as an 'acceptable and impressive illness' for men, being 'suited to a capitalist society and to the identification of masculinity with money and property'.[139] The eugenist C. W. Saleeby argued that worry was causing many mental disorders and referred to neurasthenia as the 'disease of the age' and the 'English speaking race in particular'.[140] He drew attention to the strong correlations between neurasthenia and self-consciousness, a particular characteristic of the middle-class Englishman.[141]

By the end of the nineteenth century neurasthenia had spread to another part of society. This was a period which, as Michel Foucault has highlighted, marked a critical point in the creation of a homosexual identity. Sexuality was no longer defined by particular acts, but was seen in terms of appearance, personality, even

136. Hatt, Michael, 'Muscles, Morals, Mind: The Male Body in Thomas Eakins' *Salutat*', in Adler, K. and Pointon, M. (eds), *The Body Imaged. The Human Form and Visual Culture since the Renaissance* (Cambridge: 1993).

137. Showalter, Elaine, *The Female Malady. Women, Madness and English Culture, 1830–1980* (London: 1987), p. 120.

138. Ibid., pp. 133–4.

139. Ibid.

140. Saleeby, C. W., *Worry: The Disease of the Age* (London: 1907), p. 42.

141. Ibid., p. 8.

body structure.[142] Case studies of homosexual men presented by sexologists such as Havelock Ellis in Britain and Richard von Krafft-Ebing in Austria provide an insight into the way in which homosexual men were perceived by the medical profession as well as the perceptions that homosexual men had of themselves.[143] Krafft-Ebing observed that in the case of a man presenting homosexual tendencies, 'almost invariably the existence of temporary or lasting neurasthenia may be proved'.[144] Out of Havelock Ellis's eighty case studies of homosexual men, twenty-two were described as having 'delicate health with often marked neurasthenia and unbalanced temperament', and were distinguished by an 'extremely nervous' disposition.[145]

Krafft-Ebing's case history 134 gives a perspective on the make-up and life of the neurasthenic homosexual.[146] It reports that the patient was 'mentally well endowed', and that his principal interest lay in art and literature. As a child, he was weak, nervous and subject to night terrors. He began to exhibit homosexual tendencies at an early age, and from the onset of puberty was aware of an inclination towards other males. He was attracted to young men of the lower classes wearing tight, brown trousers, and was especially drawn to cavalrymen. His ultimate desire was to press himself against such men from behind although, as Krafft-Ebing writes, the 'morality of his country did not allow such a thing'. By the age of twenty-eight he was 'neurasthenic because of excessive masturbation'. His dreams, which were of death scenes and of being attacked by dogs, were also symptomatic of his condition.[147] What was puzzling, however, was his appearance. He was 'in all respects of masculine appearance', Krafft-Ebing points out: 'In dress and manner he presented nothing that would attract attention,' and as a result, his friends and relatives had not the slightest suspicion of his sexual life.[148] The cure that Krafft-Ebing recommends is repression of the patient's homosexual feelings. He concludes: 'In the majority of cases the patient is quite satisfied when he becomes sexually neutral.'[149]

Three interesting points arise from the presentation of this case: first, the fact that the patient was sexually attracted to working-class men; second, Krafft-Ebing's observation of the effect that cultural constraints had on the patient and third, the impossibility for the doctor of seeing beyond the veil presented by the masculine composure of the body and thereby identifying with the homosexual desires of

142. Foucault, Michel, *The History of Sexuality. An Introduction. Vol. I* (London: 1990), Felski, Rita, 'Introduction', in Bland, Lucy and Doan, Laura (eds), *Sexology in Culture. Labelling Bodies and Desires* (Oxford: 1998), p. 4.

143. Felski, Rita, 'Introduction', p. 4.

144. Krafft-Ebing, Richard von, *Psychopathia Sexualis. With Especial Reference to the Antipathetic Sexual Instinct* (London: 1965), p. 223.

145. Ellis, Havelock, *Studies in the Psychology of Sex. Vol. 2 Sexual Inversion* (Philadelphia: 1917), p. 265.

146. Krafft-Ebing's case histories combined histories from the point of view of the patient and clinical observations from Krafft-Ebing himself.

147. Krafft-Ebing, Richard von, *Psychopathia Sexualis*, pp. 233–4.

148. Ibid.

149. Ibid., p. 307.

the patient. Harry Oosterhuis has argued that Krafft-Ebing, by publishing letters and autobiographies of his patients, allowed voices to be heard that were usually silenced. His medical discourse is characterised by multi-vocality: it is possible to find different, even contradictory, sets of values in Krafft-Ebing's work. Rather than viewing autobiographies as merely representations of lives as they have been lived, these life stories should be seen as a forum which gave meaning to their condition and helped to (re)construct their identity. In other words, they become what Dori Laub describes as 'testimonies'.[150] The way people experienced sexuality and gave meaning to it was determined not so much by given natural or psychological facts, but by cultural codes and symbols of social life. Homosexual identity presumed a reflexive awareness, an ability to interrogate the past from the perspective of the present, and to tell a coherent story about one's life history in the light of what might be anticipated of the future.[151] In light of this discussion the cases of shell shock recorded by the psychiatrists provided the patients with a vehicle to tell their story.

The possibility of agency that shell shock offered might explain the insistence by both medical and military authorities on dissociating sexuality from shell shock. Indeed, the debates on shell shock denied any connection between sexuality, repression and Freud's theories. As Martin Stone has argued, the major criticism of psychoanalysis that came out of the debates on shell shock was 'that Freud has been wrong in asserting that sexual factors played an all-important role in the aetiology of neurotic disorders'.[152] It was not only Rivers, whose arguments were discussed earlier, but also other eminent psychologists such as C. S. Myers and W. McDougall, who claimed that sex had little to do with shell shock.[153] As Stone argues, their accounts of shell shock's aetiology concentrated almost exclusively on the conflict between 'fear' and 'duty'. Only a few professionals drew any connection between shell shock and sexual factors. Ernest Jones, Freud's faithful follower in Britain, argued that the replacement of civilian ideals by the barbaric attitudes necessary for warfare served to bring about the return of previously repressed and long-buried sadistic impulses. In other words, the trauma of battle had 'merely served to open a can of libidinous worms'.[154]

The case studies of shell shock sufferers also reveal an unexpectedly sexual content. Case 51 was buried twice by shells. He spent forty days in a semi-confused state that was accompanied by headaches, and dreamt of the Boches wanting to behead him. Some of these dreams appeared while he was awake.

---

150. Laub, Dori, 'Truth and Testimony: The Process and Struggle', p. 63.
151. Oosterhuis, Harry, 'Richard von Krafft-Ebing's 'Step-Children of Nature'. Psychiatry and the Making of Homosexual Identity', in Rosario, Vernon (ed.), *Science and Homosexualities* (London: 1997), pp. 80–3.
152. Stone, Martin, 'Shellshock and the Psychologists', in Bynum, W. F., Porter, R. and Shepherd, M. (eds), *The Anatomy of Madness. Essays in the History of Psychiatry* (London: 1985), p. 244.
153. Myers, Charles, *Shell Shock in France, 1914–18: Based on a War Diary* (Cambridge: 1940).
154. Jones, Ernest, 'War and Individual Psychology', *Sociological Review* (London: 1915).

He had been especially troubled by 'nocturnal enuresis'.[155] Case 175 had visions of two comrades who were killed at his side during the war. There were also terrifying dreams which began with episodes at the battle front and ended with sexual experiences, which resulted in 'seminal emissions'. These added to the patient's belief that he was insane as he said he remembered literature read as a boy concerning nocturnal emissions.[156] Case 194, after a heavy bombardment, had a dreamy, bizarre sensation that he likened to a fog lying between him and his surroundings. He felt a terrible ceaseless anguish as if he were about to be executed. This fear gradually turned into a 'genital excitation'.[157] Case 342 presented another instance of dreams starting with terrible incidents at the Front and then shifting to sexual acts.[158] Case 192 had grown physically and mentally exhausted whilst serving at the Front and had been unable to concentrate. He began to neglect his uniform and was unable to keep his equipment in order. He became introspective and depressed. The case study concludes that: 'There was but one thing to do in his opinion: that was to humiliate himself by committing sodomy.'[159]

One case sums up the association between shell shock and homosexuality. The patient was a twenty-six year old man who complained of the 'terror of something lurking in the dark', especially in his bedroom, which compelled him at times to rush out in a state 'bordering upon panic'. For more than two years he had been unable to sleep without a light on and was also prone to forgetfulness and lack of concentration. Analysis revealed a traumatic war experience. During the Somme battle he remembered noticing the unburied head of a soldier, which he had to pass frequently. He had always avoided looking at the face, which 'bore an expression of extreme horror and disgust'. One night, however, despite his usual precautions not to approach the head too closely, he felt his foot touch it, and was 'instantly filled with a great revulsion of feeling', as he felt what he imagined to be the brains 'squelching' around his foot.[160]

This association of trauma with the patient's 'artistic temperament' led the analyst to establish that the patient, who was part of London's art scene, formed close attachments with men. On one occasion one of these men had invited the patient to his house and 'endeavoured to induce him to indulge in homosexual practices'. For the analyst, this event constituted the initial trauma that subsequently informed his trauma at the Front. The analyst concluded that any attempt to 'place the patient upon the heterosexual road would be impossible', because the sexual inversion was so complete. Instead, he recommended 'sublimation of the sexual energy'.[161]

155. Southard, Elmer, *Shell shock and other Neuropsychiatric Problems*, p. 63.
156. Ibid., p. 237.
157. Ibid., p. 259.
158. Ibid., p. 472.
159. Ibid., p. 257.
160. Davies-Jones, C. W. S., 'A Case of War Shock Resulting From Sex-Inversion', *International Journal of Psychoanalysis*, 1/3 (1920), p. 240.
161. Ibid., p. 244.

What becomes apparent from these cases is the associations they make between destruction, pain, disgust and desire. Sexuality no longer relies solely on desire[162] but on the possibilities of desire and the desiring self being constructed through and contingent on the extreme circumstances at the Front. The war brought together large numbers of men from different social and educational backgrounds and broke down most of the accepted codes of normative and proper social behaviour. As Santanu Das has argued, the atrocities of war, as well as 'loneliness and boredom, the strain of constant bombardment, the breakdown of language, and the sense of alienation from home, led to a new level of intimacy and intensity under which the carefully constructed morals of civilian society broke down'.[163] This, according to Das, cannot be understood solely in 'contrast to heterosexuality' and must be seen as a 'celebration of life of young men huddled against long winter nights, rotting corpses and falling shells'.[164]

In many of the memoirs the male body was particularly remembered as a source of tenderness, affection and comfort. J. S. Handley remembers the parade to camp as something grand and memorable, especially the 'huge muster of men'. The sight of six hundred men was a 'truly precious sight' and his 'blood would fire in absolute delight'.[165] Another popular memory was the sight of the men bathing. A. R. Williams remembered such a day:

> It was a glorious day. I am seated here in a wooded park. A battalion, just arrived, is having tea from the field kitchens under the trees, and the horses and transport are all lined up in an open space. There is a pond in which a lot of our chaps are having a swim. I went in this evening – my first swim in France. … it was quite an exhilarating enterprise for everyone. It would have made a fine picture for the camera man – men in khaki all along one bank, dressing and undressing.[166]

The passage is insightful in several respects. The account starts with the splendour of the day and culminates in the visual pleasure of the men bathing and swimming in the river; their bodies, in various states of undress, providing an 'exhilarating experience'. The visual pleasure could become physical as well, and A. R. Williams remembers several incidents of 'cuddling up':

> By dark we had got a couple of waterproofs to cover over the trench … Then we cuddled up close, showed one another home photographs, discussed the probabilities of the war finishing and annoyed one another by feeble joking about hot baths, clean linen and feather beds At the end of an hour we have all got the cramp.[167]

162. Foucault, Michel, *The Use of Pleasure: History of Sexuality. Vol. II* (London: 1990), p. 2.
163. Das, Santanu, '"Kiss me, Hardy": Intimacy, Gender and Gesture in World War I Trench Literature', *Modernism/Modernity*, 9/1 (2002), p. 52.
164. Ibid., p. 55.
165. Handley, J. S., IWM 92/36/1, p. 1.
166. Williams, A. R., IWM, 82/26/1, p. 69.
167. Ibid., p. 70.

The proximity of other male bodies provided comfort in the trenches and gave rise to further memories of home life, hot baths, clean linen and feather beds, all associated with the naked body and sexual activity. J. S. Handley remembers that some of his 'pleasantest hours were spent' after 'lights out', and that before going to sleep, it was possible to experience 'almost perfect joy' in the company of men.[168] Joanna Bourke, who has documented these experiences, observes that the men nursed and fed their friends when they were ill, held each other as they danced and wrapped blankets around each other, their bodies 'spooned' together in sleep.[169] For Santanu Das, these memories symbolise a 'new world of largely nongenital tactile tenderness'.[170]

Lieutenant-Colonel Hutchison's memory of his batman reinforces these experiences. Although the relationship is one of master/servant, there is a strong suggestion that it becomes something more, in the way that the batman is presented to the reader. Their first encounter is described in full detail and has all the ingredients of a romance story – a fort, the sea, and a piper appearing in the distance:

> I remember well when I first noticed him. I was whiling away an afternoon of the boredom of an orderly officer's duties ... and had strolled in the evening on the ramparts of the antiquated fortress which stands overlooking the Moray Firth. I sat upon a moss-covered wall, and idly watched the soft lapping waves as they were swept and tumbled by an unseen hand, when my thoughts were turned by the skirl of pipes, and a piper passed behind me. He turned in his beat, and continued to pace up and down the rampart. ... Then he stopped, and stood alert before me, smiling. ... That was an unusual experience for me. I asked him his name. He was pleased, and chatted away, merely an unspoilt soul. ... He played a solemn march, swinging his kilt with all the swagger of a pipe-major.[171]

Hutchison remembers the prospect of going on leave without his batman. He pleaded with the Colonel for another pass, which was finally granted: 'Peter came with me to the luxury of white sheets, bright firesides, warm baths and the mellow quietness of warm hearts.'[172] Peter was later killed in front of Hutchison: 'I held his hands a moment as a soul winged its way from that horror. Then I covered him; there was nothing man could do.'[173] Hutchison's final memory of Peter is of his perfection: 'Peter was incomparable – the friend in need, the friend of perfection.'[174] Like the Spartan saying that Hutchison used to describe his ideal machine gunner, 'How beautiful to die in perfection', Peter was his perfect friend. And the *Boy David* represents perfection, Hutchison's ideal gunner, Peter.

The description of Peter's death is, however, an idealised one. Other accounts of deaths that Hutchison witnessed at the Front, which he describes vividly in his memoirs, are filled with mutilated bodies, blood and corpses. One particular scene

168. Handley, J. S., IWM 92/36/1, p. 5.
169. Bourke, Joanna, *Dismembering the Male*, pp. 133–6.
170. Das, Santanu, '"Kiss me, Hardy"', p. 52.
171. Hutchison, Graham Seton, *Warrior* (London: 1932), p. 69.
172. Ibid., p. 70.
173. Ibid., p. 72.
174. Ibid., p. 72.

that took place at the Western Front between High Wood and Delville Wood is retold several times and becomes more elaborate each time. The scene is first described in very factual terms, in 1921. The focus is on the machine gun, particularly its anthropomorphic characteristics and its consumption of water and urine for its cooling system. The men are described as subservient to the machine and unable to match its efficiency.[175] Recalling the incident ten years later, the roles are reversed. The machine is secondary to the real focus of the description, the men. What is also more evident is the destructiveness of war, the deaths, the blood, the smells, and the chaos.[176]

Michael Roper claims that the exaggerated narratives of the war and the compulsion to tell war stories should be seen as interactions between public narratives of war and private memory.[177] These narratives, according to Roper, offer the possibility of 'managing painful experiences from the past'.[178] Hutchison's elaborate narrative needs to be seen within a framework of providing an outlet for his traumatic war experiences. Graham Dawson, however, has argued that 'traditional or recognisable forms tend to define and to limit the imaginative possibilities' of personal narratives.[179] This might offer an explanation for Hutchison's insistence, on both the atrocities of war and, on the idealised death of his batman, which is underpinned by close friendship and tangible memories of their time together. Such memories could not easily be incorporated into available heterosexual public codes and instead become incorporated into the idea of martyrdom.

The iconography of the figure of Saint Sebastian provides a possibility for incorporating a personal narrative that defies traditional incorporation. In addition it offers a narrative of martyrdom. Richard Kaye has argued that like the nineteenth century representation of the hysterical female, which provided a dramatic visual concept of medical illness for physicians, the body of Saint Sebastian furnished a series of 'imaginistically dynamic associations for the scientific conceptualisation of the homosexual'.[180] The hysterical male body, with its distorted posture, can also be compared with the figure of the Saint Sebastian.

The *Boy David* and its association with the hysterical male body becomes evident by comparing it with two drawings from Hutchison's memoir of the 33rd Battalion Machine Gun Corps. The drawings also demonstrate the difficulties in finding a distinct visual language that incorporates private memories within available public scripts. The drawing that forms the first page of the memoir (*Illustration 3.12*),

175. Hutchison, Graham Seton, *The Thirty-Third Division in France and Flanders, 1915–1919* (London: 1921), p. 20.

176. Hutchison, G. S., *Footslogger*, p. 158.

177. Roper, Michael, 'Re-remembering the Soldier Hero: the Psychic and Social Construction of Memory in Personal Narratives of the Great War', *History Workshop Journal*, 50 (2000), p. 183.

178. Ibid.

179. Dawson, Graham, *Soldier Heroes. British Adventure, Empire and the Imagining of Masculinities* (London: 1994), pp. 22–3.

180. Kaye, Richard, 'Losing his Religion. Saint Sebastian as Contemporary Gay Martyr', in Horne, P. and Lewis, R. (eds), *Outlooks. Lesbian and Gay Sexualities and Visual Culture* (London: 1996), p. 89.

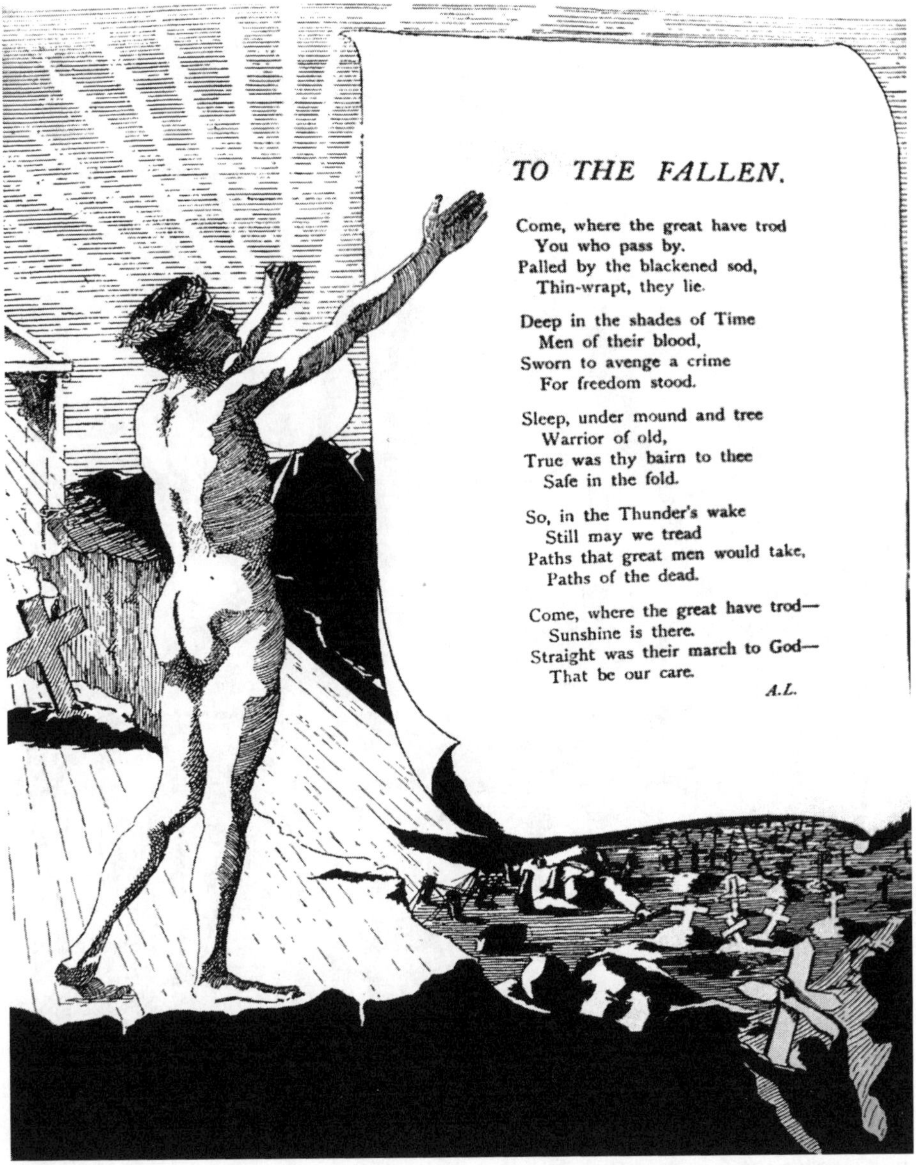

Figure 3.12 **To the Fallen. Hutchison, G. S., *History and Memoir of the 33rd Battalion Machine Gun Corps and of the 19th, 98th, 100th and 248th M.G. Companies* (London: Waterlow Brothers, 1919)**

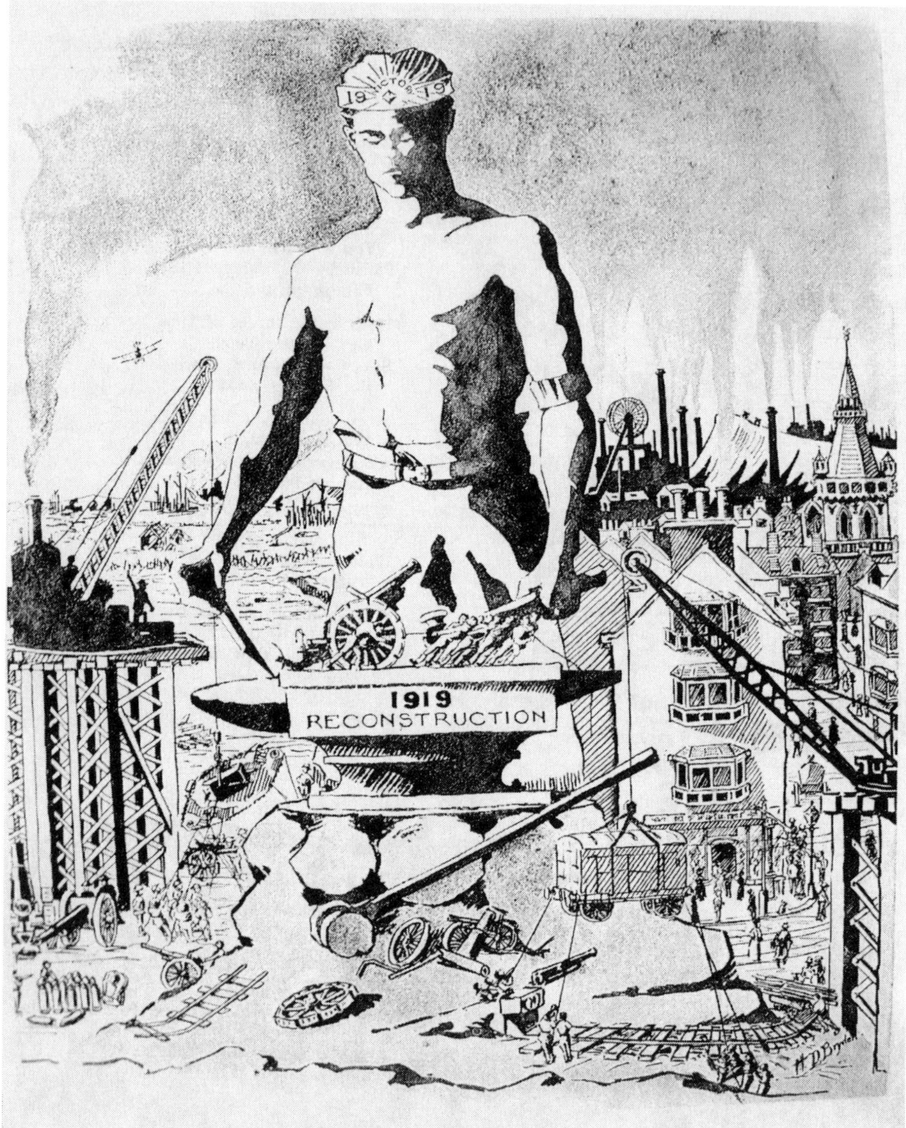

Figure 3.13 Reconstruction. Hutchison, G. S., *History and Memoir of the 33rd Battalion Machine Gun Corps and of the 19th, 98th, 100th and 248th M.G. Companies*. (London: Waterlow Brothers, 1919)

shows a male standing naked above a cemetery with his hands raised to the sky. It is possible to see similarities between the arching of the back of this figure and the *Boy David* (*Illustration 3.11*). The drawing which forms the last page of the memoir (*Illustration 3.13*), shows a gigantic man, representing victory,[181] standing in the middle of the reconstruction going on after the war. The words 'Victory 1919' (the year the memoir was written) appear across his forehead while the anvil bears the inscription '1919 Reconstruction'. The strong man of victory looks set to forge post-war manhood and provides a strong contrast with the *Boy David*, who adopts the posture and demeanour of the male youth who mourns his comrades.

The strict definitions of masculinity during and after the war, as manifested in the authorities' insistence on separating shell shock from sexuality, made it impossible for traumatised combatants who experienced different forms of masculinity at the Front to mourn their comrades. It also made it impossible for them to come to terms with the return to the pre-war codes of masculinity that the commemoration of the war attempted to impose. The result was an acting-out of masculinities in the inter-war years.

Acting-Out – The Case of Lt. Col. Graham Seton Hutchison

Hutchison's case offers a good example of the acting-out of masculinities in the inter-war years. In 1930 he began co-editing the monthly publication *The Superman*,[182] and formed the group of the Paladins. The first issue of the magazine set out the objectives of the group. In an article entitled 'Paladins. Where are the Supermen?' Hutchison wrote:

> We want Men! Never more urgently did the country require them than today. Men of proven experience, capacity, energy, understanding of industrial problems; sympathetic with the aspirations, hopes, fears, anxieties and life of the people; [...] men up-to date, progressive, neither the victims of taboos, nor the slaves of worn out dogmas; men physically fit, Spartan in habit, who will not destroy the body with an excess of food, tobacco and alcohol;

These men needed also to be eugenically fit:

> men who possess in their blood and bones the matchless tradition of the English, Scottish and Welsh countryside; men of courage, capable of sacrifice, willing to incur disfavour, social ostracism, loss of position, for a faith, for a belief, for a conviction; men to whom property, possessions, profits, material gain, mean nothing in the realm of achievement. Men who are not ashamed to testify that they believe in something bigger than life. Those would be men indeed. Supermen![183]

181. It is important to note that victory is usually shown as a female figure.

182. The journal was published between 1930 and 1941 by T. W. Standwell.

183. Hutchison, G. S., 'Paladins. Where Are the Supermen Britain's Need Today?', *The Superman Magazine*, November 1930, p. 20.

This rhetoric should firstly be seen within the political and economic conditions of the late 1920s, with rising unemployment, economic depression and discontent, especially amongst ex-servicemen.[184] The 1920s represent in the eyes of many of the commentators on the period a time when the war was 'forgotten'. It was not until the late 1920s and early 1930s that a need to remember the war emerged, which provided a cause for the collapse of the system, a 'source of explanations, justifications and alternatives to a deflated capitalist system'.[185]

Another factor needs to be taken into account which becomes clearer as Hutchison's article moves on to look at the war years. He describes the war as having deprived the country of the 'cream of a generation'. Those who survived are seen as 'damned and despoiled, slandered and thrust aside'. Instead of the war heroes being in power, the corridors of power belong to the 'same faces as before the War'. Eric Leed believes that this view can be interpreted as the fashioning of war experience into a myth of negative selection, a 'devout belief that the best had died and the worst survived'. For Leed, the burial of the dead and the commemoration of the war represented a defining moment in the consciousness of the survivors, who found themselves being compared, in most cases unfavourably, with the dead, the 'lost generation'.[186] Hutchison finds an even more important reason for the discontent amongst ex-servicemen: the notion that prevailed immediately after the Armistice that everything should 'return to normal'. According to Hutchison, 'any man of vision could have told them that, that was the one thing impossible'. How could they 'return to normal', is the implication, when they 'had suffered the anguish of wounds, the horror of bombardment, the bitterness of imprisonment, the dread of the unknown, and the shock of being uprooted from the placid peace of English life'.[187]

The example shows that it is the trauma of war that leads to the rejection of the return to normalcy and the demands of post-war life. Eric Leed argues that the 'trauma of war defines and determines the present actions and thinking of the rememberer'.[188] However, the returning soldiers are being asked to forget. They are being asked to remember sacrifice, unselfishness and heroism of the war, but to forget the actual trauma of war with all its horrors. Leed argues that the war equipped the citizen-soldiers with a double past – a pre-war past and a wartime past – linked but incommensurate with the present.[189] One could argue however that the pre-war and wartime past were incommensurate with each other, and that the same parallel existed between the heroic wartime past demanded by the commemoration of war and the traumatic, unheroic past of the combatants. The commemoration

184. Taylor, A. J. P., *English History 1914–1945* (Oxford: 1992) and Mowat, Charles, *Britain Between the Wars 1918–1940* (London: 1968).

185. Leed, Eric, 'Fateful Memories: Industrialized War and Traumatic Neuroses', *Journal of Contemporary History*, 35/1 (2000), p. 94.

186. Ibid., p. 93.

187. Hutchison, G. S., 'Paladins. Where Are the Supermen?', p. 20.

188. Leed, Eric, 'Fateful Memories', p. 87.

189. Ibid., p. 89.

creates a gap, a schism, between the traumatic experience and the integration of the individual within post-war society.

This schism is breached by comradeship. Comradeship and its idealisation provides the only way in which the pre-war and the post-war experiences can be integrated. Leed argues that the 'terrors of war detach male sexuality from reproduction and channel it to other men, friends, enemies, the machinery of war'.[190] Hutchison's article demonstrates that out of the suffering and trauma he previously described, grew comradeship: 'The men have fulfilled a comradeship and friendship so deep rooted that it cannot be destroyed.'[191] The Paladin League was to provide a means for this comradeship to develop further and be put to use within society. Hutchison viewed the League as being political, spiritual and cultural. It celebrated physical culture, the open air, preservation of the countryside, the development of crafts, and above all, 'comradeship in its highest, broadest sense'.[192] Comradeship was also a leveller of class distinctions, claimed Hutchison, who wrote: 'Paladins do not understand what is implied by "class".' Another fundamental principle of the League was to 'do away with taboos', which were seen as imposing 'ridiculous, unhealthy, indecent restrictions upon man and his commune with nature'. Its ultimate goal was to 'uphold the matchless tradition and culture of the British Race'.

The German Youth Movement, one could argue, influenced Hutchison's ideas. He visited Germany on many occasions during the 1920s and several photographs of himself with young German men adorn the pages of his biography and the magazine. He himself admitted he was influenced by Germany.[193] Harry Oosterhuis, commenting on the German Youth Movement in relation to the publication *Der Eigene*,[194] argued that the main preoccupation of this publication was the promotion of *Mannerbund,* a bond between men that was in decline because of the feminisation of society. The contributors to *Der Eigene*, including its editor, Adolf Brand, were unhappy with the Weimar democracy and more specifically with the erosion of German culture by both Bolshevism and American civilisation. American civilisation was seen as threatening the German spirit with its capitalistic consumerism and desire for luxury, accompanied by cultural feminism. *Der Eigene* saw the war generation as carrying the flag for *Mannerbund*, since they had experienced male solidarity and comradeship in the trenches. Male bonding, which was an education in manliness and 'physiological friendship', had benefits for military loyalty and sacrifice, and for war itself.[195]

---

190. Ibid., p. 97.
191. Hutchison, G. S., 'The Paladin League of Youth. Its Charter and Its Mission', *The Superman Magazine*, January 1931, p. 5.
192. Ibid.
193. Hutchison, G. S., 'Out of the Blue', *The Superman Magazine*, July 1931, p. 5.
194. The journal was published between 1896 and 1931.
195. Oosterhuis, Harry, 'Introduction', Oosterhuis, Harry and Kennedy, Hubert (eds), *Homosexuality and Male Bonding in Pre-Nazi Germany. The Youth Movement, the Gay Movement and Male Bonding Before Hitler's Rise* (New York: 1991), pp. 187–8.

The Superman Magazine. [NOVEMBER, 1930] 21

happiness determined by endless Royal Commissions and abortive Conferences which, as history has already shown, produce nothing.

Our Perilous National Position.

It is a plain fact that Great Britain is in a receding economic position. Yet this is the moment chosen by politicians to increase the benevolent services, to multiply state assistance in every department of life, and to stultify individual genius and capacity, the very genesis from which the mass of the people acquire prosperity, by strangling, crushing legislation. Rather than turn their attention to flagrant abuses of commercial usage and of personal liberty, successive Governments, by specious propaganda, have sought to impose greater restrictions on liberty, while the financial highwayman, the destroyer of industry, is free to do as he pleases. There exists no relation whatever between the capital valuation of an

industry and its productive capacity or the number of people engaged therein. The surplus wealth, capital, derivable alone from work, is diverted into companies, possessing nothing of any social value to manufacture and which often have nothing whatever to sell, which engage no labour, and which operate only to provide an opportunity for share-pushers to spoof the public.

It is absurd to suppose that it is beyond the wit of man to devise a system whereby the productive and consumptive capacity of the population shall be related. There are millions of people living below, or at starvation level: there are other millions wholly unemployed, on part time, or eking out an existence selling goods on commission or what not. Nothing stands between productive and consumptive capacity except price fixation, itself based upon credit. Money, prices, credits are arbitrary questions, controlled alone by man. It is absurd that our farmers cannot sell the produce of our land, when people are starving; it is ridiculous that thousands in Lancashire should be out of work, should be unemployed, with all the misery and anxiety involved in idleness, when there are thousands without shirts to their backs, and that miners should not get coal, with factories starved of this essential raw material. Money, perhaps, is the most useful device of civilisation, invented as a token, the medium of exchange of labour and services. It is not a commodity to be bought and sold.

Confiscation of our Most Valuable and Vital Heritage.

In the realm of public health, during the last half-century there have been sufficient abuses to fill volumes. Vested interest has deprived the public, for generations, of the discoveries and new determinations of science. Public auhorities, charged with the common weal, even to-day are so infected with the preachings of Mrs. Grundy, so fearful of the taboos, that they impose ridiculous, unhealthy, even indecent restrictions upon man and his commune with Nature, between him and the light, from which all life springs, the greatest healer in all the world of medicine.

The matchless beauty of the English countryside, its hills, its vales and woods, its flower-strewn meadows, is largely enclosed behind spiked fences and high walls, that a very few may shoot driven pheasants or perambulate pompously from one country seat to another. The legend "Trespassers will be prosecuted" should be made illegal. In our age, wherein our people are herded in cities, living

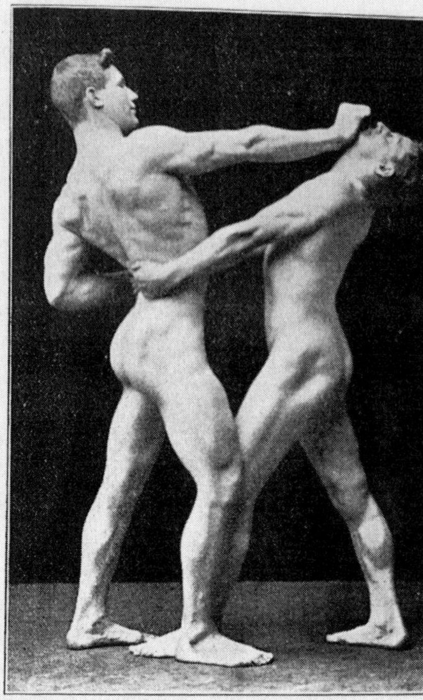

L.D.O. Marshall, who also poses for our front cover, posed with a colleague as "The Grapplers."

Figure 3.14 Nudity/Nakedness – Source: *The Superman Magazine*, November 1930

Morality and the 'foolish superstitions' were a returning theme for Hutchison's articles. He wanted to 'kill Mrs Grundy', who 'whispers in the ears' of men and women that 'all those grand emotions of love and friendship' are forbidden, and insisted that sexual instinct could not be eradicated since 'it is as fundamental as the instinct of self-preservation'. He called for a reform on sexual matters in the law.[196]

What Hutchison was particularly interested in was nakedness *(Illustration 3.14)*, which for him possessed a 'heroic and aesthetic idealism' of 'immense cultural value'. Nakedness, he asserted, had hygienic and educational properties and was a 'preventative of morbid emotion'. Its most important function was as an 'inspiration to adults'. Hutchison wrote: 'The vision of the essential and eternal human form, made in God's own image, the nearest thing to us in all the world, with its vigour, its grace, and its beauty, is without doubt the most stimulating tonic in life. More beautiful than flowers, or stars, or trees, or mountains, or sea.'[197]

Leo Bersani has commented on a scene in André Gide's novel *The Immoralist*, where Michel, the central protagonist, makes a trip to the Mediterranean and discovers nude sunbathing and swimming in Ravello. Michel, who is married and has heterosexual relationships, is drawn to the Arab boys: 'The health of that little boy was beautiful,'[198] he exclaims. This, according to Bersani, brings Michel to an 'unprecedented concentration on himself. He reaches for their bodies in his body'. They become for him a kind of sensualised alter ego. The nude sunbathing and swimming, according to Bersani, teaches Michel what it means to be a 'desiring skin': 'I felt the hard soil beneath me; the stirring grass brushed by body. Though sheltered from the wind, I trembled at each breath of air. Soon a delicious radiance enveloped me; my whole being brimmed to the surface of my skin.'[199] The uncovering of his body serves to uncover his authentic being with the result that he is 'nothing but a bodily ego' which at the same time has 'broken down the boundaries of that ego'.[200] For Bersani, Michel's desiring skin can be interpreted as homosexuality without sexuality, desire that is satisfied just by the proximity of the other, at the most by the other's touch.[201]

It is important to understand the significance of touching and the 'desiring skin' in a historical context and within the work of the sexologists at the time. The case studies presented by both Havelock Ellis and Richard von Krafft-Ebing present the reader with a close understanding of the sexual experiences of their subjects. It is perhaps surprising to find that the 'sexual act' often only meant mutual masturbation.[202] For most, 'practising pederasty', a term used at the time for anal penetrative sex, was not even a consideration. In some instances, 'ejaculation occurred when a sympathetic man laid his hands on the patient's thigh'.[203] The images displayed in Hutchison's magazine *The Superman* take on

196. Hutchison, G. S., 'The Paladin League of Youth. Mrs Grundy Exposed', *The Superman Magazine*, June 1931, pp. 5–6.
197. Hutchison, G. S., 'Nakedness', *The Superman Magazine*, September 1931, p. 23.
198. Gide, André, Trans. by David Watson, *The Immoralist* (London: 2000 [1902]), p. 24.
199. Ibid., p. 56.
200. Bersani, Leo, *Homos* (Cambridge, Massachusetts: 1995), p. 120.
201. Ibid., p. 121.
202. Krafft-Ebing Richard von, *Psychopathia Sexualis*, case 125, p. 191.
203. Ibid., case 134, p. 233.

a different meaning if considered within this framework. The idealised beauty of the photographs of naked men in the pages of the magazine provide a process by which the memory of the war and in particular the physical proximity of the male body in the trenches can be immortalised. The male nude in this instance becomes the locus of the acting-out of the trauma of the war.

Reconstructing the Man

Idealised beauty is also evident in the work of the sculptor of the *Boy David*. But behind his unblemished face lay something deeper. Englishness and beauty were key attributes in the work of Francis Derwent Wood, who sculpted the *Boy David*. His work was described as 'thoroughly national'[204] and beauty, which Kineton Parkes defined as 'an English characteristic', was at the heart of all Derwent Wood's work. According to the art critic Kineton Parkes, 'abstract beauty was a gospel' for Francis Derwent Wood and 'physical beauty a joy and the work of his hands'.[205]

Derwent Wood's memories of the war, however, are of facial disfigurement. He received a commission with the Royal Army Medical Corps in 1916, and served at the Third London Hospital, where he specialised in modelling facial masks for disfigured soldiers. Facial disfigurement constituted a traumatic memory for many of the combatants, but was a personal tragedy for many of the men who survived with these wounds. The sculptor Tait McKenzie, who also worked on facial reproductions, describes the way in which the disfigured men were perceived as 'permanent objects of repulsion to others and a grievous burden to themselves'. These men, he claimed, 'become victims of despondency, of melancholia, leading, in some cases, even to suicide'.[206] Even plastic surgery, which was in its infancy and owed its development to experimentation with disfigured combatants, could not restore the face to its original features and many of the men, according to McKenzie, remained 'nothing but a living gargoyle'. After surgery had done all it could, came sculpture. The sculptor's modelling skills were employed in creating masks which, when attached to the face, could 'hide those hideous deformities'.[207]

---

204. Parkes, Kineton, *Sculpture of Today* (London: 1921), p. 82. There is very little written about Francis Derwent Wood. His father was American and his mother English. He was brought up in Switzerland, hence the 'cosmopolitan' in Parkes' description, and then moved to England. He spent a few years in Paris. He trained under Lanteri at the National Art Training Schools (later the Royal College). He taught sculpture at the Glasgow School of Art, the Slade, Royal College and Royal Academy. He died in 1926.

205. Ibid., p. 88.

206. McKenzie, Robert Tait, *Reclaiming the Maimed. A Handbook of Physical Therapy* (New York: 1918), p. 117.

207. Ibid. McKenzie himself, worked on facial reconstructions. On the work of Tait Mackenzie see Kozar, Andrew, *Tait McKenzie. The Sculptor of Athletes* (Tennessee: 1975); Hussey Christopher, *Tait McKenzie. A Sculptor of Youth* (Philadelphia: 1930).

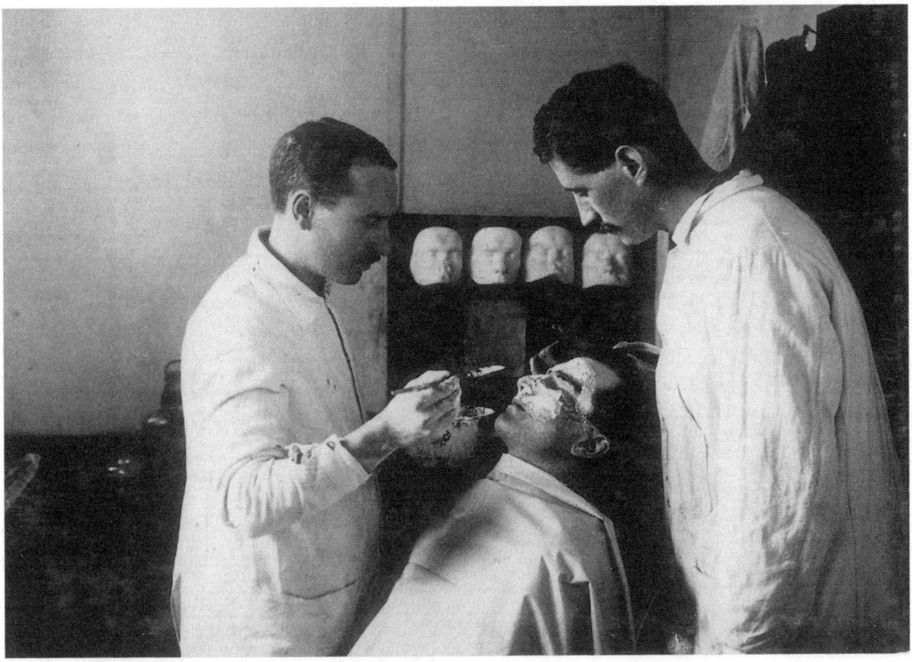

Figure 3.15 Applying First Quote of Plaster, Noses Room, 3rd London Hospital. Imperial War Museum Photographic Archive

Derwent Wood pioneered facial reconstruction at the Third London Hospital. He worked in the 'Noses Room', which was filled with photographs of the patients before their injuries, and plaster casts of what remained of their faces.[208] Tait McKenzie describes in detail the procedure adopted by Derwent Wood: 'The deformed part of the face and the surrounding regions were lubricated. A quick setting plaster was gently painted over the sound tissue, with a soft brush (*Illustration 3.15).* The plaster was strengthened and thickened, until it formed a sheet about one inch in thickness. This mould, the negative, was used to create a cast, or positive. The missing parts were modelled on the cast with reference to photographs of the patient. When the missing features had been modelled to the satisfaction of the sculptor and the patient (*Illustration 3.16),* a cast in wax was made and worked on. From these, Derwent Wood constructed delicate masks of water-thin electroplate, blending the man's own skin colour (*Illustration 3.17).* The masks were then placed on the disfigured face. If damage to the saliva glands had occurred constant discharges needed to be controlled. Absorbent pads were then placed between the mask and the face. Further masking was usually offered by the use of large spectacles and false moustaches'.[209]

208. IWM, Art Department, File 314/7, undated newspaper cutting.

209. McKenzie, Robert Tait, *Reclaiming the Maimed*, pp. 117–22.

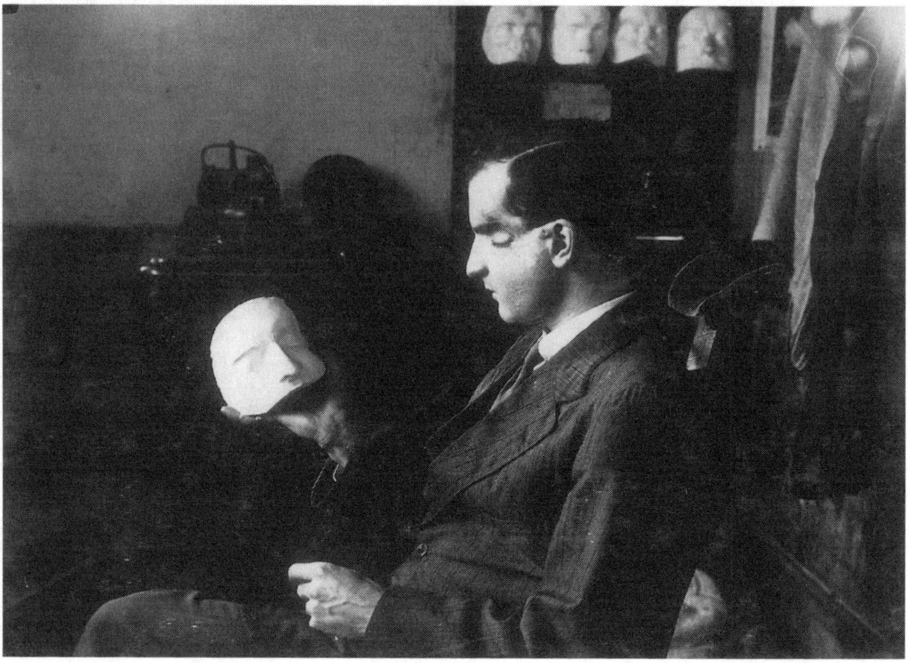

Figure 3.16 Patient Examining the Mould of his Face, Noses Room, 3rd London Hospital. Imperial War Museum Photographic Archive

The process, according to McKenzie, required a high degree of sculptural skill, with 'infinite patience in trimming down, building up, altering, and adapting'.[210] *Illustration 3.18* shows the sculptor examining the finished mask, with the patient standing in attendance. The sculptor, for whom 'physical beauty is a joy and the work of his hands',[211] is admiring his creation, the restoration of beauty. In a letter to Hamo Thornycroft, Derwent Wood wrote that he found the 'mangled faces' difficult to cope with: 'I do long for my studio and a good sculptural exercise to revel in.'[212] However, he was also aware of the power he had over the disfigured soldiers: 'I hold over their heads the great power I possess – in three strokes of my wizard's brush I can present to the public such a vision.'[213] In the photograph, Derwent Wood is not looking at the patient but is looking at the mask he has made. The patient has to cope with his trauma, which the mask is expected to erase. The French analyst Didier Anzieu argues that 'skin shields the equilibrium of our internal functioning from exogenous disruptions', but

210. Ibid., p. 123.

211. Parkes, Kineton, *Sculpture of Today*, p. 88.

212. Henry Moore Institute Archives, C 757, Letter from Derwent Wood to Thornycroft, dated 29 January 1916.

213. Ibid.

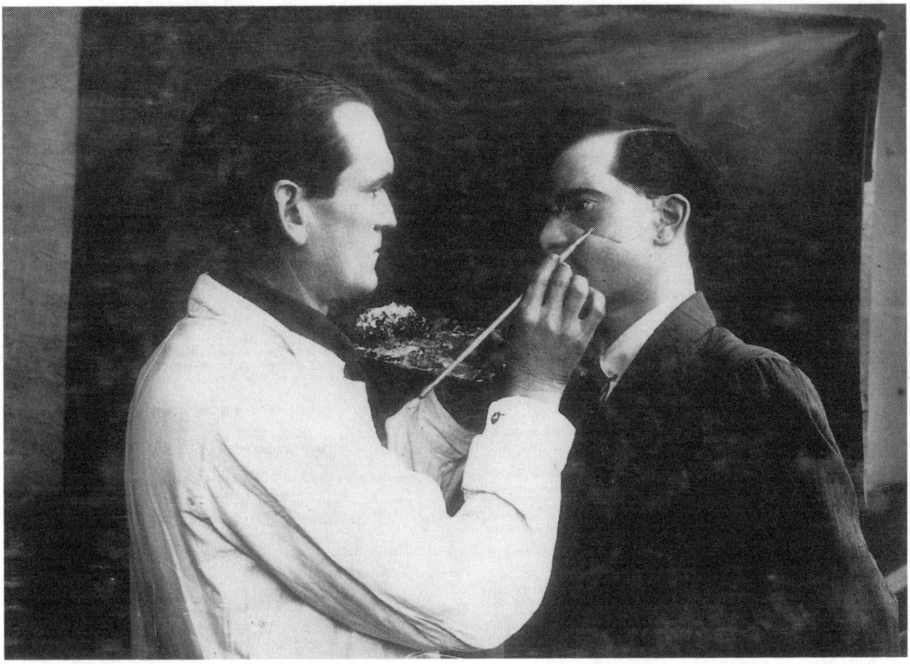

Figure 3.17 Francis Derwent Wood Painting the Plate, Noses Room, 3rd London Hospital. Imperial War Museum Photographic Archive

that in its scars, 'it preserves the marks of disruptions'.[214] The mask, like a prosthetic skin, is expected to enclose and contain the traumatic memories, erasing any marks of disruption.

How do the memories of the servicemen and the memories of the sculptor converge in the body of the *Boy David*? The memories of the combatants are of heads, feet and body parts sticking out of the mud. Many remembered bodies that were so stiff, they had to be tied on a pole before they could be removed. These men were so saturated with the sight of dead bodies that it was almost possible not to notice them any more. But the memory lingered not only visually, but also physically, with the smell of the decomposing body and the feel of the cold corpse. They could not forget the image of whole faces blown away and flies crawling over the flesh. They could not forget the surprise of being wounded, and of looking at their own torn flesh and exposed bones. It was not only the memories, but also the constant nightmares that haunted them. What Julia Kristeva describes as the abjected inside which culminates with the vision of the corpse,[215] became a daily spectacle for these men.

---

214. Anzieu, Didier, *The Skin Ego* (New Haven: 1989), p. 17.

215. Kristeva, Julia, *Powers of Horror*, p. 4.

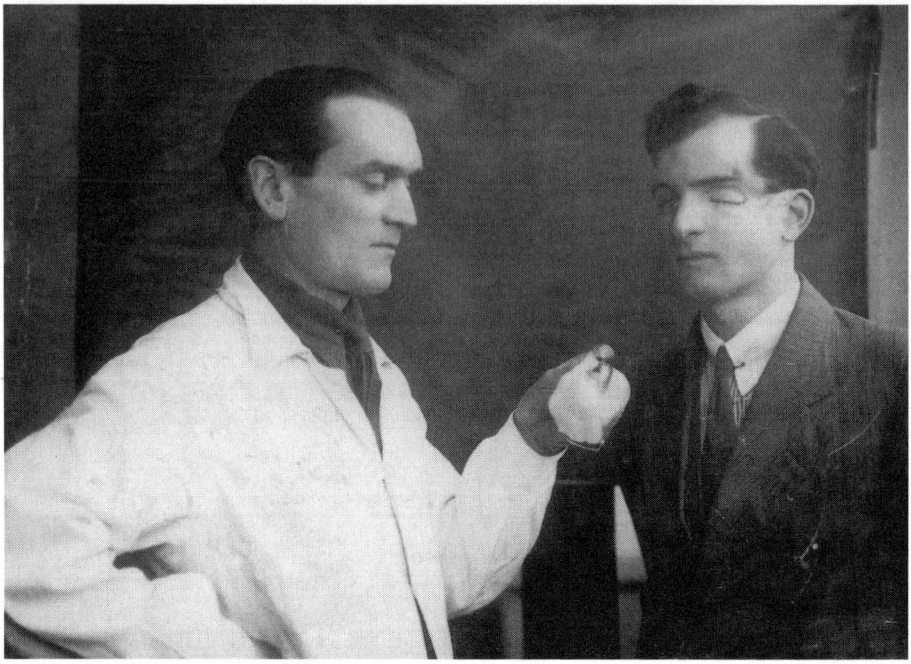

Figure 3.18 Francis Derwent Wood Examining the Finished Plate, Noses Room, 3rd London Hospital. Imperial War Museum Photographic Archive

The sculptor becomes part of the healing process. With infinite patience he trims and builds up the face in order to recreate the one that has been lost. Derwent Wood's casts of the inside of the face become the moulds for the outside. The modeller, who prefers mud instead of stone, because of its obedience and malleability, tames the horrors of mud and turns its slimy, sticky qualities into the solid bronze of the *Boy David*. The bronze becomes the skin that protects and contains the body once again. The sculpture because of its nudity, posture and positioning to the modern instruments of war offers a number of interpretations. Unlike the uniformity of the other figurative memorials that rely on military positions and uniforms for their impact, the *Boy David* relies on the male body and the memories that it embodied for the servicemen. However, the personal memories, because of the newly discovered masculinities at the Front could be problematic. Most importantly, no public scripts were available to express such private memories. This resulted in the acting-out rather than the working through of traumatic memories.

The museum space, particularly the war museum, will be discussed next, to show the interaction between private traumatic memories and the memories of war constructed within the museum space. The gigantic guns will be contrasted with the miniature artefacts created by the servicemen and the souvenirs they collected at the Front.

Chapter 4

Unveiling Polished Guns/ Veiling Fragile Masculinities

A Nation, like a man, is discovered in the critical moments of its fate.[1]

This is how the catalogue of the first exhibition of the Imperial War Museum (IWM) *(Illustration 4.1)* in June 1920 at Crystal Palace greeted visitors to the exhibition. The anthropomorphising nature of the quote and the comparison it makes between the nation and a man highlights the correlation that existed between nation and masculinity in the period following the First World War, and the role that the IWM played in maintaining such a relationship. Sue Malvern has argued that establishing the IWM was an exercise in projecting a national identity.[2] What bearing this had on the establishment of a hegemonic memory of war masculinities will be the theme of this chapter. The relationship between national identity and masculinity was complex, not to mention problematic because of the precarious position that various definitions of masculinity occupied in the aftermath of the war.

The first exhibition to be held at the IWM recognised the unstable positioning of masculinities in post-Armistice Britain. According to the catalogue, 'Great men' as they were thought to be 'shrivel into smallness', while men who were otherwise 'lost in obscurity are brought out of their hiding'. It is precisely this unpredictability that the museum sought to address. Men could not be trusted as they were subject to sudden bursts of fear and emotion; the machinery of war was able to offer a more reliable and efficient way of mapping the history of the war The IWM catalogue reads: 'The story of that efficiency in the conduct of war of which victory is ultimately born, is the story of the inspired discovery and the inspired use of rifles, each of which made its apparently insignificant contribution to the whole pattern of events, perfectly conceived.'[3]

1. IWM, *First IWM Exhibition at Crystal Palace*, Catalogue, Central Files, A 1/4, 1920, no pagination.
2. The Imperial War Museum has received very little critical attention despite the immense growth in museum studies and publications in the 1990s. Sue Malvern provides the first critical studies of the museum and its art collections. See Malvern, Sue, 'War, Memory and Museums: Art and Artefacts in the Imperial War Museum', *History Workshop Journal*, 49 (2000), pp. 177–203.
3. IWM, *First IWM Exhibition at Crystal Palace*, no pagination.

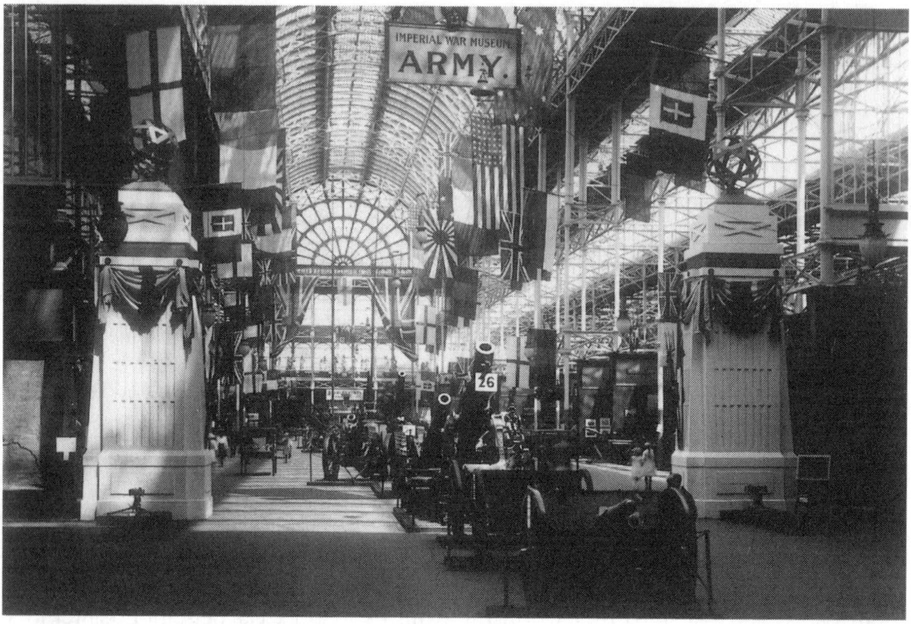

Figure 4.1 First Exhibition of the IWM at Crystal Palace, June 1920. Imperial War Museum Photographic Archive

But if it was important for the museum to demonstrate the role that machinery played in the war, what implications did exhibiting the objects of warfare, especially the 'celebration of the uncelebratory'[4] have for the ex-servicemen? Was the IWM exhibition merely transforming killing machines into aesthetic objects? Annie Coombes has observed that museums are a 'vital component in reclaiming and defining a concept of collective memory' and the reconstitution of 'certain cultural icons'. The IWM became in a sense a 'site for the nostalgic manufacture of a consensual past in the lived reality of a deeply divided present'.[5] This manufacturing of a consensual past in the public space of the museum also resulted in a 'collision of subjectivities and collectivities', according to Susan Crane, which was equally problematic.[6] In this chapter the notion of a public consensual past will be examined in more depth, and compared with the personal souvenirs compiled by the ex-servicemen, which offered a counter-point to the exhibition of war machinery at the IWM.

4. Malvern, Sue, 'War, Memory and Museums', p. 178.
5. Ibid., p. 91.
6. Crane, Susan (ed.), *Museums and Memory* (Stanford: 2000), p. 7.

Establishing the Imperial War Museum

The IWM was founded in March 1917 as the War Museum. It was the brainchild of three men: Alfred Mond, who was appointed as First Commissioner of Works in 1916, Charles ffoulkes,[7] who was later appointed first secretary of the museum, and Martin Conway, who became director of the museum. The Crawford Committee, set up by Lord Crawford, was given the remit to advise on the establishment of the museum, including the decision whether it should be a combined museum and war memorial, and its scope if it performed this dual function.[8] Martin Conway[9] submitted a memorandum to the Crawford Committee outlining his vision for the museum. His position was clear: the war museum should be regarded as *the* memorial for the war.

Conway's memorandum suggested that the museum could take the form of a Hall of Honour, 'as rich and beautiful in character as artists can devise',[10] with separate memorials for the Navy and the Army. The Hall of Honour would display portraits and sculptures of eminent individuals. In the Memorial Gallery, the name of every individual who fell in battle would be inscribed on bronze plates. Conway wrote: 'No pile of sculpture wherever set up could possibly vie for public interest or truly memorial character with this Hall and Gallery of Honour in the heart of a great War Museum.'[11]

---

7. ffoulkes insists in his autobiography that his surname is not spelled with a capital letter. See ffoulkes, Charles, *Arms and the Tower* (London: 1939).

   ffoulkes, before being appointed secretary of the IWM, was Keeper of Arms in the Tower of London. He was associated with the artistic and literary circles of Beardsley, Yeats and Simmonds. See ibid.
8. Agenda and Minutes of Committee on Imperial War Museum, 1917–1920, IWM, Central Files, A1/3.
9. Martin Conway was an MP for the combined English Universities from 1918 and was involved in the Ministry of Works. From 1917 he was the Director of the Imperial War Museum. He was also a mountaineer, he wrote a number of books on the subject, and art historian (Slade professor of fine art at Cambridge 1901 to 1904). His collection of more than 100,000 photographs of works of art was presented to the Courtauld Institute of Art. The Dictionary of National Biography describes him as someone who 'would not have welcomed the 'century of the common man', for he did not believe in the infallibility of the majority'. Amongst his publications his work on crowds, *The Crowd in Peace and War* (1915) expresses according the Dictionary of National Biography his 'mature mind' and is 'considered to be his best book'. Other publications include: Conway, Martin, *Mountain Memories. A Pilgrimage of Romance* (London: 1920); Conway, Martin, *The Domain of Art* (London: 1901); Conway, Martin, *The Sport of Collecting* (London: 1914).
10. Conway, Martin, 'Memorandum on the Scope of the National War Museum', *Agenda and Minutes of Committee on Imperial War Museum*, 1917–1920, IWM, Central Files, A1/3.
11. Ibid.

Carol Duncan claims that museums need to be seen as 'ceremonial monuments' which carry out 'political and ideological tasks'.[12] Seen from Conway's perspective, the proposed museum could become a place where a unified hegemonic memory of the war could be projected through codes of honour that promoted a self-less masculinity. The figures of eminent individuals could reflect these codes. The museum space was the only form of space that Conway felt would allow for such possibilities; other schemes proposed at the time, such as the creation of an *Empire War Memorial* or a *National War Memorial*, which Conway referred to as a 'pile of sculpture', could not have the same impact because the museum element was lacking. The Hall of Honour, for Conway, was what Duncan describes as a 'ritual site', demanding a 'particular kind of contemplation'.[13]

The Crawford Committee recommended that the War Memorial should be 'erected in juxtaposition to the War Museum building'. As to the character of the collection 'due regard should be had to the Imperial character of the exhibits', and there should be a 'tribute to the heroism of the Empire'. The nature of the museum's content was also beginning to take shape. A. Fisher MP, a member of the Crawford Committee, wrote in a letter to the Earl of Crawford:

> The museum, in a word, would be selective, not exhaustive, it would consist of paintings, engravings, drawings, maps, plans and designs of all sorts, models of armaments and instruments of war, uniforms and equipment, selected with a view to giving to the visitor an *ordered and organised conception of the war* [My italics].[14]

Conway argued that the importance of the exhibits would attract a wide range of audiences:

> Thus the sailor and soldier should be able to see models of ships, batteries, trenches, and the like in which they fought, the uniform they wore, and the weapons they used … craftsmen should be able to examine models of some of the great munitions works in which they were employed.[15]

Both Fisher and Conway placed particular emphasis on the ways in which the paraphernalia of war could become a point of attraction and interest for a wide spectrum of society. For Fisher in particular, it was the ordered organisation of such objects that would provide the visitor with the necessary appeal and attraction. Yet the orderly organisation of the objects of war provides an antithesis to the disorderly way in which the servicemen remembered them. Such display of objects in a museum, Susan Stewart suggests, seeks to replace history with classification

12. Duncan, Carol, 'The Art Museum as Ritual', in Preziosi, D. (ed.), *The Art of Art History: A Critical Anthology* (Oxford: 1998), p. 474.
13. Ibid.
14. Letter from A. Fisher to the Earl of Crawford, 20 September 1917, *Agenda and Minutes of Committee on Imperial War Museum*, 1917–1920, IWM, Central Files, A1/3.
15. Conway, Martin, 'Memorandum on the Scope of the National War Museum', in *Agenda and Minutes of Committee on Imperial War Museum*.

and order, something which is beyond the realm of temporality.[16] For Conway, the associative memories that war objects were able to convey to the ex-servicemen offered the basis for creating a particular memory of the war. This links to Susan Crane's argument that the museum fixes the memory of entire cultures by selecting which objects deserve to be kept, remembered and treasured.[17]

Professional bodies such as the Museums Association approved of the machinery of war being used to promote a particular hegemonic ordered and organised memory of the war. The editorial of the May 1917 issue of the Association's journal was dedicated to the establishment of the IWM. It applauded the government decision to set up the museum and offered ideas on ways in which the collection should function. Its central message was that deeds of devotion and bravery should be represented in the museum. The problem was in representing these deeds; in the view of the Museums Association journal, the machinery of war presented the best way forward, and these objects should be 'singled out for special prominence'. Size was also important: 'A gigantic enemy howitzer requiring two or three railway wagons to accommodate its vast bulk, would form an impressive exhibit without the aid of accessories', claimed the editorial.[18] As Susan Stewart has argued however, the miniature is more likely to offer closure, interiority and domesticity than the gigantic, which is inaccessible to lived experience.[19] The large-scale machinery of war represented a contradiction to the inclusivity of the museum that the editorial article was trying to promote: 'history and experience prove all too clearly that the common fighting-man is apt to be soon forgotten.'[20]

Some commentators found the public display of war material offensive, and called it a display of 'organised murder'.[21] Charles ffoulkes' article in the October 1918 issue of *Museums Journal* outlined the methods and principles of collecting material for the museum, and used this opportunity to respond to those who criticised the museum. He claimed that 'art invariably follows the sword', and argued that had William the Conqueror been unsuccessful in the Battle of Hastings, 'we should have had none of the magnificent Norman architecture that we possess and our artistic development would have missed the very valuable impetus that it received from its conquerors'.[22] For ffoulkes, war provided not only a means of renewal but also a way in which weapons could reveal their own aesthetic properties. The aestheticisation of the machinery of war he was proposing relied to a great extent on personal memory and association, without which, interest in the exhibits could not be sustained.[23]

16. Stewart, Susan, *On Longing. Narratives of the Miniature, the Gigantic, the Souvenir, the Collection* (London: 1993), p. 152.
17. Crane, Susan, *Museums and Memory*, p. 3.
18. Editorial, 'A National War Museum', *Museums Journal*, 16/11 (May 1917), p. 246.
19. Stewart, Susan, *On Longing*, p. 70.
20. Editorial, 'A National War Museum', *Museums Journal*, p. 243.
21. For example, Madeley, Charles, 'Local War Museums', *Museums Journal*, 18/4 (October, 1918), p. 64.
22. ffoulkes, Charles, 'War Museums', *Museums Journal*, 18/4 (October, 1918), p. 57.
23. Ibid., p. 59.

However, this did not take account of the potential problems that could arise from investing these personal associations and memories with a national character.

According to ffoulkes the purpose of the museum should be twofold: to exhibit a 'series of weapons for the student of military matters', and to appeal to 'individuals of all classes on account of the intimate personal associations collected round the several exhibits'. However, he saw a problem in the intention to include all classes: the English working classes, he believed, lacked the necessary intelligence to understand the exhibits. Charles ffoulkes made a trip to France to research the way in which they were putting together their own museum of war. On his return, he pointed out that the French working class, in comparison with their English counterparts, 'display far more intelligent appreciation of the exhibits'. The matter of the working-class museum-goer was a point which Frederic Kenyon also emphasised in his address to the museums' conference in Paris in 1921. He argued that the wave of revolutionary spirit evident at that time was due to a sense of historic discontinuity. The working classes needed to be educated in the importance of historical tradition, of a national heritage which the museums could supply.[24] This attempt at inclusivity needs to be seen within the context of the wider museological debates at the time when the museum space and exhibitions played an important role in support for class unity.[25] Nevertheless, the main consideration for both ffoulkes and Kenyon was not inclusivity but regulation and control.

A number of people feared that the use of war objects as exhibits could result in a potential collision between personal subjectivities and public objectivities. Charles Madeley, director of the Warrington Municipal Museum, warned: 'They are commonly called souvenirs and sometimes trophies, objects that have a tendency to the abnormal rather than the typical, and so cease to be historical.'[26] Henry Howorth, President Elect of the Museums Association, argued that the appeal of war relics could only be ephemeral and that the associations they carried could only last for the generation that experienced the war. He claimed that a new generation would 'neither understand the weapons nor the machines that you show them'.[27]

This opposition to the use of war material made no difference, and at the opening ceremony of the IWM the speeches from both the Chairman of the Board of Trustees of the IWM, Alfred Mond, and King George V stressed the importance of exhibiting the machinery of war. Alfred Mond's address explained that each of the chosen exhibits was linked with a specific event or incident. As such, they could become 'memorials' to the men who died amongst them:

> In the choice of war material, the endeavour has been made to select among suitable examples those to which a definite honourable history can be attached, thus making them

24. Kenyon, Frederic, 'Museums in Modern Time', *Museums Journal*, 21/2 (August, 1921), p. 29.
25. Coombes, Annie E., 'Ethnography and the Formation of National and Cultural Identities', in Hiller, Susan (ed.), *The Myth of Primitivism. Perspectives on Art* (London: 1991), p. 197.
26. Madeley, Charles, 'Local War Museums', p. 64.
27. Howorth, Henry, 'Discussion', *Museums Journal*, 18/4 (October, 1918), p. 68.

> also serve as memorials of the heroic men who served them on the field of battle and too often laid their lives beside them.[28]

The response from King George V also focused on the histories behind the chosen material:

> It was indeed a happy inspiration in selecting your exhibits not to seek mere specimens, however perfect, but to choose the very things which had played an actual part in the War and had an individual history which could be recorded and cherished.[29]

The war exhibits, or the relics or trophies as they were often called,[30] and their cherished histories, were to become the embodiment of the memories of the men and the memorials to the dead. Through their direct connection with specific incidents, the articles of war became a personification of the dead men as well as a vehicle for the memories of the survivors. Mieke Bal has argued that on the surface, objects, 'appear as the most 'pure' form of objectivity'.[31] It is this pure objectivity that the instigators of the IWM were seeking. What was overlooked, however, was the fact that attaching memories to objects of warfare was problematic because of the personal memories that these objects also carried for the servicemen; memories which did not always correlate with the heroic histories credited to them by the museum. As Annie Coombes has observed, the 'cultural object can never be an empty vessel waiting to be filled with meaning'; it can only ever be a 'repository' and is 'replete with meanings that are never imminent but always contingent'.[32]

A further point emphasised by both speakers at the opening ceremony of the IWM was the inclusivity of the exhibition. King George V took pains to reassure everybody at the ceremony that the museum was a lasting memorial to common effort and common sacrifice for the whole nation. Modern warfare, according to the King, no longer relied for its success on a few distinguished leaders, but was the result of the 'devoted and heroic work of millions of men and women', who all co-operated as 'parts of one vast living machine'. The museum was 'unique in history' because, as King George V declared: 'It records faithfully and impartially the efforts of all ranks in the field and of all classes at home, the private as well as

28. Mond, Alfred, 'Address to the King', *Third Annual Report of the Committee of the Imperial War Museum*, 1 April 1919 to 2 July 1920, p. 3.
29. King George V, 'Reply to The Address of the Chairman of the Imperial War Museum', *Third Annual Report of the Committee of the Imperial War Museum*, 1 April 1919 to 2 July 1920, pp. 3–4.
30. The terms 'relics' and 'trophies' were often used interchangeably to describe war exhibits from big artillery guns to shells and rifles. They included trophies captured from the enemy as well as British war memorabilia.
31. Bal, Mieke, 'Telling Objects: A Narrative Perspective on Collecting', in Elsner, J. and Cardinal, R. (eds), *The Cultures of Collecting* (London: 1994), p. 99.
32. Coombes, Annie E., 'The Recalcitrant Object', p. 92.

the Commander, the worker in the workshop as well as the statesman in the council chamber.'[33]

King George V was clearly attempting to promote the exhibits as representative of all cultural groups, in other words, as a consensual display that could tell a unified story of the war, and to endorse the museum as a place of equal access. As Annie Coombes has commented, such 'rhetoric of equality' declares 'objectivity at the expense of a recognition of the multiple political interests at stake'.[34] The memory of the war is fixed around the objects that are chosen to be kept, remembered and treasured, erasing both the political struggle of the returning servicemen and the traumatic memories that such objects induced. It becomes what Sharon Macdonald describes as an exercise in 'cultural objectification' which structures a 'modern way of seeing and comprehending the world, as if it were an exhibit'.[35]

Collecting souvenirs from the Front was a very common occupation. The items that servicemen collected ranged from empty shells and helmets, to rats and voles. This was also an occupation that engaged all classes of society. Susan Stewart has made the claim that the souvenir internalises external experiences and that by collecting it, 'the beast is taken home'.[36] The following passages provide some examples of this, and illustrate the significance that such souvenirs had for the collectors in containing and expressing the trauma of war.

Personal/Public: Collecting Souvenirs for the IWM

Major Beckles Willson spent the war years collecting war relics for the IWM. Although he was on an official mission, his collecting became a personal quest that reflected the problems of transposing the personal object to an object of public display, particularly when these objects were invested with his own personal memories. During his service in the Middle East he witnessed the capture of Jerusalem and acquired the white flag of surrender waved by the Turkish and German troops. The story goes that on the day the city was surrendered, Willson was riding back to his camp when he discovered a white flag at the roadside, which he took as a souvenir. Later, the Mayor of Jerusalem identified the flag as the original flag of surrender. Shortly before he died he signed it for Willson.[37] The flag, like a painting, was thus authenticated.

Major Willson's hunt for war relics continued with astonishing commitment along the road to Damascus. Between Jerusalem and Haifa he collected 'scores of

33. King George V, 'Reply to The Address of the Chairman of the Imperial War Museum', pp. 3–4.
34. Coombes, Annie E., 'The recalcitrant object', p. 105.
35. Macdonald, Sharon, 'Introduction', in Macdonald, Sharon (ed.), *The Politics of Display. Museums, Science and Culture* (London: 1998), p. 7.
36. Stewart, Susan, *On Longing*, p. 134.
37. Willson, Beckles, letter to IWM, *Major Beckles Willson Correspondence 1917–1919*, IWM Central Files, A4/4.

guns, machine-guns and some thousands of rifles'. Back on the road to Damascus, 'in order to lose no time', he 'travelled until nearly midnight although the road was very bad'. He stopped at El Kuneitra, which troops had entered a few days earlier, and found the white flag of surrender still flying from the neighbourhood citadel. With the General's permission, he removed the flag, assisted by two orderlies, and brought it to the General who at his request 'kindly certified it'.[38]

Three hours later, travelling along a road littered with Turkish corpses and carcasses of dead horses, Willson entered the suburbs of Damascus,[39] where he asked that the silver-gilt wreath and two banners which Kaiser Wilhelm II had placed on the tomb of Saladin be given to the IWM. From Damascus, he set off for Beirut in search of more trophies. On the way he witnessed yet more death and destruction.[40] After arriving in Beirut he managed to acquire six naval officer's swords, one of these, 'a beautiful little weapon of curious design'. Willson's report reveals several similar instances of juxtaposing the destruction encountered at the Front with the perceived aesthetic beauty of the war relics. The act of collecting war material seemed to provide a containment for the acts they had inflicted, cleansing them of any association with killing, and framing them within the language of aesthetics and art. Willson only ceased his frenzied criss-crossing of Mesopotamia when he contracted Spanish flu. His collection became a justification for the destruction that had surrounded him. The value he attached to the objects he collected is encapsulated in a letter to Charles ffoulkes in which he complains about the way that the items he had sent to the IWM were treated. He asserts that the relics are 'of the very greatest human and historic interest and importance' and that he was deeply astonished to find that they were not to be exhibited and would be replaced by 'official photographs and other tame repetitions and reproductions'.[41]

How can Willson's authenticating, aestheticising and de-contextualising activities be explained? His account of the battle at Ypres goes some way towards providing an answer. In his memoirs, he describes the attack as 'hell broke loose'. The noise became engrained in his memory. The blast from the detonations turned from 'stunning' to 'overwhelming' as it continued, deafening the ears and paralysing the nerves. He reports that 'dazed men groped about in the storm trying to save the surrounding earth from engulfing them', and that two shells collided in mid-air, 'with a shriek like a woman in agony'. The guns, he describes as 'merciless hidden machines belching forth fragments of insensate metal'.[42] It was one of these fragments that killed his commander, a man he much admired. 'I never saw a finer

38. Willson, Beckles, Report to Martin Conway (no date), *Major Beckles Willson Correspondence 1917–1919*, IWM Central Files, A4/4.
39. Ibid.
40. Ibid.
41. Ibid.
42. Willson, Beckles, *In the Ypres Salient. The Story of a Fortnight's Canadian Fighting. June 2–16, 1916* (London: 1916), p. 71.

death' another man told Willson. 'He looked very brave and handsome up there, outlined against the sky, the only figure on the bank above, his helmet off, and his face very pale and blazing with anger, and his right arm pointing forward.'[43]

The objects Willson collected offered a way of taming the horrors of the battlefield. Susan Stewart has argued that the 'memory of the body is replaced by the memory of the object' and that the object then becomes 'saturated with meanings that will never be fully revealed to us'.[44] The containment of the battle is achieved through the collecting of those machines and fragments of metal that caused the destruction. This explains Willson's dismay at finding out that his exhibits were 'thrown about carelessly', that they were 'wrongly labelled or with missing labels', and most alarmingly, that many of them were 'consigned to the cellars'.[45]

Collecting Mammals

The case of Philip Gosse offers another example of an attempt to contain the horrors of the battlefield. Philip Gosse volunteered as a military doctor at the outbreak of the war and his memoir provides an insight into his collection of artefacts from the Front. As with the memoirs discussed in the previous chapter, he begins his account with an apology for the absence of horrors in his text.[46] The title of his book, he explains, should have been 'A Solace of Birds', since without the birds he 'dare not think' how he should have 'got through the War at all'. A friend who read his manuscript told him that it should have included more horrors. Gosse's reply to the friend was that he could 'remember no real horrors, though of birds he could remember so much'. He continues:

> The mangled corpse is forgotten, but the warbler with its nest and eggs is remembered. I think the reason for this is largely that at the time the 'horrors' were so beastly, so ugly, that one got into the habit of putting them aside by concentrating on the birds, so that now, after so many years the memory retains the birds and to a large extent got rid of the rest.[47]

Gosse's collecting provided him with 'stability of mind'. He admitted that the situation at the Front tended to make one 'nervous and apprehensive' unless one lacked a 'tiresome imagination'. However, with Gosse, the memory of birds was not of the tranquil pastime of bird watching, but of his encounters with taxidermy. He

43. Ibid.
44. Stewart, Susan, *On Longing*, p. 134.
45. Willson, Beckles, Letter to Charles ffoulkes, 28 October 1917, *Major Beckles Willson Correspondence 1917–1919*, IWM Central Files, A4/4.
46. Gosse, Philip, *Memoirs of A Camp-Follower* (London: 1934). The memoirs were compiled from letters to his parents, which he found after their death. Philip Gosse was the son of the writer Edmund Gosse.
47. Ibid., p. xiv.

describes the first time he came across someone at the Front who was 'skinning a vole', claiming that immediately, he knew that 'here was a man after my own heart'. He subsequently contacted Oldfield Thomas of the Natural History Museum to enquire whether the museum was well provided with specimens of small mammals from Flanders. Thomas wrote back to say that they were in great need of specimens from Western Europe. He enclosed some museum labels and some arsenic soap for preserving the skins. This was to be the start of Gosse's taxidermic adventure at the Western Front.

In his memoirs, Gosse describes the procedure of catching and skinning the animal. Each evening he went out with his haversack full of traps and a piece of ration for bait. By dawn the next day he would be off again on his rounds, collecting the traps together with the captured mammals. Days of disappointment were followed by days of 'discovery', when he would 'discover some small animal the like of which you had never seen before'. On returning to the camp he would carefully examine and measure each specimen and record on a label its measurement in millimetres, taking the length from the point of the nose to the stump of the tail, noting the length of the tail, not including any hairs at the tip, and the length of the ears and paws. He would also make a note of the place and date that the animal had been caught, along with whether the animal was male or female. Having completed the label, he began the actual skinning. The most difficult part, and the part that required greatest patience and practice, was removing the bone from the tail of a mouse and inserting in its place a long thin wire on which cotton wool had been spun, which tapered in thickness to correspond with the bone that had been withdrawn. Once this had been done, the animal stuffed with army cotton wool and the skin sewn up with needle and thread, it had to be pinned out on a board to dry and a label attached to its leg. It all sounds 'very easy' wrote Gosse, but in 'taxidermy, even the skinning of mice is quite an art, or certainly a craft'.[48]

Susan Stewart, commenting on the collecting activities of the American collector Charles Wilson Peale in the eigtheenth century, observes that his interest in taxidermy 'served as an antidote to surplus meaning'.[49] The captured animal can be seen as a metaphor for the ugliness and horror of the war. The measuring and labelling of the captured animal combined with the horror of that moment provides Gosse with the power to contain that horror as well as the means to measure it. The act of skinning the animal and emptying it of its insides, the actual viscera of the war, can be compared with the act of the modeller, as discussed previously. It is interesting that Gosse does not claim taxidermy to be a science, but an art or a craft.

Further on in his memoir, Gosse recounts some horrific scenes. In one scene following a raid, a man whose face was blown off in the blast was brought to

48. Ibid., p. 9.
49. Stewart, Susan, 'Death and Life, in that Order, in the Works of Charles Willson Peale', Elsner, J. and Cardinal, R. (eds), *The Cultures of Collecting* (London: 1994), p. 211.

Gosse for medical treatment. He writes: 'It was the first time I had seen such a thing and it was very dreadful. His face was not merely skinned, but entirely gone, slashed off by a splinter of a steel shell. He died in the cellar.'[50] Gosse anticipates the question of how a surgeon could be shocked by such a sight, pointing out that the surgeon is 'no more callous than other men, but has learned to hide or suppress his feelings'. Making the first incision with his scalpel was something that he found particularly upsetting: 'I always had to glance away from that one moment. Once the first cut had been made I lost all feeling that the subject being operated on was a human being and it became simply a case a piece of living anatomy.'[51]

Gosse writes of the death of his 'dear friend McKerrow' and McKerrow's 'inseparable companion, his sergeant'. The death made him 'both angry and sad', although compared to an otherwise dense reminiscence these deaths are given only a short mention. As in the 'first incision', which he found distressing, he was compelled to look away. However, his taxidermy meant that he had to perform that 'first incision' on many occasions. Like in the cases of acting out discussed in the previous chapter, he kept repeating the act he was unable to contain within the boundaries of the self.

Gosse published an earlier memoir in 1927. This was illustrated by his wife, Sylvia, and like his later memoir, 'gave no hint of bloody warfare'. Gosse wanted the reader to 'fritter away their time on the printed page'. Moreover, he wanted the words to 'form a mere frame to the illustrations'. The book records three incidents that took place at a small French village behind the line in 1916. The first incident involves an affair between a young corporal and the female proprietor of a small cafe; the other two incidents involve stories of collecting little mammals.[52] What is interesting, is that Gosse's wife has provided the illustrations, which implies that there was a sharing of the experiences – albeit the acceptable memories – at the Front. This contradicts arguments that there was no sharing of experiences by the ex-servicemen with their families once they returned from the Front, and that there was a need to forget these experiences.[53] Rather than a deliberate lack of communication, it was often an inability to communicate the traumatic experiences of the war. In the case of Gosse, beauty has replaced the horror of the Front and a female interpretation of a very 'manly experience' has emerged, which is significant when one considers that Philip Gosse insisted that the words formed a frame for the illustrations. A similar process takes place in the narratives that follow.

---

50. Gosse, Philip, *Memoirs of A Camp-Follower*, p. 24.
51. Ibid., p. 25.
52. Gosse, Philip, *Rest Billets* (London: 1927).
53. Winter, Jay, *Sites of Memory, Sites of Mourning. The Great War in European Cultural History* (Cambridge: 1995) and Gregory, Adrian, *The Silence of Memory. Armistice Day 1919–1946* (Oxford: 1994).

Collecting, Authenticating, and Containing the Trauma of War

Lieut. G. N. Holt's letters to his parents provide us with an insight into the life of another middle-class officer at the Front.[54] He wrote to his parents after finding a case from an anti-aircraft shell, describing the shell as 'one of our own "Archies"'. He claimed that he had polished it up 'nicely' and now considered it as 'quite good souvenir'. He had even thought of the new use it could acquire in his parents' home: it 'will make a decent paper weight', he wrote. Significantly, he stressed that when his parents received the shell it 'will be just the same as it was when I picked it up'. The only difference, he pointed out, was that 'I have cleaned it up' and 'the shell part of it went off in the air'.[55] What Holt had picked up was the remains of the shell after it had reached its target of the enemy line. In polishing it, he had purified it of its original use, transforming it from a killing instrument into a desk accessory, a paperweight, and a symbol of knowledge, education and domesticity. But Holt also wanted it to remain authentic, and for his parents to know that it was still the same shell that he had picked up from enemy lines. Susan Stewart has argued that the souvenir will not 'function without the supplementary narrative discourse that both attaches it to its origins and creates a myth with regard to those origins'.[56] The authenticity of Lieut. Holt's shell is given in more detail in a letter to his parents written three days later, during which Holt describes a successful sniping incident. 'I also had some quite good "sniping" yesterday and put one Boche out for certain,' he writes. 'I hit him in the back at about 35 yards and he was clean out.'[57]

The way that the souvenir was acquired was also important for the collectors. It represented a sense of adventure, control and achievement in a landscape of destruction and chaos. Holt also sent his parents a German trench notice board, relating how he had found the object. He and his men had been on a night lighting patrol during which they crossed eight hundred yards of No-Man's-Land. Several obstacles had made the journey difficult, but he writes: 'I really enjoyed myself.'[58] The significance of the souvenir is made greater by its direct association with a genuine adventure.

Sometimes men would go to great lengths to collect souvenirs. V. E. Upton, who was on a hospital ship in the Dardanelles, was extremely anxious to get ashore

54. Holt, Lieut. G. N., IWM, Con Shelf, Letter, 6 December 1916.

    Holt comments in a letter to his parents that although it was 'bad enough' for the officer, the officer's life 'was paradise compared with that of the men's'. Holt used to get his weekly food parcels initially from Fortnum & Mason and later from Selfridges as he found Fortnum & Mason unreliable in their orders. He used to send his dirty washing back home to be laundered. For Christmas, he asked his mother to send him 'white American cloth' to cover the mess festive table.

55. Ibid., 13 December 1916.
56. Stewart, Susan, *On Longing*, p. 136.
57. Holt, Lieut. G.N., IWM, Con Shelf, Letter, 16 December 1916.
58. Ibid., 11 February 1918.

to collect 'curios' and took a 'small sack ashore' for the occasion. Writing to his wife, he describes the difficulties he had to go through. After landing on the beach and failing to find any souvenirs, he and the other men entered a communication trench. This took them to an opening where: 'The Turkish dead were lying all over the field just as they fell some with arms off, legs off etc. It was an awful sight. Everywhere round about were hundreds of Turkish shells and shrapnel. Bullets were lying about in thousands like pebbles.'[59] Amidst all this Upton managed to collect three shells and a number of spent bullets. This was despite the fact that, he points out, 'all the time we had to keep ducking down on our hands and knees as snipers were firing all the time'. He adds: 'you get used to it and take no notice'. Back at the hospital ship Upton and his fellow soldiers had to stretcher 1,116 patients on board; double the amount they were supposed to carry. Seventeen more died that night.

O. C. M. Haines was stationed in Cairo with the Royal Army Medical Corps and sent a stream of souvenirs to his parents, especially his mother. The size of the collection led him to suggest to his parents that 'you will have to get a show case to display them in and charge 1d to see them'. His souvenirs were divided into two categories: 'Orientalist curiosities' from Cairo, and war relics. In a letter to his parents he describes how he acquired a 'Sikh's bangle' which, he said, 'of course has no intrinsic value' but which he declared 'a great curio'. During the night he had gone to the mosque, where he saw a group of Sikhs 'all squatting down singing and of course it wasn't long before I was in the circle too'. Once in the circle, one of the men 'put his arm around my neck', although Haines adds in brackets, 'I felt creepy as it was dark'. He admired the bangle that the man was wearing, at which point the man promptly removed the bangle and 'forced it on my wrist saying "*backsheesh*"'. Haines translates the word for his parents as 'something for nothing'. In fact, its meaning is tip: something for services rendered. As Susan Stewart argues, the souvenir 'must remain impoverished and partial so that it can be supplemented by a narrative discourse'. What is particularly important, according to Stewart, is that this is a 'narrative discourse, which articulates the play of desire'.[60] We will never know what happened to merit Haines being given the bangle as a tip, but it is significant that he chooses to send it to his mother as if it is a love token. After relating the acquisition of the bangle, the mood of the letter changes. Haines describes the patients he has to treat every day at the hospital: 'The wounds are terrible, some with no elbow joints, some with a finger or so left and the hand all shattered. There were eleven operations today.'[61] In another letter home, he writes: 'It is nothing to see a great gaping wound as big as your fist in a man's arm, and to see the shattered bone and tendons all exposed. It doesn't upset me a bit now.'[62] He then proceeds once again with his acquisition of 'curios':

59. Upton, V. E., IWM, 81/35/1, 30 August 1915.
60. Stewart, Susan, *On Longing*, p. 136.
61. Haines, O. C. M., IWM, 95/16/1, Letter, 2 June 1915.
62. Ibid., 15 August 1915.

> This week I am sending you a curious curio. It is the scoring book of a Turkish crackshot. All in Arabic. One of the wounded gave it to me. Number 2 enclosure is a cigarette card which looks as though a little piece was torn out; well it was taken out by a piece of shrapnel casing. The man who gave it to me was wounded in the shoulder and the shrapnel passed right through his pocket case, letters, pay-book etc. and just teared [sic] this piece out.[63]

Haines often describes the curios with affection – 'such a lovely bomb',[64] or a 'lovely piece of Turkish shrapnel'[65] – and maintains in his letters that he 'longed for mother to see' them. He usually had suggestions on the new use to which the objects could be put – for example, a Turkish cartridge case could be made into a pencil case.[66]

For another serviceman, W. M. Floyd, the collection of curios went a step further. Like Haines, he was stationed at a military hospital in France and his description of wounds forms a major part of his diary. Unlike Haines, however, Floyd is from a working-class background.[67] His description of one wounded patient reveals the conflation of disgust and desire he felt:

> Had patient yesterday young chap about 19, with fair, clear skin large eyes who had bullet in neck, lying in bed with eyes wide open, lips trembling like as if going to cry every minute. Had a bandage around neck and head, and with the dim light of the candle, I thought he would make the prettiest nun I've seen. I had to look once or twice to see if it wasn't a girl.[68]

Sometimes his accounts reveal the sheer horror of the wounds he has seen:

> Side of face blown away. Oh Lord it made it look I tell you. His mouth was wide open couldn't shut it and looking down into his mouth could see all black inside … side loose could be pushed any shape when wiping mouth clean with lint and cotton wool. Got awful job to understand him when talking with mouth open. [69]

Floyd's favourite job was 'cleaning up the operating room', especially 'after taking a leg off' because it meant that he could collect souvenirs. He had a 'piece of bone' from an officer's leg that had been amputated as well as a collection of surgeon's needles.[70] When German patients were at the hospital he would retrieve buttons from

63. Ibid.
64. Ibid., 27 February 1916.
65. Ibid., 11 May 1915.
66. Ibid., 9 July 1915.
67. Floyd, W. M., IWM, 87/33/1. Transcript of original diary. During his embarkation for France at Southampton Floyd's class is evident in the following statement which appeared in his diary: 'At the station before departing for Southampton the Lord Mayor of Cardiff came up and shook hands with me. As a rule I never have much to do with this class of man.'
68. Ibid., p. 10.
69. Ibid., p. 10.
70. Ibid., p. 20.

their coats.[71] Susan Stewart has argued that the souvenirs of the 'mortal body are not so much a nostalgic celebration of the past as they are an erasure of the significance of history'. According to Stewart, souvenirs of death 'disrupt and disclaim' the continuity of personal narrative.[72]

As well as acquiring curios from his activities as a soldier, Holt also purchased a number of objects from the Front, which he sent to his parents. In one letter, he wrote: 'I have also bought a rather novel ashtray made with a Boche 77 shell fuse, which I think you will like. It is most ingenious.'[73] Holt was one of a number of men who purchased objects made out of used war material, known as Trench Art.[74] Nicholas Saunders, in an analysis of these items, comments that the broken fragmented world which the war produced found its miniature in metal Trench Art. These objects provided 'portable pieces of war made into whole items of peace'. According to Saunders, the grotesque nature of war was not denied but rather aestheticised. However, the process of aestheticising is one of denial, of de-contextualising the object from the world of war and destruction and transforming it into the sphere of art and aesthetics. This links with a further comment from Saunders, that 'the strange conglomerations of shells and bullets were modernism embodied'.[75] Modernism during the inter-war years, one could argue, was a process of de-contextualisation and disavowal.

The War Photographic Album

Souvenirs brought back from the Front were not the only vehicle for the traumatic narratives that the servicemen wanted to communicate to those around them. The photograph and the photographic album, like the souvenir, provided the means by which the narrative could unfold and become domesticated. Captain L. Gameson[76] created seven volumes of photographic albums and wrote two volumes of memoirs. He served as a medical officer in the Western Front from 1916 to 1920. In the introduction to his memoirs he outlines his writing process and its association with the photographic albums. His memoirs were based on a diary kept from 1916–18, along with other documents and letters from that period. The albums comprised photographs he had taken himself, and official photographs. Gameson began to 'order the material' and write his first draft in 1922, when his memories were 'reasonably trustworthy and he still had access

71. Ibid., p. 11.
72. Stewart, Susan, *On Longing*, p. 139.
73. Holt, Lieut. G.N., IWM, Con Shelf, Letter, 19 November 1917.
74. Only very recently have these objects been studied in detail. Nicholas Saunders was the first to offer an anthropological approach to their categorisation and understanding. See Saunders, Nicholas, 'Bodies of Metal, Shells of Memory', *Journal of Material Culture*, 5(1) (2000), 43–67.
75. Ibid., p. 62.
76. Gameson, Captain L., IWM, P396.

to a 'number of the survivors involved'. Between 1936 and 1937 he rewrote his memoirs. He then 'put the draft aside for some fifteen years' before completing it in its final form of a 'continuous, if patchwork narrative, uninterrupted by conventional chapters'. Like Lt. Col. Hutchison, Gameson's rewriting of his memoirs provided a way of acting out the trauma he had experienced. Gameson revisited his memories and in particular his photographic albums over a period of forty years. The gap in time between the actual event and the final version of the memoir provided him with the opportunity to 'reflect back on youthful naivety and liberality of autobiographical admissions', which he found 'unsettling' but 'sincere when written'.[77]

Gameson's autobiographical admissions will be discussed in more detail, particularly in relation to the structuring of the photographic album. As in the case of other combatants, his war accounts juxtaposed death and destruction with the comradeship and male companionship he had encountered. Like Gosse, he was a medical officer who was profoundly affected by the scenes he witnessed. What makes Gameson's memories intriguing is the way in which once again, death and destruction are often presented hand in hand with desire.

At the start of his memoir he writes that he is getting tired of the smell of blood, but proceeds to describe the wounds of the men in front of him:

> They lie inert, lids half open and eyeballs rolling in seemingly deliberate manner that has an unpleasant suggestion of purpose. The breathing is stertorous. It rattles the mucous that cannot be reached, with the rhythm of a machine. The toneless face is white. The flaccid cheeks and lips are sucked in and puffed out by the dreadful rhythmic stertor. Blood, that earlier had oozed from mouth and nose, is clotted to form a half-mask by the time the patients get here.[78]

The albums follow a similar structure to the memoir, that is, a continuous, patchwork narrative. Patricia Holland has argued that the photographic album in the late nineteenth century was a means of portraying 'domestic sensibility'.[79] Gameson's albums depart from this by also displaying images of death and destruction. The photographs become what Linda Haverty Rugg has described as the 'physical evidence' that 're-anchor the subject in the physical world', or an 'exertion of control over self-image'.[80]

On the first page Gameson explains that the photographs are arranged in a chronological order. He also explains that the album is there to illustrate the manuscript and not to replace it. The text that accompanies the photographs in the albums seems similarly problematic for Gameson and has been crossed through a

77. Ibid., *Memoir*, p. i.
78. Ibid., p. 12.
79. Holland, Patricia, '"Sweet is to Scan …" Personal Photographs and Popular Photography', in Wells, L. (ed.), *Photography: A Critical Introduction* (London: 2001), p. 132.
80. Haverty Rugg, Linda, *Picturing Ourselves. Photography and Autobiography* (Chicago: 1997), p. 2.

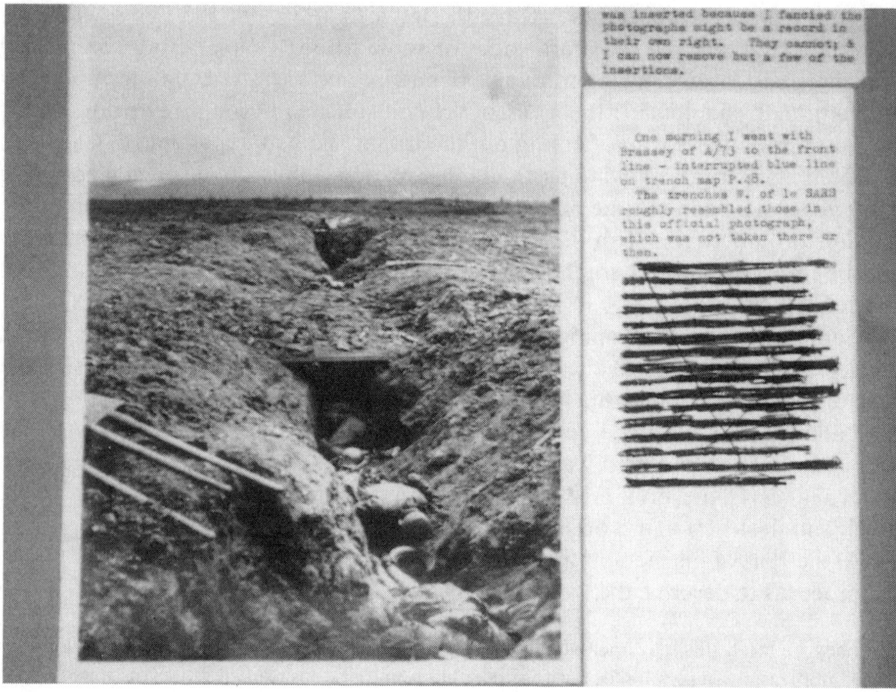

Figure 4.2 Captain Gameson, L., Photographic Album, p. 50. Imperial War Museum, Department of Documents, P396

number of times *(Illustration 4.2)*. The albums start with his work at the London hospital after his enlistment as an officer. Here, he is pictured with three female nurses, the only female figures to feature in the entire seven volumes other than his fiancée. The photo of the nurses is followed by a photograph of his batman, with whom he appears to have had a close friendship. The first and second volumes of the albums are devoted almost entirely to the destruction that Gameson witnessed at the Front. Gameson indexes each photo to a very detailed map. On page 32 *(Illustration 4.3)* the map pinpoints where to locate a series of photographs of mutilated bodies. Donna Haraway has argued that maps can be seen as fetishes and as such they make 'things seem clear and under control'.[81] By pinpointing the traumatic event on the map, Gameson is attempting to contain the event and bring it under control.

The visual is used by Gameson as a form of evidence for the narrative but also as a means by which the experience can be located, made tangible and hence contained within the boundaries of the map and the frame of the photograph. Taking private photographs at the Front was forbidden and any cameras were

81. Haraway, Donna, 'Deanimations: Maps and Portraits of Life Itself', in Brah, A. and Coombes, A. E. (eds), *Hybridity and Its Discontents. Politics, Science, Culture* (London: 2000), p. 114.

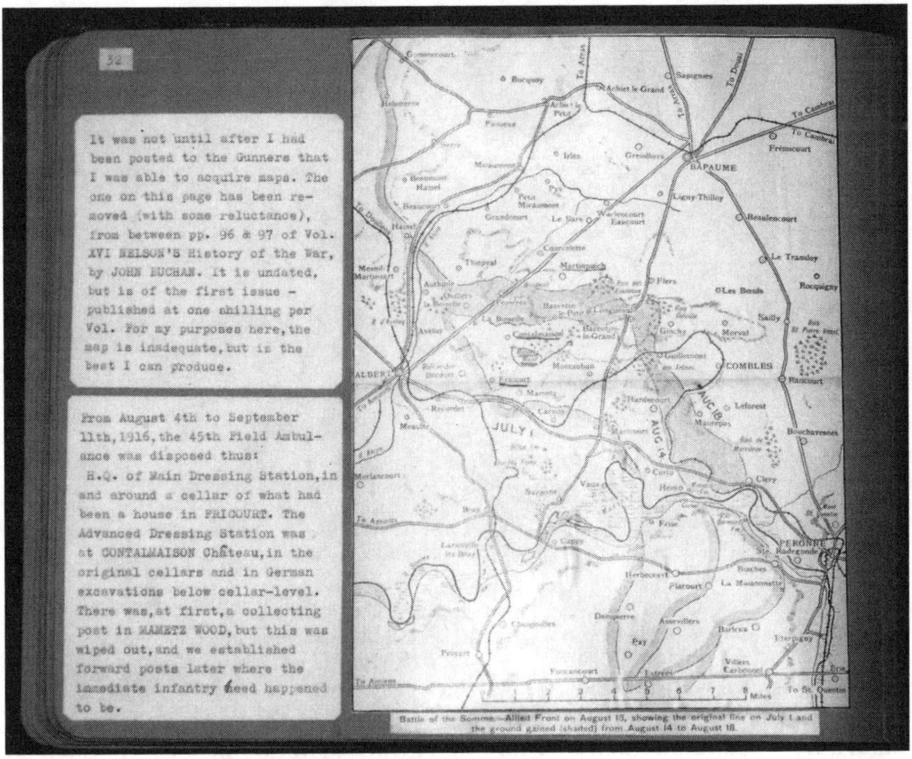

Figure 4.3 Captain Gameson, L., Photographic Album, p. 32. Imperial War Museum, Department of Documents, P396

confiscated. Like Gameson, however, the officers – and it was mostly officers who could afford to have a camera – found ways of taking private pictures. The official photograph provided a means of representing the atrocities at the Front but also, because of its official status, provides an official unquestionable proof of the events. The caption for the official photo on page 44 *(Illustration 4.4)* reads: 'One of my first domestic jobs at *Bazentin-le-Petit* was to clear an enemy dug-out for the HQ staff. The above official photo although not taken at the Somme represents things as they then were.'[82]

The photograph on page 46 was taken by Gameson. Its caption reads:

> Near the rubble of our church there was a horse with its head clean-severed from its body. It was not a practice of mine to photograph corpses and human wreckage. Most of the photos in the following books are of a mild, domestic kind. I well fancy to put in a few that hint at the less delightful aspect of war![83]

82. Gameson, Captain L., IWM, P396, *Album*, p. 44.
83. Ibid., p. 46.

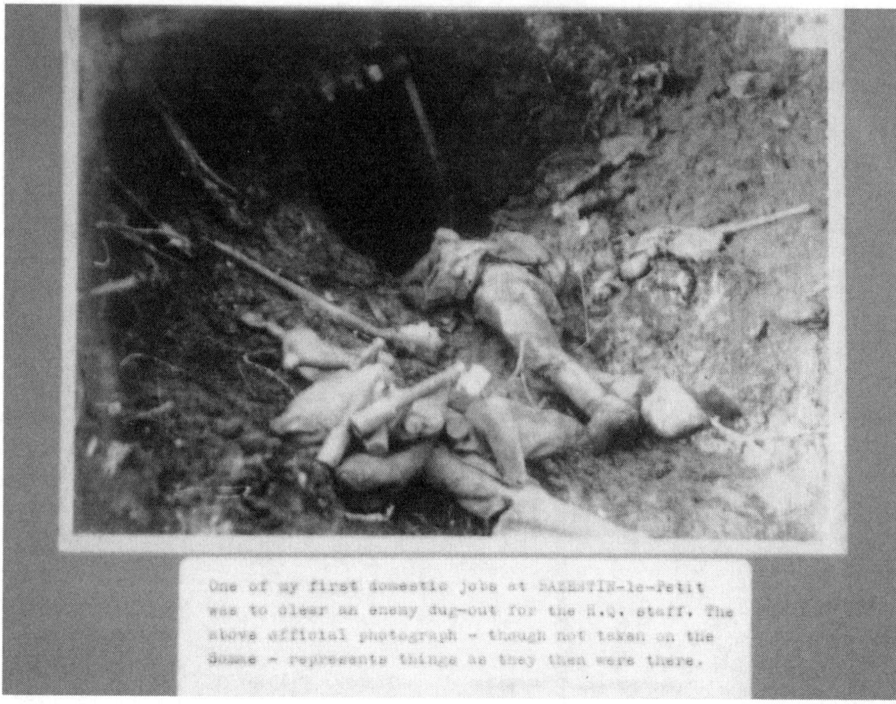

Figure 4.4 Captain Gameson, L., Photographic Album, p. 44. Imperial War Museum, Department of Documents, P396

Photos displaying the atrocities of war continue for another twenty pages after this one. Gameson then writes: 'In the next five volumes there will be no more photographs of unpleasantness. I cannot stress too strongly that only a hint has been given of the actual conditions obtaining.'[84]

The point about giving only a hint of the atrocities of the war is made in most of the memoirs. Those serving in the war needed and felt compelled to narrate the destruction, but there was always a reservation in doing so, which makes the impact of the narrative above, and in this instance, of the photograph, even greater for the reader/viewer. As Gameson promises, the pages that follow do not include any scenes of mutilation and death. Instead, there is a mixture of devastated landscapes *(Illustration 4.5)* and men in uniform in various poses *(Illustration 4.6)*. Gameson does not make such a clear distinction in the narrative between mutilation and landscapes. The visual can be compartmentalised, categorised and contained in a more tangible way, whereas in the narrative desire and disgust can coexist. Gameson writes:

84. Ibid., p. 69.

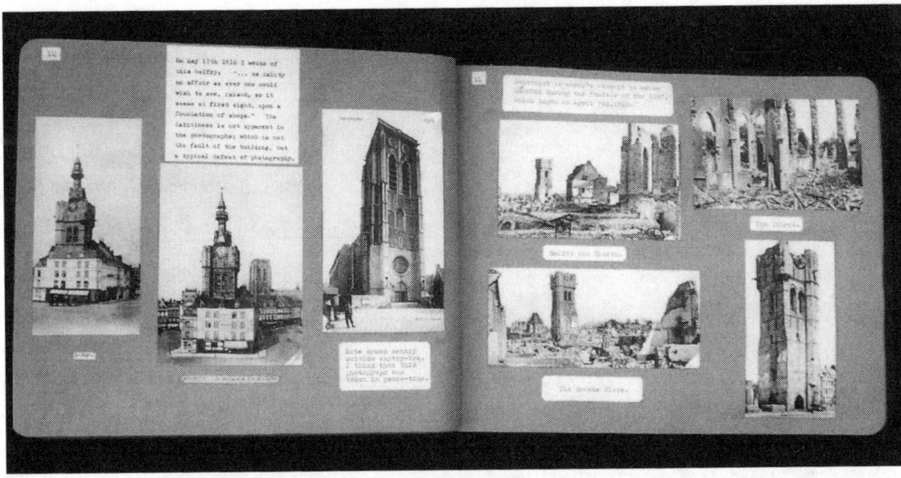

Figure 4.5 Captain Gameson, L., Photographic Album, p. 10. Imperial War Museum, Department of Documents, P396

> In the last lot [of wounded] is a surprisingly beautiful youth, as youths just occasionally can surprisingly be: long lashes, straight nose, finely finished limbs and so on. He was oozing frothing filth. Would the woman who wished him good-bye press now her lips to the clotted slime about his mouth?[85]

A special relationship develops between Gameson and another officer, the 'babe', as he calls him. They exchange little notes which are signed with phrases such as 'Your angel! Babe,' and which Gameson went on to treasure for the rest of his life. In the memoir Gameson describes his feelings of reverence and tenderness for the officer, who also appears in photos of groups of soldiers in later albums. The photographs of the men in uniform, due to Gameson's feelings for this officer, take on a special meaning. They provide what Leo Bersani has described as the 'desiring skin': the homosexuality without sexuality, desire that is satisfied merely by the proximity of the other, at the most by the other's touch.[86] The photograph with its membranous, skin-like qualities can represent the approximation of the desiring skin. As Linda Haverty Rugg has argued, 'autobiographical texts and photographs indicate both an absence of the body and presence of life; they announce life in the midst of death'.[87] For Gameson they represent the proximity of the male body and the tenderness of male sociality. They are the tactile memory traces of his desiring skin.

---

85. Ibid., *Memoir*, p. 12.
86. This concept was analysed in more detail in the Chapter 3 in relation to Lt.Col. G. S. Hutchison and the journal *The Superman.* See Bersani, Leo, *Homos* (Cambridge, Massachusetts: 1995), p. 121.
87. Haverty Rugg, Linda, *Picturing Ourselves*, p. 27.

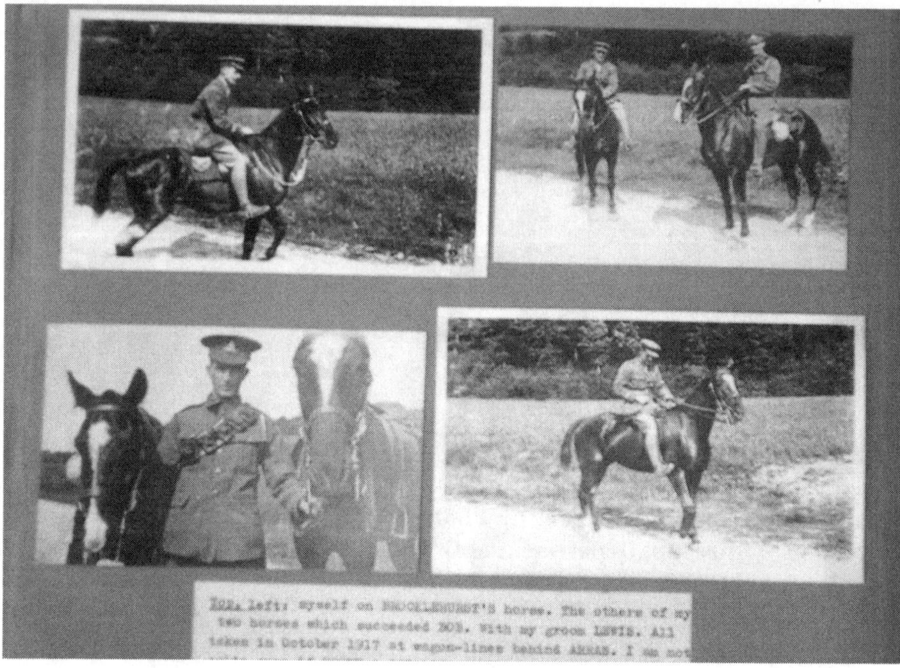

Figure 4.6 Captain Gameson, L., Photographic Album, p. 157. Imperial War Museum, Department of Documents, P396

How was the private collecting of souvenirs and photographs from the Front represented at the IWM? It is clear that the kind of objects collected by the servicemen played a very minor role in the exhibition. To this day, these items are tucked away in a corner of the museum. As we know, the objects that were favoured were large military equipment and artillery guns. According to Stewart, 'we are enveloped by the gigantic, surrounded by it, enclosed within its shadow'.[88] Seen in the museum, the guns are de-contextualised and aestheticised. The function of the collection, as Susan Stewart has argued, 'is the creation of a new context' which stands in a 'metaphorical rather than a contiguous relation to the world of everyday life'. The collection 'represents a hermetic world'.[89]

Recycling Guns

The exhibition at the IWM focused on instruments of warfare. During the war, guns and other instruments of warfare were loaned across the country to help promote the war effort and raise money. An internal report of the IWM highlights the way

88. Stewart, Susan, *On Longing*, p. 71.
89. Ibid., p. 152.

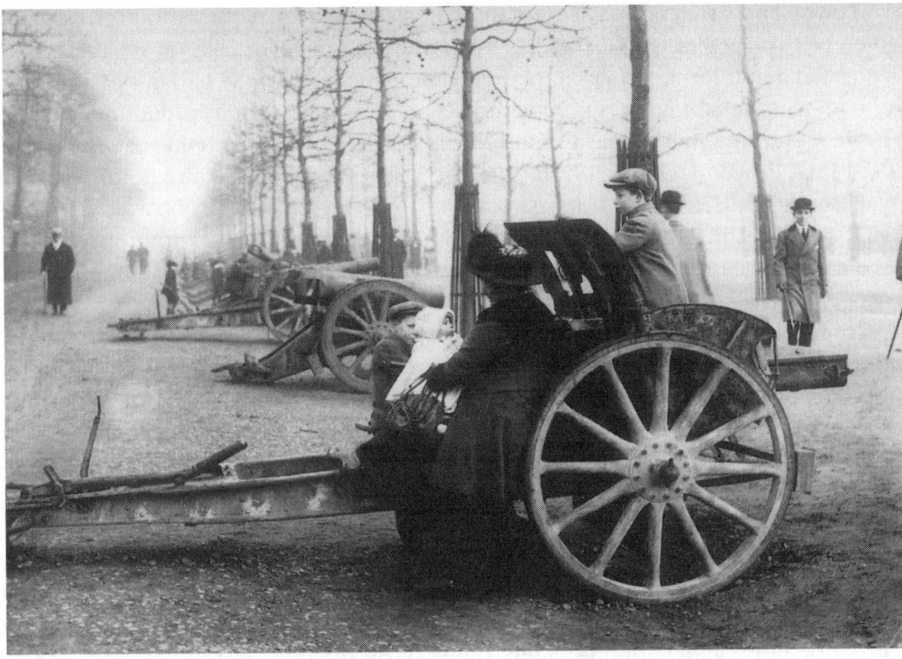

Figure 4.7 Display of War Relics along the Mall, London (no date, probably 1916–17). Imperial War Museum Photographic Archive

in which the 'souvenirs of war' had a direct appeal for the public that was 'almost magic'. The photographs from a display of artillery guns along the Mall *(Illustration 4.7)* in London gives a sense of the appeal claimed by the report. The photograph of the mother with her baby, sitting astride the field gun while her small boy climbs on its barrel, provides the viewer with a pacified image of the gun. The absence of a father figure, who was possibly killed in the war by a similar gun, is noticeable, but the children bring a sense of playfulness to the photo and the newborn baby provides a sense of hope for the future. As a result, the gun is cleansed and abstracted from its previous use and endowed with a magical appeal. The foggy London weather that forms the setting to the image contributes to the sense of the sublime.

Such images were able to arouse in the 'stay-at-home British taxpayer a more definite emotion' that was otherwise impossible with the 'cold appeal of print' alone. However, even without their histories their interest for the public was undiminished: 'Other exhibits have no history save the eloquent evidence of shattered mechanism and the mud of the battlefields. These relics are attractive in no aesthetic sense but one and all possess a grim absorbing interest.'[90]

90. Loan Exhibitions 1918–1919, IWM, Central Files, A5/2, no date. It is interesting to note that the IWM report noted some reservations as to the effectiveness of these objects on the returning servicemen.

Towns and cities across Britain also made their own requests to borrow or be given war relics that would stand as memorials to the dead. G. Stewart of Haylake requested a gun for the town to 'perpetuate the memory of the gallantry displayed' by one of its inhabitants, Sgt. Gousley REA, who had been awarded the Victoria Cross.[91] The Keighley Local Central War Savings Committee requested use of the war relics 'in connection with the specific effort to stimulate the sale of National War Bonds'.[92] Meanwhile, the secretary of the Dundee Postmen's War Memorial Fund praised the Trophies Committee on the success of its exhibition of guns: 'We had four captured guns sent from Croydon, which were the main attraction. Altogether the show was a great success financially and otherwise.'[93]

Reports from other exhibitions of war trophies endorsed their use as public attractions. The West Houghton Prisoners of War Fund reported that the 'trophies proved very attractive especially to the youths of the district'. An exhibition of war memorabilia organised in Leicester elicited the comment that the 'war relics were of a distinct help to the popularity of the exhibition, particularly the more unusual things'. The Faversham War Savings Committee reported that 'the Howitzer has proved a great attraction in our recent war savings week.[94] One of the most interesting requests came from Lord Robert's Memorial Workshops Committee. The workshops provided work for people who had been wounded during the war, and the committee asked for help to raise funds for the workshops and stimulate sales of their products.[95] War relics also served educational purposes, such as 'inculcating a larger spirit of patriotism and pride to the British Empire'. A letter from the Brigadier General of the 2nd Training Reserve Brigade to the IWM called for the loan of war relics as a 'graphic aid' to lectures given to reservists.[96]

Recycling provided a further use for the relics. In 1919 the IWM received an application from the Wolseley Memorial Committee for guns that could be melted down to provide metal for a statue of Field Marshal Wolseley.[97] There was also a request for war relics that could be melted down to produce the Victoria Cross.[98] The history of the Victoria Cross has an interesting bearing on the association between war relics, their recycling and gallantry. The Victoria Cross was instigated in 1856 by Queen Victoria because at the time there was no award for 'recognising the gallantry' of officers of the lower grades and non-commissioned officers and soldiers. Previous merits had been awarded for long service rather than for bravery in action or distinction before the enemy; the new award was for those who 'by their valour have particularly signalled themselves'. Queen Victoria's instructions

91. War Trophies Committee, IWM, Central Files, A1/4, 2 May 1918.
92. War Trophies General File IA, IWM, Central Files, A4/4, 22 February 1918.
93. Ibid., 25 July 1918.
94. Loan Exhibitions 1918–1919.
95. War Trophies, General File IA, 15 December 1917.
96. War Trophies, General File IA, 3 February 1918.
97. War Trophies Committee, 25 July 1918.
98. Ibid., 8 November 1917.

set out in detail the circumstances under which the medal was to be awarded and what constituted gallantry and valour. The medal would be in the form of a Maltese Cross, with the Royal Crest at the centre and underneath, the inscription 'For Valour'.[99] What was particularly important was that the medal was to be made from recycled metal – specifically, from bronze from a gun captured in the Crimean War. Because of the unprecedented number of medals given out during the First World War the original gunmetal had begun to run low, which accounts for the request for more guns to be recycled. In view of the large number of guns at Croydon, where the war relics and trophies were stored, and the maintenance expenses this incurred, the request came for 10,000 machine guns to be 'disposed off as scrap'.[100]

Certain groups were not permitted to receive war trophies. Sending trophies to Ireland was conditional on the items being 'unserviceable and not repairable' because of the political situation in Ireland at the time.[101] Sending trophies to ex-servicemen's organisations was considered even more dangerous. One of the associations, the Comrades of the Great War, asked for trophies for one of their fundraising events in Scotland. The application was refused. Writing to Major Pritchard of the Comrades of the Great War, Charles ffoulkes said that after having consulted with Martin Conway, the decision was that: 'In view of the present activities of all the soldiers associations and also the undoubted political activities of the other two [ex-servicemen's associations] it would be inadvisable for us to send out trophies to any of the three [associations].'[102] What this incident also points to is a contradiction between the apparent aestheticisation of the guns and their real function. It was only as objects of curiosity and, to a certain extent, admiration and de-contextualised, that they were allowed to serve a purpose.

Exhibiting Guns

The guns in the exhibition at the Imperial War Museum were displayed in the main atrium of Crystal Palace and formed the major attraction. A short film of the opening ceremony of the IWM[103] follows part of the ceremony, including the arrival of King George V and the Queen, as they walk through the galleries. On entering the main atrium, King George V stops in front of one of the field guns *(Illustration 4.8)* and points it out to the Queen. The camera then observes the other visitors who, taking the King's lead, also pause to admire the gun *(Illustration 4.9)*. Mieke Bal has argued

99. Warrant Instituting the Cross, PRO WO 98/1, quoted in Crook, Michael, *The Evolution of the Victoria Cross. A Study in Administrative History* (Kent: 1975), p. 14.
100. War Trophies Committee, IWM, Central Files, A1/4, Extra Ordinary Meeting of the War Office Trophies Committee, No date.
101. War Trophies Committee, 26 September 1918.
102. ffoulkes to Major Pritchard, Loan Exhibitions 1918–1919, Central Files, A5/2, 10 December 1918.
103. IWM film archives.

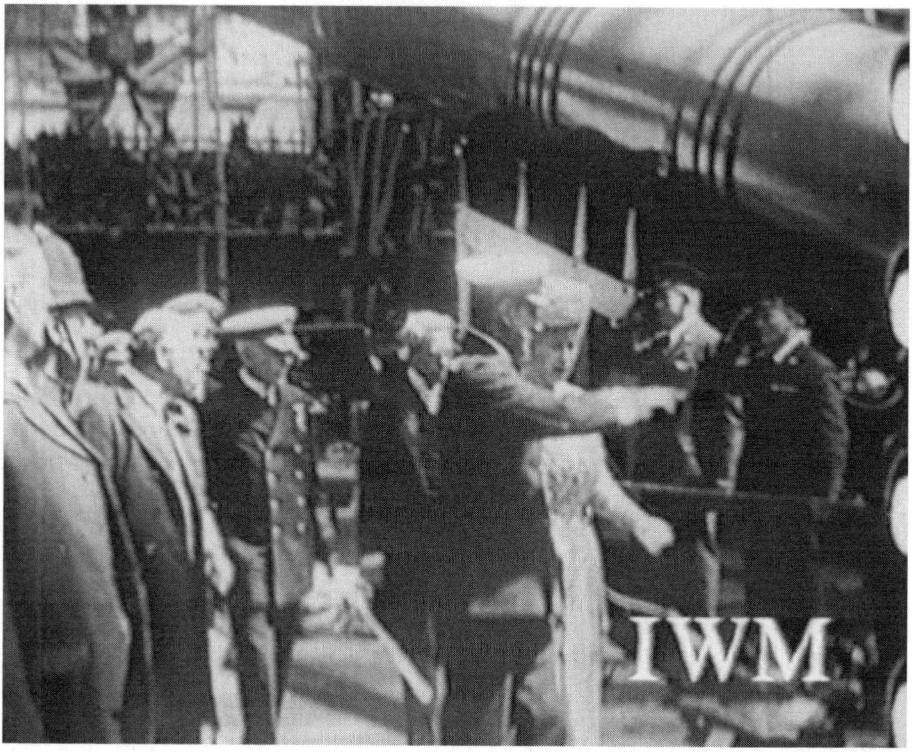

Figure 4.8 King George V pointing to one of the artillery guns, film still from a short film of the opening ceremony of the first exhibition of the IWM. Imperial War Museum Film Archive

that gestures which point to an object and seem to say 'Look', often imply 'That's how it is'. The instruction to 'look' acknowledges the visual availability of the object on view; 'that's how it is' recognises, or acknowledges the authority of the person who has pointed out the item. Singling something out for attention creates a dichotomy between subject and object, which enables the subject to make a statement about the object and the object to substantiate that statement.[104] The implied statement that King George V made in pointing to the gun was of the importance he attributed to it. The gun became imbued with meaning, ritual and majesty.

In the sequence that follows, the camera closes in on an officer who is looking at one of the guns and reading the label in front of it. None of the footage gives any prominence to the other exhibits. The press reports leading up to and following the opening of the museum saw the guns as the main attraction. *The Observer* wrote that the exhibition was not intended as a 'technical display' but

104. Bal, Mieke, *Double Exposure the Subject of Cultural Analysis* (London: 1996), p. 2.

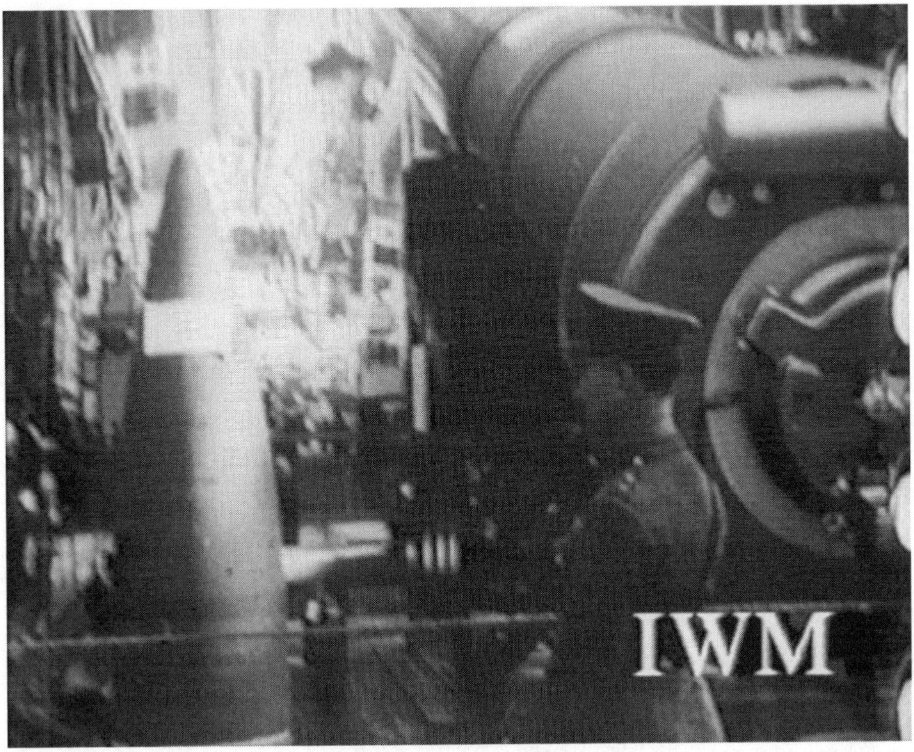

Figure 4.9 Officer looking at one of the artillery guns, film still from a short film of the opening ceremony of the first exhibition of the IWM. Imperial War Museum Film Archive

as a place where a 'father can say: 'This is the gun I used with my battery'.[105] The *Liverpool Daily Post* pointed out that the 'guns will attract the most interest', and contrasted the IWM exhibition with the Science Museum's exhibition of war material in 1914 and 1915.[106] Where the Science Museum exhibition had included models of British warships and of British and foreign aircraft with full size engines and parts, the IWM exhibition offered not only real guns of significant proportions but also avoided complicated technicalities associated with the guns. Science was being replaced by history, while technology was being replaced by aesthetics.

The *Liverpool Daily Post* wrote:

> One has not to be content with a general statement that a particular piece of cannon took its part in offence and defence. One can read in a frame beside it its complete record

105. *The Observer*, 11 April 1920.
106. *Liverpool Daily Post*, 28 May 1920.

> of service from the beginning to the end of its career and the names of the officers who served it.[107]

The reporter justified the amount of space he had given to the guns in his article by saying: 'I have dealt more fully with the guns, because of the personality which each of these monsters acquires through its printed history.'[108] The *Daily Telegraph* followed a similar line of reporting. After briefly describing the exhibition, it concluded that: 'of more fascination to the Englishman is a group of guns, whose stories will be set forth on boards standing beside them.'[109] For the *Daily Express*, the main floor of the exhibition, where all the big guns were exhibited, was a 'mammoth page in the book of world history'.[110] The *Daily Mail* initially questioned the validity of placing so much significance on the guns. Ivor Nicholson, formerly of the Ministry of Information, wrote that one might justifiably 'feel an utter sense of nausea with all the filthy paraphernalia of war', but went on to add that it would be 'selfish not to like the guns out of some personal distaste'. He wrote:

> But after all we are a nation, we are great people and not a collection of atoms living entirely to ourselves. And all these wonderful items which go to make up our War Museum are part and parcel of our own history.[111]

The *Sheffield Daily Telegraph* described the guns as 'objects that bear their tales on their faces'; most impressive of all was the 18inch howitzer, which commanded 'universal attention'.[112] The *Nottingham Journal* regarded the museum and the guns as 'the most powerful antimilitarist advertisement' one could conceive.[113]

Critics of the museum attacked it for glamorising war. They made their point particularly strongly during the House of Commons debate on the Museum Bill[114] on June 10, 1920, one day after the museum had been officially opened by the King.[115] Opponents of the Bill claimed that the museum was promoting 'propaganda of the war spirit'. They objected to the fact that the opening ceremony was advertised on posters all over London and that a public holiday had been held in celebration. The whole procedure, they claimed, 'fostered a spirit which

107. Ibid.
108. Ibid.
109. *Daily Telegraph*, 25 May 1920.
110. *Daily Express*, 5 June 1920.
111. *Daily Mail*, 7 July 1920.
112. *Sheffield Daily Telegraph*, 7 June 1920.
113. *Nottingham Journal*, 9 June 1920.
114. The Museum Bill was introduced by Alfred Mond MP and outlined the statutory powers of the IWM.
115. It appears as if the opening of the museum was rushed in order to coincide with the second reading of the Bill in the House of Commons. There is, however, no clear evidence as to this.

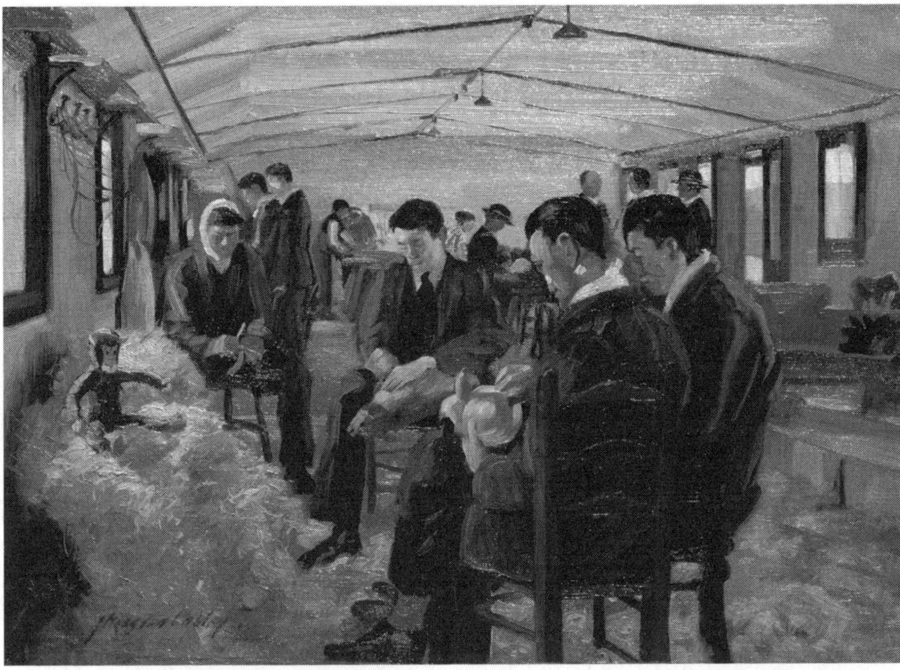

Figure 4.10 John Lobley, *The Toy-Makers' Shop* (1919). The Queen's Hospital for Facial Injuries, Frognal, Sidcup. Imperial War Museum Art Department

we all hoped will die out quickly'.[116] What was most interesting, according to the Liberal MP Lieut. Commander Kenworthy was the fact that the museum avoided the horrors of war. He was referring to the Royal Army Medical Corps (RAMC) section of the exhibition, which had been relegated to a small corner of the upper gallery. This section included, amongst other works, paintings by John Lobley of soldiers at Sidcup Hospital with facial disfigurements *(Illustration 4.10).*[117] Responding to Kenworthy's criticisms, Alfred Mond said that the positioning of the RAMC exhibits was due to simple logistics, as heavy objects needed to go to the ground floor and smaller, light exhibits needed to be placed in the galleries.[118] Kenworthy suggested that instead of attaching a history to each of the guns, the 'price of manufacture of every gun, aeroplane, mine-thrower, gas-projector and all the rest of them should be marked on it in plain figures'. He continued:

116. Lieut. Commander Kenworthy MP, 'Museum Bill – Second Reading', *Hansard*, cl.702, 10 June 1920.
117. It is also symptomatic that the majority of the RAMC paintings were disposed by the IWM following the first exhibition.
118. Mond, Alfred, MP, *Hansard*, cl.705, 10 June 1920.

> Let Democracy know what it costs to go in for war, and know that besides the pomp and the ceremony and the suffering and the disease and the demoralisation, it is also a costly business.[119]

MPs taking part in the discussion were also concerned about the effect that the exhibition would have on the minds of the young. Myers MP (Liberal) argued that the effect of the relics upon the 'young mind is such that we are going to familiarise them with all the barbarism of warfare'; instead, he maintained, 'we ought to be proclaiming the virtues of peace'.[120] Alfred Mond responded by pointing out that at the opening ceremony the previous day, when he had accompanied King George V and other officials around the exhibits, 'all felt that the museum expressed the terror and horror of war'.[121] Also supporting the exhibition was Martin Conway MP, who highlighted the role that museums could play when it came to Britain's increased reliance on the tourist trade. The museum would make its contribution to the economy through the tourist industry, he maintained: 'The tourist industry in the immediate future will be one of our great paying industries. Every year it increases in value, and our museums have a direct relationship to it, quite as much as have hotels or any other factors of that kind.'[122]

The press reporting of the opening ceremony highlighted a number of issues connected with class division and labour unrest. A major strike which threatened to postpone the opening of the exhibition was sparked by objections from the trade unions to the fact that IWM attendants were carrying out work that could have been undertaken by unemployed ex-servicemen. The Annual Report of the IWM noted that 'the labour question on several occasions assumed somewhat serious proportions' and the matter was settled by the museum taking on casual labourers for the heavy work and keeping the museum attendants for the lighter and more technical work. These labour difficulties, the IWM stated in its Annual Report, 'recurred almost every week'. Fortunately, by 'the exercise of a certain amount of tact and compromise, serious trouble never materialised'.[123]

The *Morning Post* regarded the IWM as a potential resolution to the conflict between the workforce and the economy in the way that it offered a place for 'contemplation of the great struggle' and a 'record of heroism'.[124] *The Times* editorial saw the opening of the exhibition as a chance to 're-establish the war spirit of fellowship'.[125] The principle founders of the museum, Mond, Conway and ffoulkes, as well as the King in his opening address, all tried to maintain that the museum

---

119. Lieut. Commander Kenworthy, MP, *Hansard*, cl.703, 10 June 1920.
120. Myers, MP, 'Museum Bill – First Reading', *Hansard*, cl.1468, 12 April 1920.
121. Mond, Alfred, MP, 'Museum Bill – Second Reading', *Hansard*, cl.706, 10 June 1920.
122. Conway, Martin, MP, 'Museum Bill – Second Reading', *Hansard*, cl.710, 10 June 1920.
123. *Third Annual Report of the Committee of the Imperial War Museum*, 1 April 1919 to 2 July 1920, p. 5.
124. *Morning Post*, 10 June 1920.
125. *The Times*, 'Editorial', 10 June 1920.

was a permanent record of the efforts of all ranks and classes, but the *Daily Herald* argued that the 'working-class element was not conspicuous in the assembly'.[126]

The guns, however, remained the main focus of the exhibition. Only a few press reports mentioned the art section. Other than one remark by the *Liverpool Daily Post* on John Singer Sargent's *Gassed*, and by *The Times* on Gilbert Roger's *Stretcher Bearers* – both paintings singled out because they were 'horribly real' – the reviewers seemed to concentrate on the machinery of war. Sue Malvern has argued that the museum's art collections enabled contrary meanings to leak into the homogeneous and continuous space of the displays of war material, rupturing the rhetoric of national redemption'.[127] By contrast, the 'solid exhibits', as *The Times* described the war relics, provided the 'text' out of which the 'history of the war in concrete hieroglyphs' could be written.[128] At the luncheon that followed the opening, Winston Churchill gave an address in which he acknowledged that the war relics were 'grim and fierce' but that in the future, they would become sacred: 'Those sombre relics of war would be looked upon, not merely with wonder and astonishment by future generations, they would be regarded as the sacred objects which represented the sacrifice of one splendid generation.'[129]

The stories attached to the guns provide a further example of the way in which they were singled out for attention. The guns that were chosen for display – some of which are still on display at the Imperial War Museum in London – were those to which it was possible to attach 'an honourable history'. Concentrating on some of these histories, one could gain a sense of the hegemonic memory that was being imposed on visitors to the exhibition.

The 'L' Battery Royal Household Artillery Gun, also known as 'Nery',[130] first saw action near Audringiers in August 1914. The following description was printed on its label for the exhibition:

> In September of that year it assisted against the attack that was opened by the Germans. The battery was heavily shelled and suffered severe casualties, three guns only being in action. Captain Bradbury and Sergeant Nelson took one gun, Lieut. Gifford another, and Lieut. Campbell and Mundy the third. This last gun was immediately silenced by a direct hit. At about 5.30am Lieut. Gifford was severely wounded and all his detachment killed or wounded leaving only Captain Bradbury's gun in action. Lieut. Campbell and Mundy went to his assistance, and gunner Derbyshire and Driver Osborne served the gun with ammunition from a nearby wagon. Lieut. Campbell was killed immediately. The gun was heavily shelled by the German Division at 800 yards and about 6.30am Lieut. Mundy and Sergeant Nelson were seriously wounded. About 7.15am Battery Sgt. Major Dorrell reached the gun and on arrival Captain Bradbury was mortally wounded in bringing ammunition from the wagon. By this time the German attack had been held up,

126. *The Daily Herald*, 10 June 1920.
127. Malvern, Sue, 'War, Memory and Museums', p. 192.
128. *The Times*, 19 August 1920.
129. Churchill, Winston, *The Times*, 10 June 1920.
130. The guns were usually given female names such as 'Mother'.

> and about 7.30am as the reinforcements arrived the gun fired its last two rounds. During the action it accounted for three German guns at the least before it ceased firing.[131]

What emerges from this account is the way in which the gun acquires its own heroic qualities. The men and their deaths become less important. The same idea permeates through the *Royal Artillery War Commemoration Book*. The frontispiece states that the book is dedicated to those who laid down their lives 'in the service of the Guns'. The men commemorated in the book were awarded the Victoria Cross for saving the guns from destruction. Major Ernest Wright Alexander, for example, 'handled his battery against overwhelming odds with such conspicuous success that all guns were saved, notwithstanding that owing to heavy casualties, they had to be withdrawn by hand by himself and three other men'.[132]

Another of the guns exhibited at the IWM, the 'Lone Howitzer', provides further evidence of the status accorded to the guns once the war was over.[133] A section of the *Royal Artillery War Commemoration Book* is dedicated to the gun because the 'services of the guns themselves are overlooked'. The 'Lone Howitzer' represented something 'more than a cold, lifeless piece of steel'. Most importantly: 'Many men have died round it in its service; as time goes on those still left who have tended it and fought it will pass away; but the gun, their master, will remain.'[134]

The 'Lone Howitzer', was given a name, an identity, and was polished and exhibited. The memories attached to it were filtered and expressed through its scarred but shiny surface. Shiny surfaces reflect rather than absorb, and the memories of those who visited bounced off the shiny surface of the gun as polished and newly restored memories. The IWM also promoted the idea of the guns as memorials. For each gun there was an annual service when the regiment and other interested individuals could place a wreath on the gun. As Winston Churchill had envisaged, guns became sacred. The wreaths placed on them were believed to have acquired special blessings. ffoulkes received a letter requesting the wreath on 'Nery' to be handed over so that it could be sent to Gallipoli and placed on the grave of a relation.[135] The request was refused, as it was customary to 'destroy by fire' the weathered wreaths.[136] Members of the public also requested photographs of the guns or asked permission to reproduce the guns in model form.[137] 'Nery' was even

131. 'L' Battery RHA Nery, Guns Army, IWM, Central Files, A2/4.
132. Royal Artillery Commemoration Fund, *The Royal Artillery War Commemoration Book. A Pilgrimage Record Written and Illustrated for the Most Part by Artillery Men While Serving in Line During the Great War* (London: 1920), no pagination.
133. Lone Howitzer, Guns Army, IWM, Central Files, A2/4.
134. Royal Artillery Commemoration Fund, *The Royal Artillery War Commemoration Book*, p. 172.
135. ffoulkes to J. A. Darbyshire, 'L' Battery RHA Nery, Guns Army, IWM, Central Files, A2/4, 11 September 1923.
136. ffoulkes to J. A. Darbyshire, 'L' Battery RHA Nery, Guns Army, IWM, Central Files, A2/4, 13 September 1923.
137. ffoulkes to Commanding Officer, 'L' Battery RHA Nery, Guns Army, IWM, Central Files, 12 September 1923 and 1 November 1923.

wheeled outside the confines of the museum to attend the unveiling ceremony of the *Royal Artillery Memorial* in Hyde Park Corner in October 1925. Charles ffoulkes wrote in his memoir:

> So battered was this splendid but pathetic relic that it could not be moved by horse transport and we patched up the wheels and man-handled it up Queen's Gate and Knightsbridge to Hyde Park Corner. The word must have gone before us, for I saw men en route raise their hats to this gallant relic which lay at the foot of the Memorial during the dedication ceremony.[138]

It was significant that the Royal Artillery memorial committee, responsible for the design of the *Royal Artillery Memorial*, should ask for a realistic gun to be incorporated into the monument. Lutyens and Derwent Wood, who had initially submitted designs in the form of a cenotaph, refused, and so the committee turned to Charles Jagger. Their instructions were that it should be 'a war memorial' and include all the accoutrements, equipment and details of active service. Jagger, who had been a non-commissioned officer for the infantry during the First World War, was known to respect the Artillery for their 'terrific power' and the 'last word in force'.[139]

In 1926 the *Evening News* printed an article about 'Nery' under the title 'Polished Old Veteran':

> It is a battered gun but very spick and span too. The brass hubs of the gun wheels shine so you could almost do map reading by them on a dark night. There is a dent in the muzzle of the gun. It is the dent by which the gun got its final knock out from German fire. But we all remember how smart a scarred warrior the gun looked when it was taken to Hyde Park Corner that Sunday last October when the RA memorial was unveiled.[140]

A series of photographs from the unveiling of the *Royal Artillery Memorial* provide a visual tableau of the importance of the guns in relation to masculinity. The first photograph *(Illustration 4.11)* shows Charles ffoulkes and the sculptor Charles Jagger standing in front of the veiled memorial. Both are dressed in morning suit and top hat and present an imposing picture. Between them, the two men created and orchestrated the pageantry and ceremonial that was to follow. What the photograph also reveals is the class specificity of the masculinities promoted by the commemoration of the First World War. Their masculinities were those of the establishment and a particular circle of men with very specific connections to the corridors of hegemonic power at the time.

Charles Jagger held the view that a sculptor needed to be strong because 'his mistress is without mercy and she will demand every ounce of vitality he possesses and more'. The demanding mistress could, however, also offer satisfaction:

138. ffoulkes, Charles, *Arms and the Tower*, p. 146.
139. Stevens Curl, James, 'The Royal Artillery Memorial at Hyde Park Corner', in Compton, Ann (ed.), *Charles Sargeant Jagger. War and Peace Sculpture* (London: 1985), pp.84–5; On Jagger's sculptural work, see Compton, Ann, 'Sculptural Biography', in Compton, Ann (ed.), *Charles Sargeant Jagger*.
140. *Evening News*, 7 June 1926.

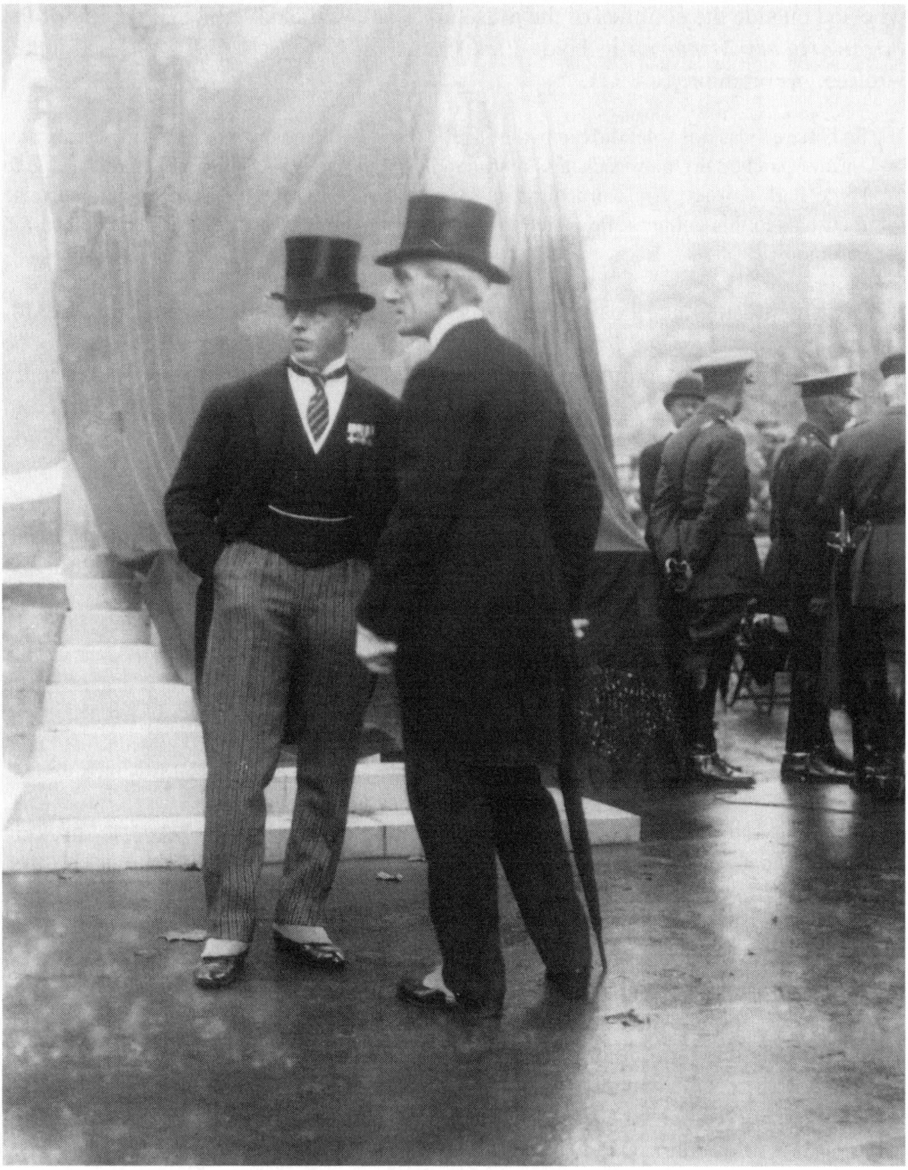

Figure 4.11 Charles ffoulkes (right) and Charles Jagger in front of the veiled *Royal Artillery Memorial* (1925). Imperial War Museum Photographic Archive

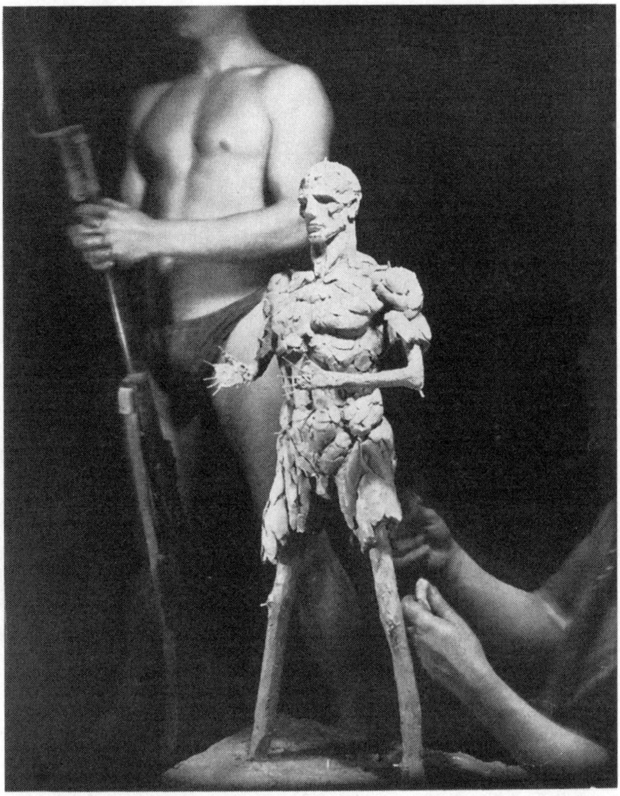

Figure 4.12 Charles Jagger modelling the figures for the *Royal Artillery Memorial* from a life model – Source: Jagger, Charles, 'Modelling and Sculpture in the Making', The Studio. 'How to Do it Series', London, 1933, p. 10

'When body and soul are satiated or have outlived the transitory pleasures and diversions of life, she will be by his side, filling his imagination with pictures of loveliness. She alone will remain with him to the grave. For this, no man can want more.'[141] Jagger's description of the sculpture as a mistress provides an escape from the constraints of contemporary modern society and the codes of masculine behaviour imposed on him by society.

In the photograph of Jagger *(Illustration 4.12)* the sculptor is seen creating a model of the soldiers for the *Royal Artillery Memorial*. He has based the clay model on a soldier who is standing in front of him naked, holding a gun complete with bayonet. The sculptor inspects the 'ideal' body of the model, who is posed standing to attention. Jagger's work was described as possessing a 'realism', and a quote from

141. Jagger, C. S., *Modelling and Sculpture in the Making* (London: 1933), p. 9.

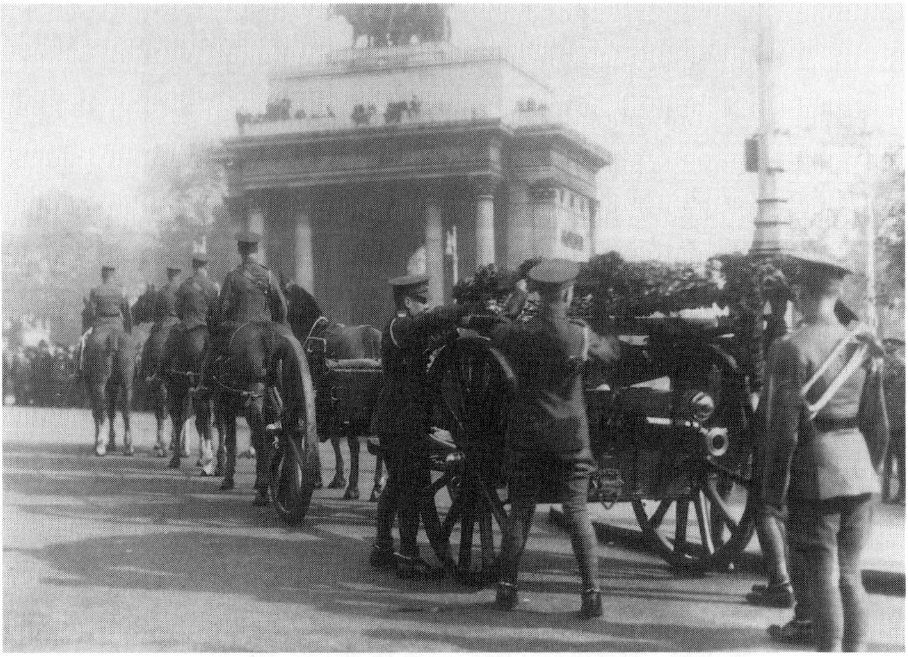

Figure 4.13 Artillery Gun 'Nery' at the unveiling of the *Royal Artillery Memorial* (1925). Imperial War Museum Photographic Archive

a gunner at the time of the unveiling is often cited to support this.[142] However, the faces and bodies of the gunners were less important than the equipment they carried. More importantly, their military uniform hides or submerges any individuality. It armours the body.[143] The unveiling of the memorial therefore revealed a further veiling: the veiling of the fragile male body. It was the gun, Nery, that was wheeled out for the ceremony *(Illustration 4.13)* that presented the real embodiment of courage, endurance and sacrifice.

The Memorial to the Fallen

The plans for the museum included mounting a centrepiece called *Memorial to the Fallen* which would incorporate photographs of all those who had died during the war. Each photograph was to be accompanied by a short biographical note. To gather

142. 'See that man carrying the shells. He is real. All the green men are real.' *Manchester Guardian*, 9 October 1925, p. 10, quoted in Glaves-Smith, John, 'Realism and Propaganda in the Work of Charles Sargeant Jagger and their Relationship to Artistic Tradition', in Compton, Ann (ed.), *Charles Sargeant Jagger*, p. 52.

143. Foster, Hal, 'Armour Fou', *October*, 56 (1991): 64–97.

the photographs for this giant memorial, adverts were placed in all the national and local newspapers. This elicited a huge response.[144] The correspondence relating to the photographs shows how their relatives sought some form of solace from the act of sending the photographs of their loved ones to the museum. One of the bereaved, Cathleen Cooke, wrote: 'I should feel so pleased to think that his name was put amongst all the other brave fellows who have died for their country.'[145] Some felt that sending photos offered a way of expressing the enormity of their loss, like the mother who lost two of her sons in two consecutive days.[146] For some, writing to the museum also represented a means of appealing for help in tracing the graves of their friends and relatives.[147]

The act of sending something that belonged to the dead or related to their death seems to have been very important for most of the correspondents. Frederick Pattern made a memorial tablet to the memory of his son; 'something new', which 'has never been seen before'. The tablet was a mosaic that could 'stand on the table' or as 'an ornament on the wall'. Pattern wanted the museum to have this memorial tablet 'for a month or two' so that it could 'hang up to his memory'. The museum politely refused the tablet, although it suggested that he could send a photograph of the tablet.[148] Sarah Bisson had only one document relating to her son's death, which she wanted to send to the museum. She wrote: 'I am enclosing my dear son's photo and a letter from his commanding officer. I have no other papers.'[149] The letter from Mrs M. Collett to the museum enclosing her son's photograph encapsulates how many saw the compilation of photographs as a form of honouring the dead. She wrote: 'I have sent you his photo and letter I received from the Priest. ... He was my eldest son by my first husband and better son a mother ever [sic] had. I am only glad to do anything to honour him.'[150]

Once they had parted with their photographs, correspondents were anxious to find how they would be displayed.[151] The curator of the museum wrote back, saying that the photographs would be kept in 'special boxes alphabetically for ease of reference'. This was important because of the lack of permanent accommodation for the museum. His letter continued: 'The ultimate arrangement will be decided upon

144. The photographs are still held in storage at the IWM. At present there are approximately 15,000 photographs. These have never been exhibited. This information was provided by Hilary Roberts from the photographic section of the museum. The correspondence with the relatives of the dead who sent photographs to the museum is held in the museum's central files.
145. Cathleen Cooke to IWM, 'Memorial to the Fallen', Central Files, IWM, 4 September 1917.
146. Mrs Herbison to IWM, ibid., 28 July 1917.
147. Sarah Bisson to IWM, ibid., 31 May 1918.
148. Frederick Pattern to IWM, ibid., 31 May 1918.
149. Sarah Bisson to IWM, ibid., 31 May 1918.
150. M. Collette to IWM, ibid., 17 July 1918.
151. Mrs Gibson to IWM, ibid., 27 February 1918.

when the Museum building is settled.'[152] The photographs were to remain in their boxes to the present day in a storage space at Duxford.

In some instances the museum responded with a rather personal touch. Correspondence was mostly dealt with by the Keeper of Photographs, E. Sikes, who had two sons in the army and for whom the letters provided a constant reminder of what could have happened to his own sons. To one correspondent who forwarded a memoir of his nephew, Sikes wrote that he found it so interesting that 'I have rather neglected my duty, in order to read some part of it.'[153] Sikes' comforting responses combine the personal with the official. The letters were also an opportunity for Sikes to express his feelings on pacifism. In a letter marked 'Not for Publication' he elaborated his strong dislike not only of the German race but more importantly, of the 'perverted pacifists' who advocated kindness:

> It passes one's comprehension to imagine how, with this and innumerable other evidences of the frightfulness that is characteristic of the whole German Nation, there are still found in our country spineless and perverted pacifists who advocate kindness to Germany. The whole race is utterly vile.[154]

The correspondence accompanying the photographs conveyed a sense of the loss and an attempt to provide a closure to the grief by idealising the dead. One correspondent wrote that her son was 'ideal in every way'. His life was perfect in 'everything that gives to make a man and a gentleman'. He was a man whom 'any man could envy' and 'wherever he was he would have led'.[155] Such idealisation could be attributed to the bereavement process that the correspondent was going through, but was also characteristic of the middle and upper classes and the way in which they saw their role as leaders especially in relation to devotion, selflessness, and a sense of duty. Another correspondent described the life of his dead son as an example of 'unselfish devotion to duty'.[156] One mother wrote that her son 'underwent a painful operation' in order to make him fit for service. She praised him for being 'self-denying and anxious to do his best for others', and concluded by saying: 'I do not know if I have said too much but he was everything to me.'[157] This letter provides a striking contrast with another from a correspondent whose son had almost completed his apprenticeship as a blacksmith before joining the Army. The soldier's mother wrote: 'He died on June 18th 1917, after serving over two years out in France. The Government have never appreciated the sacrifice these grand young men made who went so willing at the beginning of the war.'[158]

152. Charles ffoulkes to Mrs Gibson, ibid., 2 March 1918.
153. Sikes to Sir James, ibid., 10 July 1918.
154. Sikes to Mrs C. Bennett, ibid., 14 November 1918.
155. Mrs Richardson to IWM, ibid., 18 October 1918.
156. Mr Bracklehurst to IWM, 'Memorial to the Fallen', Central Files, IWM, 24 November 1918.
157. Mrs Torey to IWM, ibid., 6 December 1918.
158. Mrs Rawcliffe to IWM, ibid., 3 December 1918.

Whereas the middle- and upper-class families often resorted to an idealisation of the dead men, the working class appeared to derive comfort from drawing to attention the inability of the government to provide an appreciation of the sacrifice of the dead men.

The idealisation of the dead men is also prevalent in the memoirs that accompanied the photographs,[159] such as the memoir of Lieut. Col. A. H. James (Archie).[160] This memoir was compiled by James's uncle, Ferdinand Baker, from letters sent to him during the war, and printed for private circulation. The letters are juxtaposed with personal observations by Baker on James's character and abilities whilst managing his uncle's plantations in India. The publication also quotes official letters from James's superiors concerning his injury and subsequent death, and eulogies from the parish priest and other 'officials' at home. James's own letters are few and far between. One letter describes a near escape at the Front when he tried to help a man who had been shot next to him and as a result was hit by an enemy bullet which passed through his breast pocket, through his field glasses and bore a hole in his steel whistle. Baker chose this unselfish act as a symbol of James's character. In a testimony on James's life in India, Baker writes:

> As a tea-planter, Archie had a fine reputation and greatly increased the productiveness of the estate, which he managed mainly owing to the excellent discipline and organisation, which he maintained amongst the overseers and labourers.[161]

James's managerial abilities and sporting prowess led to a degree of fearlessness which was particularly evident on hunting expeditions:

> Archie was a brilliant sportsman, and was ignorant of fear. He commenced his career in India when barely seventeen by pursuing a wounded bear into some bushes, and was severely torn by the engaged animal. … On one occasion he tackled a wounded bear in a cave, armed only with a revolver. He also killed chamois, and other local wild beasts.[162]

James's hunting prowess extended to Africa, where he 'succeeded in killing, single-handed, a huge male elephant' and 'two very large male wild buffalo'. This capacity for killing was praised by the military authorities. His Major contributed a eulogy paying tribute to James's fearlessness, unselfishness and ability to lead his men. He wrote that James was 'always in the thick of it, encouraging and urging his men'.[163] The vicar wrote along similar lines, describing James as 'an excellent shot and rider', a man of 'strong character' and a 'strict disciplinarian'. He particularly remembered a lecture that James gave to the Boy Scouts on the 'Big Game', shortly before the war started, and

159. The majority of these have been lost with only a few exceptions.

160. Baker, Ferdinand, *A Short Memoir of Lieut. Col. A. H. James DSO* (Exeter: 1918), p. 40.

161. Ibid., p. 41.

162. Ibid.

163. Ibid., p. 36.

he also recalled the mug James had presented to his godson bearing the words 'Be bold and fear not'. The vicar observed that although James was unmarried, he possessed a great love for children and his 'constant care and kindness for his men was very conspicuous'.[164]

To those who sent photos and mementos to the Imperial War Museum, the official reasons given to explain why it was not possible to display all the memorabilia appeared contradictory. Charles ffoulkes claimed that owing to the enormous number of photographs received, it was impossible to display them all.[165] Martin Conway, however, claimed that insufficient photographs had been received, despite widespread publicity of the project.[166]

Several issues arise from the correspondence received for the *Memorial to the Fallen*. By sending personal details to the IWM, the relatives were seeking a channel for their grief; a chance to justify the deaths of their loved ones and to give a meaning to those deaths. For some, it was a way of voicing their dissatisfaction at the treatment they had received from the government. For others, it was a way of re-establishing the significance of the life that had been lost. This element was entrenched in the codes of acceptable masculinities, which included unselfishness, fearfulness, strength and discipline. In this respect, the museum during the run-up to the project of the *Memorial to the Fallen* offered an opportunity to express multiple views. As Andreas Huyssen has commented, no matter how much the museum consciously and unconsciously produces and affirms the symbolic order, there is always a surplus of meaning that opens spaces for reflection and counter-hegemonic memory.[167] Perhaps it was this fear of the possibility of a counter-hegemonic memory which led to the photographs and the *Memorial to the Fallen* itself being confined to the storage space of the museum, where it remains to this day.

The establishment and inauguration of the IWM provided a platform from which a national identity could be established, but most importantly, it provided a forum in which a hegemonic memory of war masculinities could be promoted. As this book has argued, the establishment of such masculinities was problematic because of the uncertain position that various definitions of masculinity occupied as a result of civil unrest, shell shock and new forms of male sociality at the Front. The establishment of hegemonic forms of masculinity relied on the establishment of certain cultural icons, the machinery of war, which in the museum space were de-contextualised and imbued with importance, ritual and majesty. It was these objects that became the memorials to the war, over-shadowing the unstable nature of masculinities at the time.

164. Ibid., pp. 44–45.

165. ffoulkes to C. Campion, 'Memorial to the Fallen', Central Files, IWM, 22/02/1921. I thank Gill Smith of the Directorate Service of the IWM for bringing this letter to my attention.

166. Conway, Martin, *Museums Journal*, 20/2 (July 1920), p. 27.

167. Huyssen, Andreas, *Twilight Memories. Marking Time in a Culture of Amnesia* (London: 1995), p. 14.

Conclusion

The new Imperial War Museum North (IWM North) opened in July 2002. It was designed by Daniel Libeskind, who designed a number of key museums worldwide,[1] and links the previously derelict landscape of the Salford Quays in Manchester with regeneration and culture. It is also the first purpose-built building to house the IWM eighty-five years after the idea for such a memorial to the war was first conceived.

The architect's vision was to create a 'striking emblem that in an instant illuminates both tradition and the new', but also 'brings together culture and regeneration'. The building consists of three fragments or 'shards'. These are the fragments of a 'shattered world', which are reassembled 'as a fundamental emblem of conflict'. The shards, which could also represent 'traces of history', are there to create a new landscape in which the participatory experience of the public will 'begin long before the visitors enter through the actual doors'. They also take their cue from the environment to represent earth, air and water. It could be said that they represent the Army, Air Force and Navy. The Earth Shard forms the main museum space and 'signifies the open earthly realm of conflict and war. The Air Shard houses the projection and the educational space, and also serves as a 'dramatic entry into the museum'. The Water Shard forms the platform for viewing the canal and houses the restaurant, café and performance space. What is essential is the way in which the three shards come together:

> These three shards together, Earth, Air, and Water, concretise twentieth century conflict, which has never taken place on an abstract piece of paper but has been fought on dramatic terrain by the infantry, in the skies by the air force and on the sea by the battleships.[2]

For the architect, the space provides an arena in which the 'personal histories of the people of the North' can be shown in a 'concrete and visible form'. These personal histories, however, serve yet another purpose. The museum space is seen by Libeskind as a 'cultural dynamo' which transforms the past into a new era and is underscored by the recreation of the region in the form of urban regeneration and tourist spending. Martin Conway's prophetic comments to the House of Commons

---

1. The most famous of which are the Jewish Museum, Berlin, 1988–99 and The Boiler House Extension, V&A Museum, 1996–Present,
2. Libeskind, Daniel, 'Earth/Time', in Libeskind, Daniel, *Daniel Libeskind: The Space Encounter* (London: 2001), p. 62.

on the future importance of the museum industry could not have been better realised.[3] More importantly, the previously derelict site of Salford Quays has been re-cycled from its previous industrial use to become a cultural heritage landscape,[4] with immense possibilities for economic regeneration. The guns that were first exhibited in 1920 to contain the unpredictable emotions of the men who fought the First World War, and create stability in the social and economic reconstruction of the 1920s, are being used once again to provide for economic regeneration. This time their polished surfaces are housed under the shining, aluminium-clad surfaces of the IWM North. Shine abstracts, dematerialises, cleanses and creates an object that is untouchable, autonomous and outside any time and place. As such, the shattered world that the three shining shards represent is outside the realm of war and traumatic memory and inside the realm of regeneration and global capitalism.

What is absent from Libeskind's vision is the idea of the trauma of war; it is only in his projects relating to the Holocaust that trauma is evident. Although one cannot deny the immensity of that experience in terms of the suffering and loss it caused, one also needs to recognise that war in every form entails destruction, loss and trauma. In a lecture in Berlin entitled 'Trauma', Libeskind argued the (im)-possibility of representing the trauma of the Holocaust. He saw traumatic experiences relating to the Holocaust as having created a void which needed to be experienced historically in terms of the relationship between what the void is and the absence of a generation from history. Libeskind interpreted that absence as catastrophic. He believed that it was impossible to simply interpret trauma and that here, trauma found expression in the void of architectural space since the void is a space, the 'space of being and non-being'.[5] The concept of the architectural void is reflected in his design for the Jewish Museum Berlin and forms its central feature. The void is contained within fragmented lines, zigzags instead of spheres, which incorporate the names of the dead. The zigzags form sixty-two sections, each of which represents one of the 'Stations of the Star' described by Walter Benjamin in *One-Way Street*.[6] Once again the external and internal surfaces are clad in shining aluminium but in the Jewish Museum Berlin they incorporate the names of the dead and the void they left behind. The same void has not been recreated for in the IWM North. Instead, the guns form the focus of attention.

In 2002 another war museum was unveiled, this time in Nicosia, Cyprus, when the National Museum of Struggle (NMOS) moved to its new building. The museum commemorates the four-year war of independence (1955–59) from British rule and

3. The National Lottery Heritage Fund twice rejected the funding application for the new museum. The original cost had to be reduced from £40 million to £28.5 million financed by the Trafford Metropolitan Council, Peel Holdings plc, developers of the area, the European Regional Development Fund and the Board of Trustees of the IWM. The opening of the museum received very little publicity in the press.

4. The Lowry Centre is amongst the other developments as well as the Manchester United Football Ground.

5. Libeskind, Daniel, 'Trauma', in Libeskind, Daniel, *Space Encounter*, pp. 202–205.

6. Benjamin, Walter, *One-Way Street and Other Writings* (London: Verso, 2000).

its exhibits are strictly confined to that period, despite the fact that the history of the island is a continuous history of war.[7] The way in which war is represented at the NMOS differs significantly from the way it is represented at the two IWMs. Wyndham Lewis comments on the IWM in his autobiography:

> For your reconstruction you would have to admit Death there as well. You would have to line the trenches with bodies freshly killed that morning. No hospital could provide it.[8]

The NMOS has managed to fill the majority of its space with photographs of dead bodies. A spiral walkway leads the visitor through the four levels of the museum. The first level provides an introduction to the war of independence and connects the history of Cyprus with the ancient Greek civilisation, thus establishing a firm historical background. The second level provides an iconography of the demonstrations that were an almost daily occurrence during the period of the war. The third level provides a very different visual picture which details guerrilla-style warfare and its consequences. Photographs of the mutilated bodies of the dead line the wall. This procession of the dead bodies leads to the last level, which has been transformed into a shrine to all those that died. A candle burns in front of each photograph. Three ropes hang from the centre of the space. These represent the ropes used by the British Colonial troops to hang those involved in the struggle. The IWM also has its own monument to the war of independence. In a small glass case lies a collection of various items of war used during the struggle. There are no dead, mutilated bodies here. There are no dead mutilated bodies anywhere in the IWM.

Writing during the outbreak of the first Gulf War more than ten years ago, Judith Butler noted the absence of the human body from the reporting of the war. Instead of images of human beings at war, the media presented images of a war carried out by machines. Body counts were replaced by weapon counts. The only bodies that featured in the coverage of the war were the bodies of reporters and the single, sanitised body of the American military. American masculinity was re-inscribed through the hyper-masculine weaponry. Bodies of any kind, marked by race, gender or the fragility of flesh, were invisible in the spectacular images of the Gulf War. Viewing spectacle necessitated the absence of any associations with death:

---

7. See for example, Mavratsas, V., 'The ideological contest between Greek-Cypriot nationalism and Cypriotism 1974–1995: Politics, Social Memory and Identity', *Ethnic and Racial Studies*, 20/4 (1997), pp. 713–37; Cassia, Paul, 'Martyrdom and Witnessing: Violence, Terror and Recollection in Cyprus', *Terrorism and Political Violence*, 11/1 (1999), pp. 22–54; Anthias, F., 'Ethnicity and Class in Cyprus', *Race and Class*, 25 (1983), pp. 59–76; Panayiotopoulos, P., 'The Emergent Post-colonial State in Cyprus', *Commonwealth and Comparative Politics*, 37/1 (1999), pp. 31–55; Papadakis, Yiannis, 'The National Struggle Museums of a Divided City', *Ethnic and Racial Studies*, 17/3 (1994), pp. 400–19; Bryant, Rebecca, *Imaging the Modern. The Cultures of Nationalism in Cyprus* (London: 2004).
8. Lewis, Wyndham, *Blasting and Bombardiering. An Autobiography (1914–1926)* (London: 1937), p. 134.

> The so called 'smart bomb' records its target as it moves in to destroy it – a bomb with a camera attached in front, a kind of optical phallus; it relays that film back to a command control and that film is re-filmed on television effectively constituting the television screen and the viewer as the extended apparatus of the bomb itself.[9]

It was after the invasion of Iraq by the Allied forces that images of the tortured naked body of the 'enemy' started emerging in the media. These images were often characterised as pornographic, voyeuristic, a carnivalesque spectacle which glorified violence and which provided an index for the torture committed by the Allied forces in Iraq. What the images also revealed were the boundaries of the acceptable representation of the human body, especially of the male body in war, and the shock that the sight of the tortured, dead, mutilated body creates in the Western World.

As this book has demonstrated, the commemoration of the First World War faced the same boundaries of acceptability and relied on another spectacle, the perfectly formed spectacle of the unveiling ceremonies. The mutilated bodies of the war were absent. Only the sanitised and aestheticised body of the 'picturesque soldier' was evident, and masculinity was inscribed on the machinery of war. By concentrating on the relationship between masculinity and national identity, this book has investigated the kinds of masculinities that were projected by the commemoration of the war and the power relations across male sociality that the commemoration attempted to re-establish after the war. Fundamental to this were class relations and the new forms of male sociality that emerged at the Front.

The commemoration of the First World War in general and its memorials in particular have often been described as inclusive and as a means of facilitating the resolution of the grief of the bereaved. This argument can be challenged on two fronts: the idea of simplicity was a class specific aesthetic, and the grief and trauma of the ex-servicemen was to a very great extent ignored. During the post-Armistice period the notion of simplicity in the commemoration of the First World War was an aesthetic idea that was embedded in middle- and upper-class artistic sensibilities. As such, simplicity in the design of war memorials cannot be seen as providing a universal language for the expression of grief but needs to be seen within the broader perspective of the commemoration of the war.

---

9. Butler, Judith, 'Contingent Foundations: Feminism and the Question of Postmodernism', in Butler, J. and Scott, J. (eds), *Feminists Theorise the Political* (London: 1992), pp. 11–12.
   For similar views see Virilio, Paul, *Desert Screen. War at the Speed of Light* (London: 2002); Mirzoeff, Nicholas, *Watching Babylon. The War in Iraq and Global Visual Culture* (London: 2005).

Bibliography

Archival Sources

Henry Moore Institute Archives, Letter from Francis Derwent Wood to Hamo Thornycroft, C 757.

IWM, Abbot, S. B., 78/36/1.

IWM, Abraham, A. J., P191.

IWM, Adam, H. L., 83/50/1.

IWM, Agenda and Minutes of Committee on Imperial War Museum, 1917–1920, Conway, Martin, 'Memorandum on the Scope of the National War Museum', Central Files, A1/3.

IWM, Annual Reports, London 1919–1921.

IWM, Arbroath War Memorial Committee, Ephemera, Memorials, Box C.

IWM, Art Department, File 314/7.

IWM, Atkins, A. L., P267.

IWM, Balydon War Memorial Committee, Ephemera, Memorials, Box C.

IWM, 'L' Battery RHA Nery, Guns Army, Central Files, A2/4.

IWM, Beater, Captain O. L., 86/65/1.

IWM, Bradbury, S., 81/35/1.

IWM, Butt, H. R., 97/26/1.

IWM, Caseby, A., 78/4/1.

IWM, Crompton Memorial Committee, Ephemera, Memorials, Box C.

IWM, Ellis, A. E., 88/18/1.

IWM, 'The Empire War Memorial for Westminster', Art Department, 480/11.

IWM, Floyd, W. M., 87/33/1.

IWM, Gameson, Captain L., P396.

IWM, Gateshead War Memorial Committee, *Gateshead and the Great War. A Retrospective and a Reminder* (Gateshead: 1922), Ephemera, Memorials, Box C.

IWM, Haines, O. C. M., 95/16/1.

IWM, Handley, J. S., 92/36/1.

IWM, Holt, G. N., Con Shelf.

IWM, Jameson, 2nd Lieut. A. M., 98/13/1.

IWM, King George V, 'Reply to The Address of the Chairman of the Imperial War Museum', Third Annual Report of the Committee of the Imperial War Museum, 1st April 1919 to 2nd July 1920.

IWM, Lambert, R. E., 88/18/1.

IWM, Leicester Memorial Committee, Ephemera, Memorials, Box C.

IWM, Lillywhite, Colonel G., 76/19/1.

IWM, Loan Exhibitions 1918–1919, Central Files, A5/2.

IWM, Lone Howitzer, Guns Army, Central Files, A2/4.

IWM, Major Beckles Willson Correspondence 1917–1919, Central Files, A4/4.

IWM, Memorial to the Fallen, Central Files.

IWM, Mond, Alfred, 'Address to the King', *Third Annual Report of the Committee of the Imperial War Museum*, 1 April 1919 to 2 July 1920.

IWM, Murray, Reverend M. W., 77/106/1.

IWM, Nurse, E. G., 81/23/1.

IWM, Paviere, Major H. O., 8/19/1.

IWM, Pearson, R., 87/51/1.

IWM, Pegler, Captain D. H., 82/7/1.

IWM, Skirling Memorial Committee, Ephemera, Memorials, Box C.

IWM, Smithens, Captain, 77/142/1.

IWM, Taylor, Captain Norman Austin, 90/28/1.

IWM, Tickle, E., 88/65/1.

IWM, Upcher, Lieut. C., 98/2/1.

IWM, Upton, V. E., 81/35/1.

IWM, War Trophies Committee, Central Files, A1/4.

IWM, War Trophies General File IA, Central Files, A4/4.

IWM, Westmacott, Major T. H., 87/13/1.

IWM, Williams, 2nd Lieut. A. R., 82/26/1.

IWM, Woolard, Bertie William, 86/48/1.

MSS, 127/NU/6/IN 16 The Glasgow and District Railwaymen's Strike Bulletin, 30 September 1919.

MSS, 127/NU/MV7/3/5A Circular letter by the Secretary of the Kingston on Thames Labour Party, 6 December 1919.

MSS, 127/NU/NV7/3/5A Circular from J. H. Thomas to the members of the NUR, 30 September 1919.

MSS, 127/LC/4/2/1/1 'To the Class that Holds the Future in its Hands', Leaflet published by the Central Labour College.

MSS, 127/LC/4/3/1 Central Labour College Prospectus.

NIWM, Southwark Memorial Committee, File 2120.

Parliamentary Reports, 'A Collection of Reports on Bolshevism in Russia, No.1 (1919), Cmd8, Vol. Liii, April 1919.

PRO, Cab 24/68, GT6195, 'Suggestions to Prevent the Spread of Revolutionary Ideas in the UK'.

PRO, Cab 24/96, CP462, 'A Survey of Revolutionary Feeling in the Year 1919', Directorate of Intelligence, Special Report No.13.

PRO, Cab 52/27, 'Peace Celebrations'.

PRO, Cab 52/27, 'War Cabinet Peace Celebrations Committee', Minutes of meeting, 1 July 1919.

PRO, RAIL 2868, Euston Memorial.

PRO, WORK 20/146, Machine Gun Corps Memorial.
PRO, WORK 20/39, Cenotaph.
PRO, WORK 21/74, Peace Celebrations.
Royal Academy of Arts, *Annual Report*, London, 1918.
Royal Academy of Arts, *War Memorial Exhibition*, Exhibition Catalogue (London: 1919).
Science Museum, *Annual Report,* London, 1915.
Victoria & Albert Museum Archives, Internal Memo from the curator, A. Kendrick to Cecil Smith, 2 June 1919, Nominal File, Exhibition of War Memorials, July–Oct. 1919.

Newspapers And Periodicals

Church Family Newspaper
Country Life
Daily Express
Daily Herald
Daily Mail
Daily Mirror
Daily Telegraph
Evening News
Hansard's Parliamentary Debates
Illustrated London News
L&NWR Railway Gazette
Liverpool Daily Post
Machine Gun Corps Magazine
Morning Post
National Review
Nottingham Journal
The Observer
The Plebs
Railway Magazine
Railway Review
Sheffield Daily Telegraph
Sunday Times
The Call
The Superman
The Times
Tribunal
Vigilante
Westminster Gazette

Primary Sources

Aldington, Richard, *Death of Hero* (London: Hogarth, 1929).

Anon., *What Every Soldier Ought to Know* (Oxford: Oxford University Press, 1915).

Anon., *Practical Collecting, The New Culture Library* (London: Hodder & Stoughton, 1922).

Armstrong-Jones, Robert, 'The Mental Effects of the War and their Lessons in Regard to Medical and Social Reconstruction', *Journal of the Royal Society of Arts*, LXVI (1918).

Baker, Ferdinand, *A Short Memoir of Lieut. Col. A. H. James DSO* (Exeter: William Pollard & Co, 1918).

Barbusse, Henri, *Under Fire* (London: Dent, 1988 [1916]).

Bayes, Gilbert, *Modelling for Sculpture. A Book for the Beginner* (Harrow: Winsor & Newton, Ltd, 1930).

Benjamin, Walter, 'The Work of Art in the Age of Mechanical Reproduction', *Illuminations* (London: Pimlico, 1973).

Benjamin, Walter, *One-Way Street and Other Writings* (London: Verso, 2000).

Benson, A. C., *Lest We Forget* (London: Civic Arts Association, 1917).

Blunden, Edmund, *The Bonadventure. A Random Journal of an Atlantic Holiday* (London: Duckworth, 1922).

Blunden, Edmund, *Undertones of War* (London: Penguin, 1928).

Bohun, Lynch, *Collecting. Being one of a series of essays edited by J. B. Priestley and entitled: These Diversions* (London: Jarrolds, 1928).

Bostock, J., *The Machine Gunners' Handbook. Including the Maxim, Lewis, and Colt Automatic Machine Guns* (London: W. H. Smith & Son, 1916).

Clutton-Brock, A., *On War Memorials* (London: Civic Arts Association, 1916).

Conway, Martin, *The Domain of Art* (London: John Murray, 1901).

Conway, Martin, *The Sport of Collecting* (London: Fisher Unwin, 1914).

Conway, Martin, *The Crowd in Peace and War* (London: Longmans, 1915).

Conway, Martin, *Mountain Memories. A Pilgrimage of Romance* (London: Cassell, 1920).

Courtney, W. L., *Is it a New World? A series of Articles and Letters contributed by Correspondents to the Daily Telegraph, August–September, 1920* (London: Hodder & Stoughton, 1920).

Craik, William, 'The Railway Strike', *The Plebs*, XI/10 (November, 1919).

Dauntesey, C. B., *Drill & Training Remembrancer* (London: Gale & Polden Ltd, 1919).

Davies-Jones, C. W. S., 'A Case of War Shock Resulting From Sex-Inversion', *International Journal of Psychoanalysis*, 1/3 (1920), 240–4.

Ellis, Havelock, *Studies in the Psychology of Sex. Vol. 2 Sexual Inversion* (Philadelphia: F. A. Davies, 1917).

Evans, Howard, *Sir Randal Cremer. His Life and Work* (London: Fisher and Unwin, 1909).

Ewart, Wilfrid, 'The Young Men of England', *The Nineteenth Century*, DXIII (November, 1919).

Ferenczi, S., Abraham, K., Simmel, E., Jones, E., *Psychoanalysis and the War Neurosis* (London: The International Psychoanalytic Press, 1921).

ffoulkes, Charles, *Arms and the Tower* (London: John Murray, 1939).

ffoulkes, Charles, 'War Museums, *Museums Journal*, 18/4 (October, 1918).

Freud, S., 'Mourning and Melancholia', 1917 [1915] in Strachey, J., *The Standard Edition of the Complete Psychological Works of Sigmund Freud*, Vol. 14 (London: Penguin, 1991).

Freud, S., 'Thoughts for the Time on War and Death' (1915), in Strachey, J., *The Standard Edition of the Complete Psychological Works of Sigmund Freud*, Vol. 14 (London: Penguin, 1991).

Fuller, J. F. C., *Training Soldiers for War* (London: Hugh Rees, 1914).

Garratt, V. W., *A Man in the Street* (London: J. M. Dent & Sons, 1939).

Gibbs, Philip, *The New Man. A Portrait Study of the Latest Type* (London: Sir Isaac Pitman, 1913).

Gide, André, Trans. by David Watson, *The Immoralist* (London: Penguin, 2000 [1902]).

Glover, Edward, *War, Sadism and Pacifism* (London: George Allen & Unwin, 1933).

Gosse, Philip, *Rest Billets* (London: Dalau & Co, 1927).

Gosse, Philip, *Memoirs of A Camp-Follower* (London: Longmans, 1934).

Gramsci, Antonio, Hoare, Q. and Nowell Smith, G. (eds), *Selections from the Prison Notebooks* (London: Lawrence & Wishart, 1971).

Graves, Robert, *Goodbye to All That* (London: Penguin, 1988 [1929]).

Green, Second Lieut., 'Manufacturing Machine Gunners', *Machine Gun Corps Magazine*, Vol. I (November, 1916).

Halbwachs, Maurice, *The Collective Memory* (London: Harper & Row, 1980 [1950]).

Hamilton, Ian, *The Soul and Body of an Army* (London: Edward Arnold & Co, 1921).

Hankey, Donald, *A Student in Arms* (London: Andrew Melrose Ltd, 1917).

Hayden, Arthur, *Bye-Paths in Curio Collecting* (London: Fisher and Unwin, 1919).

Head, Henry, *Studies in Neurology* (London: Hodder & Stoughton, 1920).

Herford, Travers, *Realities and Reconstruction* (London: Lindsay Press, 1920)

Holmes, Edmond, 'Religion as the Basis of Social Reconstruction', *The Nineteenth Century and After* (November, 1919).

Hopkinson, Alfred, *Rebuilding Britain. A Survey of Problems of Reconstruction after the World War* (London: Cassell, 1918).

Howorth, Henry, 'Discussion', *Museums Journal*, 18/4 (October, 1918).

Hurst, Sidney, *The Silent Cities. An Illustrated Guide to the War Cemeteries and Memorials to the 'Missing' in France and Flanders: 1914–1918* (London: Methuen & Co, 1929).

Hussey, Christopher, *The Fairy Land of England* (London: Country Life, 1924).

Hussey, Christopher, *Tait McKenzie. A Sculptor of Youth* (Philadelphia: J. Lippincott Co, 1930).

Hussey, Christopher, *The Life of Sir Edwin Lutyens* (London: Country Life, 1950).

Hutchison, Graham Seton, *History and Memoir of the 33rd Battalion Machine Gun Corps and of the 19th, 98th, 100th and 248th M. G. Companies* (London: Waterlow Brothers & Layton Ltd, 1919).

Hutchison, Graham Seton, *The Thirty-Third Division in France and Flanders, 1915–1919* (London: Waterlow & Sons, 1921).

Hutchison, Graham Seton, 'Paladins. Where Are the Supermen Britain's Need Today?', *The Superman Magazine* (November, 1930).

Hutchison, Graham Seton, 'The Paladin League of Youth. Its Charter and Its Mission', *The Superman Magazine* (January, 1931).

Hutchison, Graham Seton, 'The Paladin League of Youth. Mrs Grundy Exposed', *The Superman Magazine* (June, 1931).

Hutchison, Graham Seton, 'Out of the Blue', *The Superman Magazine* (July, 1931).

Hutchison, Graham Seton, 'Nakedness', *The Superman Magazine* (September, 1931).

Hutchison, Graham Seton, *Footslogger. An Autobiography* (London: Hutchinson & Co, 1931).

Hutchison, Graham Seton, *Warrior* (London: Hutchinson & Co, 1932).

Hutchison, Graham Seton, *Meteor* (London: Hutchinson & Co, 1933).

Hutchison, Graham Seton, *Challenge* (London: Hutchinson & Co, 1934).

Hutchison, Graham Seton, *Pilgrimage* (London: Rich & Cowan Ltd, 1935).

Hutchison, Graham Seton, 'Man and Mechanics. Training a Soldier', *Army Quarterly*, XXXV/2 (1938).

Hutchison, Graham Seton, *Machine Guns. Their History and Tactical Employment. (Being also a History of the Machine Gun Corps, 1916–1922)* (London: Macmillan & Co., 1938).

Hutchison, Graham Seton, *The V Plan* (London: Eyre and Spottiswoode, 1941).

Imperial War Graves Commission, *Annual Report, 1920–21* (London: HMSO, 1921).

Ingram, Arthur, *Rebuilding the Walls* (London: Darton & Co, 1922).

IWM, *First IWM Exhibition at Crystal Palace*, Catalogue (London: 1920).

Jagger, C. S., *Modelling and Sculpture in the Making* (London: The Studio. 'How to Do it Series', 1933).

Jones, Ernest, 'War and Individual Psychology', *Sociological Review* (London, 1915).

Kenyon, Frederic, 'Museums in Modern Time', *Museums Journal*, 21/2 (August, 1921).

Kernot, C. F., *British Public Schools War Memorials* (London: Roberts & Newton, 1927).

Krafft-Ebing, Richard von, *Psychopathia Sexualis. With Especial Reference to the Antipathetic Sexual Instinct* (London: Mayflower-Dell, 1965 [1886]).

Lake, Chas, 'My Experience as a Volunteer Engine-Man on the Great Western Railway During the Strike', *The Railway Magazine*, 269 (November, 1919).

Lansbury, George, 'The Class War', *Daily Herald* (4 October, 1919).

Le Bon, Gustave, *The Crowd. A Study of the Popular Mind* (London: Ernest Benn, 1930 [1896]).

Legge, R. F. (Major), *Mainly About Discipline* (London: Gale & Polden Ltd, 1914).

Leverhulme Lord, *Reconstruction after the War* (Port Sunlight: Lever Brothers Ltd, 1919).

Lewis, Wyndham, *Blasting and Bombardiering. An Autobiography (1914–1926)* (London: John Calder, 1937).

Lloyd George, David, *Peace and Retrenchment. The Prime Minister's Call to the Nation,* London: W. H. Smith, 1919).

Longstaff, F. V. and Atteridge, A., *The Book of the Machine Gun* (London: Hugh Press Ltd, 1917).

Lord Montagu of Beaulieu, 'On the Foot-plate', *The Nineteenth Century and After*, Vol. LXXXVI (November, 1919).

Lord Sydenham, 'The Mental Effects of the War and their Lessons in Regard to Medical and Social Reconstruction – Discussion', *Journal of the Royal Society of Arts*, LXVI (1918).

Lutyens, Robert, *Sir Edwin Lutyens. An Appreciation in Perspective – By His Son* (London: Country Life, 1942).

MacCurdy, John, *The Psychology of War* (London: William Heinemann, 1917).

Macpherson, W. G., Herringham, W. P., Elliott, T. R. (eds), *History of the Great War, Medical Services. Diseases of the War* (London: 1923).

Madeley, Charles, 'Local War Museums', *Museums Journal*, 18/4 (October, 1918).

Marx, K. and Engels, F., *The Communist Manifesto* (London: Lawrence & Wishart, 1933).

Masterman, Charles, *England After the War. A Study* (London: Hodder & Stoughton, 1922).

Maurice, Major General, 'Esprit de Corps – Its True Basis', *Machine Gun Corps Magazine*, Vol. II (October, 1918).

Maxwell, W. N., *A Psychological Retrospect of the Great War* (London: George Allen & Unwin, 1923).

McDougall, William, *An Introduction to Social Psychology* (London: Methuen, 1919 [1908]).

McDougall, William, *The Group Mind, A Sketch of the Principles of Collective Psychology with some Attempt to Apply them to the Interpretation of National Life and Character* (Cambridge: Cambridge University Press, 1926 [1920]).

McKenzie, Robert Tait, *Reclaiming the Maimed. A Handbook of Physical Therapy* (New York: Macmillan Co, 1918).

Ministry of Reconstruction, *The Aims of Reconstruction* (London: HMSO, 1918).

Ministry of Reconstruction, *The Demobilisation and Resettlement of the Army* (London: HMSO, 1918).

Ministry of Reconstruction, *Art and Industry* (London: HMSO, 1919).

Ministry of Reconstruction, *The Mission of the British Army* (London: HMSO, 1919).

Morris, A., 'Esprit de Corps', *Machine Gun Corps Magazine*, Vol. I (February, 1917).

Mottram, R. H., *Ten Years Ago. Armistice and Other Memories* (London: Chatto and Windus, 1928).

Mottram, R. H., *Through the Menin Gate* (London: Chatto & Windus, 1932).

Mottram, R. H., *Journey to the Western Front. Twenty Years After* (London: G. Bell & Sons, 1936).

Mottram, R. H., 'A Personal Record' in Mottram, R. H., Easton, John, Partridge, Eric, *Three Personal Records of the War* (London: Scholartis Press, 1929).

Myers, Charles, *Shell shock in France, 1914–18: Based on a War Diary* (Cambridge: Cambridge University Press, 1940).

National Council of Labour Colleges, *History, Report and Directory* (London: 1924).

Nordau, Max, *Degeneration* (Lincoln: University of Nebraska, 1993 [1895]).

Parkes, Kineton, *Sculpture of Today* (London: Chapham and Hall, 1921).

Plebs Textbook Committee, *An Outline of Psychology* (London: Plebs League, 1921).

Pratt, Edwin, *War Record of the London and North Western Railway* (London: Selwyn & Bount, 1922).

Procter, T. H., 'The Motives of the Soldier', *International Journal of Ethics*, XXXI (October, 1920).

Rivers, W. H. R., *Kinship and Social Organisation* (London: Constable & Co, 1914).

Rivers, W. H. R., 'The Repression of War Experience', *Lancet*, 2 (February, 1918).

Rivers, W. H. R, 'War Neurosis and Military Training', *Mental Hygiene*, II/4 (1918).

Rivers, W. H. R., *Conflict and Dream* (London: Kegan Paul, 1923).

Royal Artillery Commemoration Fund, *The Royal Artillery War Commemoration Book. A Pilgrimage Record Written and Illustrated for the Most Part by Artillery Men While Serving in Line During the Great War* (London: Bell & Sons, 1920).

Royal Society of British Sculptors, *Modern British Sculpture* (London: Academy, 1921).

Saleeby, C. W., *Worry: The Disease of the Age* (London: Cassell, 1907).

Seton, Graham, *The W Plan* (London: Butterworth, 1929).

Shaw, Norman, 'The Home and Its Dwelling Rooms', in Sparrow, Shaw (ed.), *The British Home of Today. A Book of Modern Domestic Architecture and the Applied Arts* (London: Hodder & Stoughton, 1904).

Shaw, Norman, 'The Modern Home', in Sparrow, Shaw (ed.), *The British Home of Today. A Book of Modern Domestic Architecture and the Applied Arts* (London: Hodder & Stoughton, 1904).

Shirley, W., *Morale. The Most Important Factor in War* (London: Sifton, Praed & Co., 1916).

Skinner, S. 'Reminiscences of the Nine Days', *The Railway Review* (10 October, 1919).

Southard, Elmer, *Shell shock and other Neuropsychiatric Problems: Presented in Five Hundred and Eighty-Nine Case Histories from the War Literature 1914–18* (Boston: W. M. Leonard, 1919).

Thomson, G. C., *An Address to Recruits on The Duties of a Soldier* (London: Gale & Polden, 1917).

Thomson, G. C., *The Spirit of Discipline* (London: Gale & Polden, 1918).

Toft, Albert, *Modelling and Sculpture. A Full Account of the Various Methods and Processes Employed in These Arts* (London: Seeley & Co, 1911).

Victoria & Albert Museum, *Inscriptions Suggested for War Memorials* (London: HMSO, 1919).

W. R. B. 'A National War Museum', *Museums Journal*, 16/11 (May, 1917).

War Office, *Training and Manoeuvre Regulations* (London: HMSO, 1913).

War Office, *Field Artillery Training* (London: HMSO, 1914).

War Office, *Bayonet Fighting. Instruction with Service Rifle and Bayonet* (London: HMSO, 1915).

War Office, *Platoon Training* (London: HMSO, 1918).

War Office, *Filed Service Regulations. Vol II. Operations* (London: HMSO, 1920).

War Office, *Small Arms Training Vol. I* (London: HMSO, 1924).

Warren E., 'War Memorials', *Architectural Review*, Vol. 38 (November, 1915).

Warren E., *War Shrines* (London: Civic Arts Association, 1917).

Warren E., *War Memorials* (London: Civic Arts Association, 1919).

Weaver, Lawrence, *House and Gardens by Sir Edwin Lutyens RA* (London: Country Life, 1925 [1913]).

Weaver, Lawrence, *Memorials and Monuments. Old and New: Two Hundred Subjects Chosen from Seven Countries* (London: Country Life, 1915).

Weaver, Lawrence, *The Scottish National War Memorial. A Record and Appreciation* (London: Country Life, 1927).

Willson, Beckles, *In the Ypres Salient. The Story of a Fortnight's Canadian Fighting. June 2–16, 1916* (London: Simpkin, Marshall, Hamilton Kent & Co., 1916).

Secondary Sources

Ackrell, P. G., *My Life in the Machine Gun Corps* (Devon: Arthur Stockwell Ltd, 1966).

Anderson, Benedict, *Imagined Communities. Reflections on the Origins and Spread of Nationalism* (London: Verso, 1994).

Anthias, F., 'Ethnicity and Class in Cyprus', *Race and Class*, 25 (1983), pp. 59–76.

Antze, Paul and Lambek, Michael (eds), *Tense Past. Cultural Essays in Trauma and Memory* (London: Routledge, 1996).

Anzieu, Didier, *The Skin Ego* (New Haven: Yale University Press, 1989).

Ashplant, T. G., Dawson, G. and Roper, M. (eds), *The Politics of War Memory and Commemoration* (London: Routledge, 2001).

Aslet, Clive, *The Last Country Houses* (London: Yale University Press, 1982).

Babington, Anthony, *Shell-Shock: A History of the Changing Attitudes to War Neurosis* (London: Leo Cooper, 1997).

Bagwell, Philip, *The Railwaymen. The History of the National Union of Railwaymen* (London: George Allen & Unwin, 1963).

Bal, Mieke, *Double Exposure the Subject of Cultural Analysis* (London: Routledge, 1996).

Bal, Mieke, 'Telling Objects: A Narrative Perspective on Collecting', in Elsner, J. and Cardinal, R. (eds), *The Cultures of Collecting* (London: Reaktion, 1994).

Bal, M., Crewe, J., Spitzer, L. (eds), *Acts of Memory. Cultural Recall in the Present* (New England: Dartmouth College, 1999).

Barker, Pat, *Regeneration* (London: Viking, 1991).

Barthes, Roland, *Mythologies* (London: Vintage, 1993).

Beattie, Susan, *The New Sculpture* (New Haven and London: Yale University Press, 1983).

Bennett, Tony, 'The Exhibitionary Complex', in Greenberg, R., Ferguson, B., Nairne, S. (eds), *Thinking About Exhibitions* (London: Routledge, 1996).

Bentley, Gilbert, *British Social Policy, 1914–1939* (London: Batsford, 1970).

Bermingham, Ann, *Landscape and Ideology: The English Rustic Tradition, 1740–1860* (Berkeley: University of California Press, 1987).

Bersani, Leo, *Homos* (Cambridge, Massachusetts: Harvard University Press, 1995).

Bland, Lucy, *Banishing the Beast. English Feminism and Sexual Morality 1885–1914* (London: Penguin, 1995).

Bland, Lucy, 'Trial by Sexology? Maud Allan, Salome and the "Cult of the Clitoris" Case', in Bland, Lucy and Doan, Laura (eds), *Sexology in Culture. Labelling Bodies and Desires* (Oxford: Polity, 1998).

Bogacz, Ted, 'War Neurosis and Cultural Change in England, 1914–22: The Work of the War Office Committee of Enquiry into "Shell-Shock"', *Journal of Contemporary History*, 24/2 (1989), 227–256.

Bourdieu, Pierre, *Distinction: A Social Critique of the Judgment of Taste* (Cambridge Mass.: Harvard University Press, 1984).

Bourke, Joanna, *Working-Class Cultures in Britain, 1890–1960* (London: Routledge, 1994).

Bourke, Joanna, *Dismembering the Male. Men's Bodies, Britain and the Great War* (London: Reaktion, 1996).

Bourke, Joanna, *An Intimate History of Killing. Face-to-Face Killing in Twentieth Century Warfare* (London: Granta Books, 1999).

Boxwell, David, 'The Follies of War: Cross-Dressing and Popular Theatre on the British Front Lines, 1914–18', *Modernism/Modernity*, 9/1 (2002), 1–20.

Bracco, Rosa Maria, *Merchants of Hope. British Middlebrow Writers and the First World War* (Oxford: Berg, 1992).

Branson, Noreen, *Britain in the Nineteen Twenties* (London: Weidenfield & Nicolson, 1975).

Brod, Harry and Kaufman, Michael (eds), *Theorising Masculinities* (London: Sage, 1994).

Brower, Brady M., 'Strategic Remembering. The Boundary Politics of Mourning in Post-Great War France', *Rethinking History*, 1/1 (1997), 21–33.

Bryant, Rebecca, *Imaging the Modern. The Cultures of Nationalism in Cyprus* (London: I. B. Tauris, 2004).

Burstein, Jessica, 'Warship Segments: Lewis, Prosthesis, Fascism', *Modernism/Modernity*, 4/2 (1997), 139–164.

Burwick, Frederick, *The Crisis of Modernism* (Cambridge: Cambridge University Press, 1992).

Bushaway, Bob, 'Name Upon Name: The Great War and Remembrance', in Porter, R. (ed.), *Myths of the English* (Oxford: Polity Press, 1992).

Butler, Judith, 'Review Essay: Spirit in Ashes', *History and Theory*, 27/1 (1988).

Butler, Judith, *Gender Trouble: Feminism and the Subversion of Identity* (London: Routledge, 1990).

Butler, Judith, 'Contingent Foundations: Feminism and the Question of Post-modernism', in Butler, J. and Scott, J. (eds), *Feminists Theorise the Political* (London: Routledge, 1992).

Butler, Judith, *Bodies that Matter: On the Discursive Limits of 'Sex'* (London: Routledge, 1993).

Butler, Judith, 'Melancholy Gender/Refused Identification', in Berger, M. *et al.* (eds), *Constructing Masculinity* (London: Routledge, 1995).

Butler, Judith, *Excitable Speech. A Politics of the Performative* (London: Routledge, 1997).

Butler, Judith, *The Psychic Life of Power. Theories in Subjection* (Stanford: Stanford University Press, 1997).

Caesar, Adrian, *Taking it Like A Man. Suffering, Sexuality and the War Poets* (Manchester: Manchester University Press, 1993).

Cannadine, David, 'War and Death, Grief and Mourning in Modern Britain', in Whaley, J. (ed.), *Mirrors of Mortality. Studies in the Social History of Death* (London: Europa Publications Ltd, 1981).

Casey, Edward, *Remembering. A Phenomenological Study* (Indianapolis: Indiana University Press, 1987).

Cassia, Paul, 'Martyrdom and Witnessing: Violence, Terror and Recollection in Cyprus', *Terrorism and Political Violence*, 11/1 (1999), 22–54.

Castells, Manuel, *The Power of Identity* (Oxford: Blackwell, 1997).

Chamberlin, Edward and Gilman, Sander (eds), *Degeneration. The Dark Side of Progress* (New York: Columbia University Press, 1985).

Chambers, Emma, *Henry Tonks: Art and Surgery*, Exhibition Catalogue (London: University College, 2002).

Compton, Ann (ed.), *Charles Sargeant Jagger. War and Peace Sculpture* (London: Imperial War Museum, 1985).

Condell, Diana, *The Imperial War Museum 1917–1920. A Study of the Institution and Its Presentation of the First World War*, Unpublished MPhil Thesis (London: Imperial War Musem: 1985).

Connell, R. W., *Masculinities* (Oxford: Polity, 1995).

Connell, R. W., 'The Social Organisation of Masculinity', in Whitehead, S. and Barrett, F. (eds), *The Masculinities Reader* (Oxford: Polity, 2001).

Connerton, Paul, *How Societies Remember* (Cambridge: Cambridge University Press, 1989).

Coombes, Annie E., 'Ethnography and the Formation of National and Cultural Identities', in Hiller, Susan (ed.), *The Myth of Primitivism. Perspectives on Art* (London: Routledge, 1991).

Coombes, Annie E., *Reinventing Africa. Museums, Material Culture and Popular Imagination in Late Victorian and Edwardian England* (New Haven and London: Yale University Press, 1994).

Coombes, Annie E., 'The Recalcitrant Object: Culture Contact and the Question of Hybridity', in Barker, F., Hulme, P., Iversen, M. (eds), *Colonial Discourse/Postcolonial Theory* (Manchester: Manchester University Press, 1994).

Coombes, Annie E., 'The Art of Memory', *Third Text* (Summer, 2000).

Coombes, Annie E., 'Translating the Past: Apartheid Monuments in Post-Apartheid South Africa', in Brah, A., and Coombes, A. E. (eds), *Hybridity and Its Discontents. Politics, Science, Culture* (London: Routledge, 2000).

Cork, Richard, *A Bitter Truth: Avant Garde Art and the Great War* (New Haven and London: Yale University Press, 1994).

Cornforth, John, 'Lutyens and Country Life', in *Lutyens. The Work of the English Architect Sir Edwin Lutyens (1869–1944)*, Exhibition Catalogue, Hayward Gallery (London: Arts Council of Great Britain, 1981).

Craik, William, *The Central Labour College, 1909–29. A Chapter in the History of Adult Working Class Education* (London: Lawrence & Wishart, 1964).

Crane, Susan (ed.), *Museums and Memory* (Stanford: Stanford University Press, 2000).

Crellin, Sarah, 'Hollow Men: Francis Derwent Wood's Masks and Memorials, 1915–1925', *The Sculpture Journal*, Vol. 6 (2001), 75–88.

Crook, Michael, *The Evolution of the Victoria Cross. A Study in Administrative History* (Kent: Midas Books, 1975).

Curtis, Penelope, *Sculpture 1900–1945* (Oxford: Oxford University Press, 1999).

Das, Santanu, '"Kiss me, Hardy": Intimacy, Gender and Gesture in World War I Trench Literature', *Modernism/Modernity*, 9/1 (2002), 51–74.

Davidoff, Leonore, *Worlds Between. Historical Perspectives on Gender and Class* (Oxford: Polity, 1995).

Davidoff, Leonore and Hall, Catherine, *Family Fortunes: Men and Women of the English Middle Class, 1780–1850* (London: Hutchinson, 1987).

Dawson, Graham, *Soldier Heroes. British Adventure, Empire and the Imagining of Masculinities* (London: Routledge, 1994).

Debord, Guy, *The Society of Spectacle* (New York: Zone Books, 1994).

Dollimore, Jonathan, *Sex, Literature and Censorship* (Oxford: Polity, 2001).

Douglas, Mary, *Purity and Danger. An Analysis of Concepts of Pollution and Taboo* (London: Routledge, 2002 [1996]).

Duncan, Carol, *The Aesthetics of Power. Essays in Critical Art History* (Cambridge: Cambridge University Press, 1993).

Duncan, Carol, 'The Art Museum as Ritual', in Preziosi, D. (ed.), *The Art of Art History: A Critical Anthology* (Oxford: Oxford University Press, 1998).

Eagleton, Terry, *The Ideology of the Aesthetic* (Oxford: Blackwell Publishing, 1990).

Edwards, Brian, *Goddards. Sir Edwin Lutyens* (London: Phaidon, 1996).

Edwards, Deborah, 'Race, Death & Gender in the Anzac Memorial', in Bulbeck, S. (ed.), *Occasional Paper No. 5*, Institute for Cultural Policy Studies (Queensland: Griffith University, 1988).

Eksteins, Modris, *Rites of Spring. The Great War and the Birth of the Modern Age* (Oxford: Papermac, 2000 [1989]).

Ellis, John, *The Social History of the Machine Gun* (Baltimore: Johns Hopkins University Press, 1986).

Elsner, John and Cardinal, Roger (eds), *The Cultures of Collecting* (London: Reaktion, 1994).

Englander, David, 'Troops and Trade Unions in 1919', *History Today*, 37 (1987), 8–13.

Englander, David, 'The National Union of Ex-Servicemen and the Labour Movement, 1918–1920', *History*, 76/246 (1991), 24–42.

Evans, Jessica and Hall, Stuart (eds), *Visual Culture. The Reader* (London: Sage, 1999).

Fedorowich, Kent, *Unfit for Heroes. Reconstruction and Soldier Settlement in the Empire Between the Wars* (Manchester: Manchester University Press, 1995).

Feldman, David, *Englishmen and Jews: Social Relations and Political Culture, 1840–1914* (New Haven and London: Yale University Press, 1994).

Felski, Rita, 'Introduction', in Bland, Lucy and Doan, Laura (eds), *Sexology in Culture. Labelling Bodies and Desires* (Oxford: Polity, 1998).

Fentress, James and Wickham, Chris, *Social Memory* (Oxford: Blackwell, 1992).

Ferguson, Niall, *The Pity of War* (London: Penguin, 1998).

Forty, Adrian and Kuchler, Susanne (eds), *The Art of Forgetting* (Oxford: Berg, 1999).

Foster, Hal, 'Armour Fou', *October*, 56 (1991), 64–97.

Foster, Hal, 'Prosthetic Gods', *Modernism/Modernity*, 4/2 (1997), 5–38.

Foucault, Michel, *The History of Sexuality. An Introduction. Vol. I* (London: Penguin, 1990 [1976]).

Foucault, Michel, *The Use of Pleasure: History of Sexuality. Vol. II* (London: Penguin Books, 1990 [1976]).

Foucault, Michel, *Discipline and Punish. The Birth of the Prison* (London: Penguin, 1991 [1975]).

Fuss, Diana (ed.), *Inside/Out. Lesbian Theories, Gay Theories* (London: Routledge, 1991).

Fussell, Paul, *The Great War and Modern Memory* (Oxford: Oxford University Press, 1975).

Garber, Marjorie, *Symptoms of Culture* (London: Penguin, 1999).

Gilbert, Sandra, 'Soldier's Heart: Literary Men, Literary Women, and the Great War', in Higonet, Margaret *et al.*, *Behind the Lines. Gender and the Two World Wars* (New Haven and London: Yale University Press, 1987).

Gillis, John (ed.), *Commemorations* (Princeton: Princeton University Press, 1994).

Gilman, Sander, *Disease and Representation. Images of Illness from Madness to AIDS* (Ithaca and London: Cornell University Press, 1989).

Gilman, Sander, *Making the Body Beautiful: A Cultural History of Aesthetic Surgery* (Princeton: Princeton University Press, 1999).

Glaves-Smith, John, 'Realism and Propaganda in the Work of Charles Sargeant Jagger and their Relationship to Artistic Tradition', in Compton, Ann (ed.), *Charles Sargeant Jagger. War and Peace Sculpture* (London: Imperial War Museum, 1985).

Gorman, John, *Banner Bright. An Illustrated History of the Banner of the British Trade Union Movement* (London: Allen Lane, 1973).

Greenberg, Allan, 'Lutyens's Cenotaph', *Journal of the Society of Architectural Historians*, XLVIII (March, 1989), 5–23.

Gregory, Adrian, *The Silence of Memory. Armistice Day 1919–1946* (Oxford: Berg, 1994).

Gronberg, Tag, *Designs on Modernity. Exhibiting the City in 1920s Paris* (Manchester: Manchester University Press, 1998).

Grosz, Elizabth, in Wright, Elizabeth (ed.), *Feminism and Psychoanalysis. A Critical Dictionary* (Oxford: Blackwell, 1992).

Hall, Donald (ed.), *Muscular Christianity: Embodying the Victorian Age* (Cambridge: Cambridge University Press, 1994).

Hall, Stewart, 'Cultural Identity and Diaspora', in Rutherford, J. (ed.), *Identity: Community, Culture, Difference* (London: Lawrence & Wishart, 1990).

Hamacher, Werner, 'Afformative, Strike. Benjamin's 'Critique of Violence', in Benjamin, Andrew and Osborne, Peter (eds), *Walter Benjamin's Philosophy. Destruction & Experience* (London: Clinamon Press, 2000).

Haraway, Donna, 'Deanimations: Maps and Portraits of Life Itself', in Brah, A., and Coombes, A. E. (eds), *Hybridity and Its Discontents. Politics, Science, Culture* (London: Routledge, 2000).

Haste, Cate, *Keep the Home Fires Burning: Propaganda in the First World War* (London: Allen Lane, 1977).

Hatt, Michael, 'Muscles, Morals, Mind: The Male Body in Thomas Eakins' *Salutat*', in Adler, K. and Pointon, M. (eds), *The Body Imaged. The Human Form and Visual Culture since the Renaissance* (Cambridge: Cambridge University Press, 1993).

Hatt, Michael, 'Physical Culture: The Male Nude and Sculpture in Late Victorian Britain', in Prettejohn, E. (ed.), *After the Pre-Raphaelites. Art and Aestheticism in Victorian England* (Manchester: Manchester University Press, 1999).

Hatt, Michael, 'Race, Ritual and Responsibility: Performativity and the Southern Lynching', in Jones, A. and Stephenson, A. (eds), *Performing the Body/Performing the Text* (London: Routledge, 1999).

Haverty Rugg, Linda, *Picturing Ourselves. Photography and Autobiography* (Chicago: University of Chicago Press, 1997).

Hawkins, Peter, 'Naming Names. The Art of Memory and NAMES Project AIDS Quilt', in Greenberg, R., Ferguson, B., Nairne, S. (eds), *Thinking About Exhibitions* (London: Routledge, 1996).

Hebdige, Dick, 'The Impossible Object: Towards a Sociology of the Sublime', *New Formations*, 1 (1987), 47–76.

Hewitt, Andrew, *Political Inversions. Homosexuality, Fascism and the Modernist Imaginary* (Stanford: Stanford University Press, 1996).

Higonnet, M., Jenson, J., Michel, S., Collins Weitz, M. (eds), *Behind the Lines. Gender and the Two World Wars* (New Haven and London: Yale University Press, 1987).

Higonnet, Margaret, 'Authenticity and Art in Trauma Narratives of World War I', *Modernism/Modernity*, 9/1 (2002), 91–107.

Higson, Andrew, *Waving the Flag: Constructing a National Cinema in Britain* (Oxford: Clarendon Press, 1995).

Hirsch, Marianne, 'Projected Memory: Holocaust Photographs in Personal and Public Fantasy', in Bal, M., Crewe, J. and Spitzer, L. (eds), *Acts of Memory. Cultural Recall in the Present* (New England: Dartmouth College, 1999).

Hobsbawm, Eric, *Industry and Empire* (London: Harmondsworth, 1969).

Hobsbawm, Eric, *The Age of Capital 1848–1875* (London: Abacus, 1995).

Hobsbawm, Eric, *The Age of Empire. 1875–1914* (London: Abacus 1997).

Hobsbawm, E. and Ranger, T. (eds), *The Invention of Tradition* (Cambridge: Cambridge University Press, 2000).

Holland, Patricia, '"Sweet is to Scan …" Personal Photographs and Popular Photography', in Wells, L. (ed.), *Photography: A Critical Introduction* (London: Routledge, 2001)

Hondagneu-Sotelo, P. and Messner, M., 'Gender Displays and Men's Power', in Brod, H. and Kaufman, M. (eds), *Theorising Masculinities* (London: Sage, 1994).

Howkins, Alun, 'The Rural World and Its Representation', Beckett, J. and Cherry, D. (eds), *The Edwardian Era* (London: Phaidon Press, 1987).

Huyssen, Andreas, *Twilight Memories. Marking Time in a Culture of Amnesia* (London: Routledge, 1995).

Huyssen, Andreas, *After The Great Divide: Modernism, Mass Culture and Postmodernism* (London: Macmillan, 1998).

Huyssen, Andreas, 'Monumental Seduction', in Bal, M., Crewe, J. and Spitzer, L. (eds), *Acts of Memory. Cultural Recall in the Present* (New England: Dartmouth College, 1999).

Hynes, Samuel, *The Edwardian Turn of Mind* (Princeton: Princeton University Press, 1968).

Hynes, Samuel, *A War Imagined. The First World War and English Culture* (London: Pimlico, 1990).

Inglis, Ken, 'War Memorials: Ten Questions for Historians', *Guerres Mondiales et Conflicts*, 42/167 (1992), 5–21.

Inglis, Ken, 'The Homecoming: The War Memorial Movement in Cambridge, England', *Journal of Contemporary History*, 27 (1992), 583–605.

Inglis, Ken, 'Entombing Unknown Soldiers: From London and Paris to Baghdad', *History and Memory*, 5/1 (1993), 7–31.

Jay, Martin, 'Against Consolation: Walter Benjamin and the Refusal to Mourn', in Winter, J. and Sivan, E. (eds), *War and Remembrance in the Twentieth Century* (Cambridge: Cambridge University Press, 1999).

Johnson, Geraldine, 'Sculpture, Photography, and the Politcs of Public Space. Serra's Tilted Arc and Lin'sVietnam Veteran's Memorial', in Johnson, G. (ed.), *Sculpture and Photography, Envisioning the Third Dimension* (Cambridge: Cambridge University Press, 1998).

Jordanova, Ludmilla, 'Objects of Knowledge: A Historical Perspective on Museums', in Vergo, P. (ed.), *The New Museology* (London: Reaktion, 1989).

Jordanova, Ludmilla, *Sexual Visions: Images of Gender in Science and Medicine between the Eighteenth and Twentieth Centuries* (London: Harvester, 1989).

Karp, Ivan, *Museums and Communities. The Politics of Public Culture* (Washington DC: Smithsonian Institution, 1992).

Kavanagh, Gaynor, *Museums and the First World War. A Social History* (Leicester: Leicester University Press, 1994).

Kavanagh, Gaynor, 'Museum as Memorial: The Origins of the Imperial War Museum', *Journal of Contemporary History*, 23/1 (1988), 77–97.

Kavanagh, Gaynor (ed.), *Making Histories, Making Memories* (Leicester: Leicester University Press, 1996).

Kaye, Richard, 'Losing his Religion. Saint Sebastian as Contemporary Gay Martyr', in Horne, P. and Lewis, R. (eds), *Outlooks. Lesbian and Gay Sexualities and Visual Culture* (London: Routledge, 1996).

Kent Kingsley, Susan, *Making Peace. The Reconstruction of Gender in Interwar Britain* (Princeton: Princeton University Press, 1993).

King, Alex, *Memorials of the Great War. The Symbolism and Politics of Remembrance* (Oxford: Berg, 1998).

King, Alex, 'Remembering and Forgetting in the Public Memorials of the Great War', in Forty, A. and Kuchler, S. (eds), *The Art of Forgetting* (Oxford: Berg, 1999).

Kozar, Andrew, *Tait McKenzie. The Sculptor of Athletes* (Tennessee: University of Tennessee Press, 1975).

Kristeva, Julia, *Powers of Horror. An Essay on Abjection* (New York: Columbia University Press, 1982).

Kristeva, Julia, 'Revolt Today?', in Kearny, R. and Cooley, M. (eds), *Questioning Ethics. Contemporary Debates in Philosophy* (London: Routledge, 1999).

LaCapra, Dominick, *Representing the Holocaust. History, Theory, Trauma* (Ithaca: Cornell University Press, 1994).

Laclau, Ernesto, 'Identity and Hegemony: The Role of Universality in the Constitution of Political Logics', in Butler, J., Laclau, E. and Zizek, S. (eds), *Contingency, Hegemony, Universality. Contemporary Dialogues on the Left* (London: Verso, 2000).

Laqueur, Thomas, 'Memory and Naming in the Great War', in Gillis, John (ed.), *Commemorations* (Princeton: Princeton University Press, 1994).

Laub, Dori, 'Truth and Testimony: The Process and Struggle', Caruth, C. (ed.), *Trauma. Explorations in Memory* (Baltimore: Johns Hopkins University Press, 1995).

Leed, Eric, *No Man's Land: Combat and Identity in World War I* (Cambridge: Cambridge University Press, 1979).

Leed, Eric, 'Fateful Memories: Industrialized War and Traumatic Neuroses', *Journal of Contemporary History*, 35/1 (2000), 85–100.

Leese, Peter, 'Problems Returning Home: The British Psychological Casualties of the Great War', *The Historical Journal*, 40/4 (1997), 1055–1067.

Libeskind, Daniel, *Daniel Libeskind: The Space Encounter* (London: Thames & Hudson, 2001).

Light, Alison, *Forever England. Femininity, Literature and Conservatism between the Wars* (London: Routledge, 1991).

Llewellyn, Nigel, *The Art of Death: Visual Culture in the English Death Ritual c.1500–c.1800* (London: Reaktion, 1991).

Lloyd, David, *Battlefield Tourism. Pilgrimage and the Commemoration of the Great War in Britain, Australia and Canada, 1919–1939* (Oxford: Berg, 1998).

Lodder, Christina, 'Lenin's Plan for Monumental Propaganda', in M. Cullene-Brown and B. Taylor (eds), *Art of the Soviets. Painting, Sculpture and Architecture in a One-Party State 1917–1992* (Manchester: Manchester University Press, 1993).

Lutyens, Mary, *Edwin Lutyens by his daughter Mary Lutyens* (London: John Murray, 1980).

Macdonald, Sharon (ed.), *The Politics of Display. Museums, Science and Culture* (London: Routledge, 1998).

Macdonald, Sharon and Fyfe, G. (eds), *Theorising Museums. Representing Identity and Diversity in a Changing World* (Oxford: Blackwell, 1996).

MacKenzie, John, *Propaganda and Empire. The Manipulation of British Public Opinion, 1880–1960*, (Manchester: Manchester University Press, 1985).

MacKenzie, John, 'The Imperial Pioneer and Hunter and the British Masculine Stereotype in Late Victorian and Edwardian Times', in Mangan, J. A. and Walvin, J. (eds), *Manliness and Morality. Middle Class Masculinity in Britain and America* (Manchester: Manchester University Press, 1987).

Malvern, Sue, *Modern Art, Britain and the Great War: Witnessing, Testimony and Remembrance* (New Haven and London, Yale University Press, 2004).

Malvern, Sue, 'Things to Come. Eric Kennington's "War God"', *Henry Moore Institute Essays on Sculpture*, No.33 (Leeds, 2001).

Malvern, Sue, 'War, Memory and Museums: Art and Artefacts in the Imperial War Museum', *History Workshop Journal*, 49 (2000), 177–203.

Mangan, J. A., *Athleticism in the Victorian and Edwardian Public School: the Emergence and Consolidation of an Educational Ideology* (Cambridge: Cambridge University Press, 1981).

Mangan, J.A. and Walvin, J. (eds), *Manliness and Morality. Middle Class Masculinity in Britain and America* (Manchester: Manchester University Press, 1987).

Mansfield, Nick, 'Class Conflict and Village War Memorials, 1914–24', *Rural History*, 6/1 (1995), 67–87.

Marcus, Laura, *Auto/biographical Discourses. Theory, Criticism, Practice* (Manchester: Manchester University Press, 1994).

Marwick, Arthur, *The Deluge: British Society and the First World War* (London: Pelican, 1967).

Marwick, Arthur, 'Two Total Wars, the Cold War and Postmodernism: the Arts in Europe, 1910–2000', in Emsley, C. (ed.), *War, Culture and Memory* (Milton Keynes: Open University Press, 2003).

Mavratsas, V., 'The ideological contest between Greek-Cypriot nationalism and Cypriotism 1974–1995: Politics, Social Memory and Identity', *Ethnic and Racial Studies*, 20/4 (1997), 713–37.

McClelland, Keith, 'Masculinity and the Representative Artisan in Britain, 1850–80', in Roper, M. and Tosh, J. (eds), *Manful Assertions. Masculinities in Britain since 1800* (London: Routledge, 1991).

McKernan, Michael, *Here is their Spirit. A History of the Australian War Memorial* (Queensland: University of Queensland Press, 1991).

McKibbin, Ross, *The Ideologies of Class. Social Relations in Britain 1880–1950* (Oxford: Clarendon Press, 1990).

McKibbin, Ross, *Classes and Cultures. England 1918–1951* (Oxford: Oxford University Press, 1998).

McLaren, Angus, *The Trials of Masculinity. Policing Sexual Boundaries, 1870–1930* (Chicago: University of Chicago Press, 1997).

Medd, Jodie, '"The Cult of the Clitoris": Anatomy of a National Scandal', *Modernism/Modernity*, 9 /1 (2002), 21–49.

Michalski, Sergiusz, *Public Monuments. Art in Political Bondage 1870–1997* (London: Reaktion, 1998).

Miller, Jonathan, 'The Dog Beneath the Skin', *The Listener* (20 July, 1972).

Mirzoeff, Nicholas, *Watching Babylon. The War in Iraq and Global Visual Culture* (London: Routledge, 2005).

Mitchell, Claudine, 'Facing Horror: Women's Work, Sculptural Practice, and the Great War', in Mainz, V. and Pollock, G. (eds), *Work in Modern Times. Visual Mediations and Social Processes* (Aldershot: Ashgate, 2000).

Mitchell, Juliet, *Mad Men and Medusas. Reclaiming Hysteria and the Effects of Sibling Relations on the Human Condition* (London: Penguin, 2000).

Morgan, David, 'Theatres of War: Combat, the Military and Masculinities', in Brod, H. and Kaufman, M. (eds), *Theorising Masculinities* (London: Sage, 1994).

Morgan, Kenneth, *Consensus and Disunity. The Lloyd George Coalition Government 1918–1922* (Oxford: Clarendon Press, 1979).

Moriarty, Catherine, 'The Absent Dead and Figurative First World War Memorials', *Transactions of the Ancient Monument Society*, 39 (1995), 7–40.

Moriarty, Catherine, *Narrative and the Absent Body: The Mechanics of Meaning in First World War Memorials*, D.Phil. Thesis (University of Sussex, 1995).

Moriarty, Catherine, 'Private Grief and Public Remembrance: British First World War Memorials', in Evans, M. and Lunn, Ken (eds), *War and Memory in the Twentieth Century* (Oxford: Berg, 1997).

Moriarty, Catherine, 'The Material Culture of Great War Remembrance', *Journal of Contemporary History*, 34 /4 (1999), 653–62.

Mort, Frank, *Dangerous Sexualities: Medico-moral Politics in England since 1830* (London: Routledge, 2000).

Mosse, George, *Nationalism and Sexuality. Respectability and Abnormal Sexuality in Modern Europe* (Madison: University of Wisconsin Press, 1988).

Mosse, George, *Fallen Soldiers. Reshaping the Memory of the World Wars* (Oxford: Oxford University Press, 1990).

Mosse, George, *The Image of Man. The Creation of Modern Masculinity* (Oxford: Oxford University Press, 1996).

Mosse, George, 'Shell-shock as a Social Disease', *Journal of Contemporary History*, 35/1 (2000), 101–108.

Mowat, Charles, *Britain Between the Wars 1918–1940* (London: University Paperbacks, 1968).

Mulvey, Laura, *Visual and Other Pleasures* (London: Macmillan, 1989).

Nead, Lynda, *The Female Nude. Art, Obscenity and Sexuality* (London: Routledge, 1992).

Nora, Pierre, 'Between Memory and History: *Les Lieux de Mémoire*', *Representations*, 26 (1989), 7–25.

Nye, Robert, *The Origins of Crowd Psychology. Gustave Le Bon and the Crisis of Mass Democracy in the Third Republic* (London: Sage, 1975).

Nye, Robert, *Masculinity and Male Codes of Honour in Modern France* (Oxford: Oxford University Press, 1993).

Oosterhuis, Harry, 'Richard von Krafft-Ebing's "Step-Children of Nature". Psychiatry and the Making of Homosexual Identity', in Rosario, Vernon (ed.), *Science and Homosexualities* (London: Routledge, 1997).

Oosterhuis, Harry and Kennedy, Hubert (eds), *Homosexuality and Male Bonding in Pre-Nazi Germany. The Youth Movement, the Gay Movement and Male Bonding Before Hitler's Rise* (New York: Haworth Press, 1991).

Oram, Gerard, *Worthless Men. Race, Eugenics and the Death Penalty in the British Army During the First World War* (London: Francis Boutle Publishers, 1998).

Panayiotopoulos, P., 'The Emergent Post-colonial State in Cyprus', *Commonwealth and Comparative Politics*, 37/1 (1999), 31–55.

Papadakis, Yiannis, 'The National Struggle Museums of a Divided City', *Ethnic and Racial Studies*, 17/3 (1994), 400–19.

Parker, A., Russo, M., Sommer, D. and Yaeger, P. (eds), *Nationalisms and Sexuality* (London: Routledge, 1992).

Penny, Nicholas, 'English Sculpture and the First World War', *Oxford Art Journal*, 4/2 (1981), 36–42.

Peters Corbett, David, *The Modernity of English Art, 1914–1930* (Manchester: Manchester University Press, 1997).

Peters Corbett, David and Perry, Lara (eds), *English Art 1860–1914. Modernities and Identities* (Manchester: Manchester University Press, 2000).

Pick, Daniel, *Faces of Degeneration* (Cambridge: Cambridge University Press, 1989).

Pick, Daniel, *War Machine. The Rationalisation of Slaughter in the Modern Age* (New Haven and London: Yale University Press, 1993).

Porter, Roy (ed.), *Myths of the English* (Oxford: Polity, 1992).

Potts, Alex, 'Male Phantasy and Modern Sculpture', *Oxford Art Journal*, 15/2 (1992), 38–48.

Potts, Alex, '"Constable Country" Between the Wars', in Raphael, Samuel (ed.), *Patriotism: The Making and the Unmaking of British National Identity. Vol. 3, National Fictions* (London: Routledge, 1989).

Prettejohn, Elizabeth, *After the Pre-Raphaelites. Art and Aestheticism in Victorian England* (Manchester: Manchester University Press, 1999).

Radstone, Susannah, *Memory and Methodology* (Oxford: Berg, 2000).

Rappaport, Roy, 'Ritual Sanctity and Cybernetics', *American Anthropologist*, 73/1 (1971), 59–76.

Rappaport, Roy, 'Concluding Comments on Ritual and Reflexivity', *Semiotica*, 30(1/2) (1980), 181–93.

Reeves, Nicholas, *The Power of Film Propaganda. Myth or Reality?* (London: Cassell, 1999).

Richards, Jeffrey, '"Passing the love of women": Manly Love and Victorian Society', in Mangan, J. A. and Walvin, J. (eds), *Manliness and Morality. Middle Class Masculinity in Britain and America* (Manchester: Manchester University Press, 1987).

Ricoeur, Paul, 'Memory and Forgetting', in Kearney, Richard and Dooley, Mark (eds), *Questioning Ethics. Contemporary Debates in Philosophy* (London: Routledge, 1999).

Roberts, Julian, 'The Aesthetics of Conflict', *New Formations*, 20/2 (1993), 157–66.

Rogoff, Irit and Sherman, Daniel (eds), *Museum Culture. Histories, Discourses, Spectacles* (London: Routledge, 1994).

Roper, Michael, 'Re-remembering the Soldier Hero: the Psychic and Social Construction of Memory in Personal Narratives of the Great War', *History Workshop Journal*, 50 (2000), 181–204.

Roper, Michael and Tosh, John (eds), *Manful Assertions. Masculinities in Britain since 1800* (London: Routledge, 1991).

Rosenthal, Michael, *The Character Factory: Baden-Powell and the Origins of the Boy Scout Movement* (New York: Pantheon, 1986).

Rowlands, Michael, 'Memory, Sacrifice and the Nation', *New Formations*, 30/3 (1996), 8–17.

Rowlands, Michael, 'Remembering to Forget: Sublimation as Sacrifice in War Memorials', in Forty, A. and Kuchler, S. (eds), *The Art of Forgetting* (Oxford: Berg, 1999).

Rowlands, Michael, 'Heritage, Politics and Memory', in Buchli, V. (ed.), *The Material Culture Reader* (Oxford: Berg, 2002).

Rutherford, Jonathan, *Forever England. Reflections on Masculinity and Empire* (London: Lawrence & Wishart, 1997).

Sauerteig, Lutz, 'Sex, Medicine and Morality During the First World War', in Cooter, *et al.* (eds), *War, Medicine and Modernity* (London: Sutton Publishing, 1998).

Saunders, Nicholas, 'Bodies of Metal, Shells of Memory', *Journal of Material Culture*, 5(1) (2000), 43–67.

Scarry, Elaine, *The Body in Pain. The Making and the Unmaking of the World* (Oxford: Oxford University Press, 1985).

Scott, Joan, 'The Evidence of Experience', in Abelove, H., Barale, M. and Halperin, D. (eds), *The Lesbian and Gay Studies Reader* (London: Routledge, 1993).

Searle, Geoffrey, *Eugenics and Politics in Britain, 1900–1914* (Leyden: Noordhoff International Publishing, 1976).

Searle, J. R., *Speech Acts* (Cambridge: Cambridge University Press, 1969).

Sedgwick Kosofsky, Eve, *Between Men: English Literature and Male Homosocial Desire* (New York: Columbia University Press, 1985).

Sedgwick Kosofsky, Eve, *Epistemology of the Closet* (London: Penguin, 1990).

Segal, Lynn, *Slow Motion. Changing Masculinities, Changing Men* (London: Virago, 1990).

Shafer, Stephen, *British Popular Films 1929–1939. The Cinema of Reassurance* (London: Routledge, 1997).

Sheffield, Gary, *Officer-Man Relations, Morale and Discipline in the British Army 1902–22*, Unpublished PhD Thesis (University of London, 1994).

Sherman, Daniel, 'Monuments, Mourning and Masculinity in France after World War I', *Gender & History*, 8/1 (1996), 82–107.

Sherman, Daniel, 'Art, Commerce, and the Production of Memory in France after World War I', in Gillis, John (ed.), *Commemorations* (Princeton: Princeton University Press, 1994).

Showalter, Elaine, *The Female Malady. Women, Madness and English Culture, 1830 –1980* (London: Virago, 1987).

Showalter, Elaine, *Sexual Anarchy. Gender and Culture at the Fin de Siècle* (London: Virago, 1990).

Sider, Gerald and Smith, Gavin (eds), *Between History and Histories: The Making of Silences and Commemorations* (Toronto: University of Toronto Press, 1997).

Silver, Kenneth, *Esprit de Corps. The Art of the Parisian Avant-Garde and the First World War, 1914–1925* (London: Thames & Hudson, 1989).

Simpson, Keith, 'The British Soldier on the Western Front', in Liddle, Peter, ed., *Home Fires and Foreign Fields. British Social and Military Experience in the First World War* (London: Pergamon, 1985).

Sinfield, Alan, *The Wilde Century. Effeminacy, Oscar Wilde and the Queer Moment* (Cassell: London, 1994).

Slobodin, Richard, *Rivers* (London: Sutton Publishing, 1997).

Solomon-Godeau, Abigail, 'Mourning or Melancholia: Christian Boltanski's Missing House', *Oxford Art Journal*, 21/2 (1998), 1–20.

Soloway, Richard, *Demography and Degeneration. Eugenics and the Declining Birthrate in Twentieth-Century Britain* (Chapel Hill: University of North Carolina Press, 1990).

Sontag, Susan, *On Photography* (London, Penguin, 1979).

Sontag, Susan, *Illness as Metaphor. AIDS and Its Metaphors* (London: Penguin, 1991).

Springhall, John, 'Building Character in the British Boy: The Attempt to Extend Christian Manliness to Working Class Adolescents, 1880–1914', in Mangan, J. A. and Walvin, J. (eds), *Manliness and Morality* (Manchester: Manchester University Press, 1987).

Steadman, Jones, *Languages of Class. Studies in English Working Class History* (Cambridge: Cambridge University Press, 1983).

Steedman, Carolyn, *Past Tenses: Essays on Writing, Autobiography and History* (London: Rivers Oram, 1992).

Stevens Curl, James, 'The Royal Artillery Memorial at Hyde Park Corner', in Compton, Ann (ed.), *Charles Sargeant Jagger. War and Peace Sculpture* (London: Imperial War Museum, 1985).

Stewart, Susan, *On Longing. Narratives of the Miniature, the Gigantic, the Souvenir, the Collection* (London: Duke University Press, 1993).

Stewart, Susan, 'Death and Life, in that Order, in the Works of Charles Willson Peale', in Elsner, J. and Cardinal, R. (eds), *The Cultures of Collecting* (London: Reaktion, 1994).

Stone, Martin, 'Shellshock and the Psychologists', in Bynum, W. F., Porter, R., Shepherd, M. (eds), *The Anatomy of Madness. Essays in the History of Psychiatry* (London: Tavistock, 1985).

Storr, Mell, 'Transformations: Subjects, Categories and Cures in Kraft-Ebing's Sexology', Bland, Lucy and Doan, Laura (eds), *Sexology in Culture. Labelling Bodies and Desires* (Oxford: Polity, 1998).

Sturken, Marita, *Tangled Memories. The Vietnam War, the AIDS Epidemic, and the Politics of Remembering* (Berkeley: University of California Press, 1997).

Sturken, Marita, 'Narratives of Recovery: Repressed Memory as Cultural Memory', in Bal, M., Crewe, J. and Spitzer, L. (eds), *Acts of Memory. Cultural Recall in the Present* (New England: Dartmouth College, 1999).

Tagg, John, *The Burden of Representation* (London: Macmillan, 1987).

Tate,Trudi, *Modernism, History and the First World War* (Manchester: Manchester University Press, 1998).

Taylor, A. J. P., *English History 1914–1945* (Oxford: Oxford University Press, 1992).

Taylor, Martin (ed.), *Lads. Love Poetry of the Trenches* (London: Constable, 1989).

Terdiman, Richard, 'Deconstructing Memory: On Representing the Past and Theorising Culture in France since the Revolution', *Diacritics*, 15/4 (1985), 13–36.

Thomson, Alistair, *Anzac Memories: Living with the Legend* (Oxford: Oxford Univeristy Press, 1994).

Tickner, Lisa, *The Spectacle of Women. Imagery of the Suffrage Campaign 1907–14* (London: Chatto & Windus, 1987).

Tosh, John, *A Man's Place. Masculinity and the Middle-Class Home in Victorian England* (New Haven and London: Yale University Press, 1999).

Tosh, John, 'Domesticity and Manliness in the Victorian Middle Class. The Family of Edward Benson', in Roper, M. and Tosh, J. (eds), *Manful Assertions. Masculinities in Britain since 1800* (London: Routledge, 1991).

Tweweleit, Klaus, *Male Fantasies II. Male Bodies: Psychoanalysing the White Terror* (Oxford: Polity, 1989).

Virilio, Paul, *War and Cinema. The Logistics of Perception* (London: Verso, 1989).

Virilio, Paul, *Desert Screen. War at the Speed of Light* (London: Continuum, 2002).

Waites, Bernard, *A Class Society at War. England 1914–1918* (Oxford: Berg, 1987).

Walker, Lynne, 'Architecture and Design. Heart of Empire/Glorious Garden: Design, Class and Gender in Edwardian Britain', in Beckett, J. and Cherry, D. (eds), *The Edwardian Era* (London: Phaidon Press, 1987).

Walker, Pamela, '"I live but not yet I for Christ Liveth in Me". Man and Masculinity in the Salvation Army, 1865–90', in Roper, M. and Tosh, J. (eds), *Manful Assertions. Masculinities in Britain since 1800* (London: Routledge, 1991).

Warren, Allen, 'Sir Robert Baden-Powell, the Scout Movement and Citizen Training in Great Britain, 1900–1920', *English Historical Review*, 101/399 (1986), 376–98.

Weeks, Jeffrey, *Sex, Politics and Society. The Regulation of Sexuality since 1800* (London: Longman, 1981).

Whaley, Joachim (ed.), *Mirrors of Mortality. Studies in the Social History of Death* (London: Europa London, 1981).

Whitehead, S. and Barrett, F. (eds), *The Masculinities Reader* (Oxford: Polity, 2001).

Williams, Raymond, *Marxism and Literature* (Oxford: Oxford University Press, 1977).

Winter, Denis, *Death's Men. Soldiers of the Great War* (London: Penguin, 1978).

Winter, Jay, *Sites of Memory, Sites of Mourning. The Great War in European Cultural History* (Cambridge: Cambridge University Press, 1995).

Winter, Jay, 'Shell-Shock and the Cultural History of the Great War', *Journal of Contemporary History*, 35/1 (2000), 7–11.

Wood, Jon, 'Shine: Sculpture and Surface in the 1920s and 1930s. An Introduction', *Henry Moore Institute Essays on Sculpture*, 36 (Leeds: Henry Moore Institute, 2002).

Wright, Patrick, *On Living in an Old Country. The National Past in Contemporary Britain* (London: Verso, 1985).

Wright, Patrick, *Tank. The Progress of a Monstrous War Machine* (London: Faber and Faber, 2000).

Wright, Patrick, 'Dropping Their Eggs', *London Review of Books*, 23/16 (23 August, 2001).

Wright, Patrick and Bommes, Michael, '"Charms of Residence": the Public and the Past', Richard Johnson *et al.* (eds), *Making Histories: Studies in History Writing and Politics* (London: Hutchinson, 1982).

Young, James, *Writing and Rewriting the Holocaust. Narrative and the Consequences of Interpretation* (Indianapolis: Indiana University Press, 1988).

Young, James, *The Texture of Memory. Holocaust Memorials and Meaning* (New Haven and London: Yale University Press, 1993).

Young, James, *At Memory's Edge. After-Images of the Holocaust in Contemporary Art and Architecture* (New Haven and London: Yale University Press, 2000).

Index

(References to images are in **bold**)